Poesis and Poetic Tradition

in the Early Works of Saint-Amant

Poesis and Poetic Tradition

in the Early Works of Saint-Amant

Four Essays in Contextual Reading

by

Edwin M. Duval

French Literature Publications Company
York, South Carolina
1981

320117

Naso magister erat

I am pleased to have this occasion to express my gratitude to the American Council of Learned Societies for a research grant without which this book could not possibly have been written.

TABLE OF CONTENTS

A NOTE ON EDITIONS

The text of Saint-Amant's poems upon which the present study is based is that of the only critical edition: *Oeuvres,* ed. Jean Lagny and Jacques Bailbé, STFM, 4 vols. (Paris: Didier, 1967-1971). All references and textual quotations are from this edition, with one exception: since the fifth and final volume of the Lagny-Bailbé edition has yet to appear, references concerning the *Moÿse sauvé* and its preface are to the earlier standard edition, the *Oeuvres complètes de Saint-Amant,* ed. Ch.-L. Livet, 2 vols. (Paris: Jannet, 1855).

The text of Ronsard's poetry adopted here is the one which was reproduced in every posthumous edition of the complete works, and which Saint-Amant and his readers were consequently most likely to know: that of the 1587 (first posthumous) edition. All quotations from Ronsard's poetry, then, are from this edition as it is reproduced in *Les Oeuvres de Pierre de Ronsard: Texte de 1587,* ed. Isidore Silver, CNRS, 8 vols. (Chicago: University of Chicago Press, 1966-1970). In the case of poems removed by Ronsard from the 1587 edition but reprinted in all subsequent editions of the *Oeuvres* and in the many posthumous editions of the *Recueil des pièces retranchées,* I have adopted Laumonier's text with the appropriate variants. For the sake of convenience I have provided cross-references to the two other standard editions of Ronsard's complete works: that of Paul Laumonier (revised and completed by I. Silver and R. Lebègue) based on first editions—STFM, 19 vols. (Paris: Hachette-Droz-Didier, 1914-1974)—and that of Gustave Cohen based on the 1584 edition—Bibliothèque de la Pléiade, 2 vols. (Paris: Gallimard, 1950). References to Ronsard in the footnotes are simplified to consist only of the volume and page number in each of these three editions, identified simply by the names of their respective editors: Laumonier, Cohen and Silver.

All classical texts quoted in the original are, unless otherwise indicated, those of the Loeb Classical Library.

INTRODUCTION

...volet haec sub luce videri,
Iudicis argutum quae non formidat acumen.
—Horace

Saint-Amant, the "victim of Boileau," was rescued from two centuries of virtual oblivion by the Romantics, who saw in him a fellow spirit and a precursor. In 1844 he was rehabilitated as a "grotesque" by the author of *Le Capitaine Fracasse,* and some of his sonnets were soon after imitated by the author of *Les Fleurs du mal.* In 1855 Ch.-L. Livet published an edition of his complete works, the first since 1668. Ever since the mid-nineteenth century Saint-Amant's poetry has been anthologized, read, admired and loved, perhaps more than that of any other non-curricular French poet.

We owe a great debt to the Romantics for their re-evaluation of the poetic past, and for their literary archaeology which unearthed so many important poets whom classical doctrine had at length succeeded in burying. But the Romantic rewriting of literary history was a highly tendentious one, and the nature of its discoveries was often intentionally distorted in order to disparage the esthetics and ideals of Classicism, and promote those of the Romantic revolt. In the case of Saint-Amant, particularly, the Romantics' admiration was based almost enirely on a profound and perhaps willful misunderstanding of the poet and his works. The currency of this misunderstanding even today is proof both of the enormous impact of the Romantic revolution on the art and science of reading, and of the inadequacies of the Romantic reformation of critical paradigms. Even the important re-appraisal of the age of Henri IV and Louis XIII brought about by Baroque studies in the 1950's has done little to correct, or even to alter, the Romantic reading of this poetry. Though the critical vocabularies and general orientations of the mid-nineteenth and mid-twentieth centuries are ostensibly quite different, both are predicated upon an idea of poetry which is utterly incompatible with that shared by Saint-Amant and his contemporaries, and which was virtually inconceivable before the French Revolution.

Whether he is read as a pre-Romantic by Romantics or a baroque poet by more recent critics, Saint-Amant is almost always, to one degree or another, characterized in the following manner:

1.   He is *spontaneous*. What for Théophile Gautier and his disciples is a kind of Romantic *élan* which rules and norms are powerless to contain, is for Françoise Gourier and others a form of "baroque" freedom of inspiration and contempt for composition and formal unity:

> Il comprend que le génie n'est que l'ivresse de la raison, et il s'enivre le plus souvent qu'il peut.—Certains hommes ont le don de pouvoir dégager quand ils veulent leur rêve de la réalité et de se séparer complètement du milieu qui les environne, comme La Fontaine, qui dormit debout toute sa vie; d'autres sont obligés de recourir à des moyens factices, au vin ou à l'opium, pour assoupir la geôlière de la prison et faire prendre sa volée à la folle du logis. Saint-Amant est de ceux-là; le rayon lui arrive bien plus étincelant et coloré à travers le ventre vermeil d'un flacon de vin. Sa métaphore jaillit plus hardiment avec le bouchon de la bouteille et va frapper le plafond en même temps que lui. Quelle ardeur de touche! quelle vivacité! quel entrain!—Ce n'est plus le même homme, c'est comme un autre poète dans le poète.[1]

> . . . .si Saint-Amant avait beaucoup réfléchi sur son art, il n'en était point devenu le maître; une fois la plume en main, il ne se souvenait guère de ses propres préceptes; c'est un homme d'inspiration et de premier mouvement.[2]

> Quelles que soient les circonstances qui le conduisent à prendre la plume, le poète la laisse généralement courir avec une grande liberté. Il ne se soucie guère de donner au poème une composition ordonnée.[3]

2.   He is *original*. Saint-Amant is an intransigent modernist who refuses imitation at all costs. Thus, his descriptions—that part of poetry which the poet himself considered to

be both the quintessence of the art, and his own particular forte
—are all drawn either from direct observation of reality or from
his own fertile imagination. Gautier was the first to state this
explicitly, branding Saint-Amant as "un homme qui avait vu tant
de choses et qui peignait avec ses propres couleurs ce qu'il avait
vu de ses yeux," and claiming that in *La Solitude* in particular
"la nature y est étudiée immédiatement et non à travers les
oeuvres des maîtres antérieurs."[4] Saint-Amant still passes for a
careful observer of nature today. As late as 1964 Saint-Amant's
erudite and cautious biographer read the descriptions of *La
Solitude* in precisely the same way that Gautier had done: "Tout
cela est pris sur le vif, par un écrivain qui a toujours recherché
la description exacte (jusque dans un poème épique) à côté de
ce que sa 'fantaisie' lui suggérait pour embellir cette description."[5]

3.   He is *ignorant.* Saint-Amant never studied, knew no
Greek or Latin, and consequently had no direct contact with
the Classics. If he ever read at all, it was only in vernacular works
of contemporaries (Cervantes and Marino) or recent writers
(Berni, Rabelais and Régnier) of a like temperament. In any
case, his reading was not *serious;* he was not a student of literature. Emile Faguet speaks for both earlier and later critics in
asserting that Saint-Amant "eut une éducation infiniment négli-
gée. . . . Pour le latin et le grec, il s'en est complètement passé,
et cela explique ses théories littéraires."[6]

This traditional caricature of Saint-Amant as a spontaneous
and undisciplined poet who never studied Classical languages or
literature and who resolutely refused to imitate either ancient
or contemporary authors is based ultimately on the persona
and critical remarks contained in the poet's works themselves.
The idea of unrestrained spontaneity is derived from the persona
of "le bon Gros Saint-Amant," a Rabelaisian *goinfre* who is
always to be found drinking with his friends in the cabarets of
Paris. The verse of such a bard would appear to be simply the
artless and uncontrolled effusion of a convivial genius. As for
his alleged originality, Saint-Amant makes this claim explicitly
in the *Avertissement au Lecteur* of the first edition of his collected works in 1629, blaming

   . . .ceux qui au lieu d'essayer à faire quelque chose d'eux-mesmes s'amusent non seulement à imiter, mais à prendre laschement tout ce qu'on void dans les autres Autheurs. . . . Pour moy, si j'estois suject à ce vice, je ne m'arresterois point à desrober des pensées, je voudrois faire quelque bon larcin qui me peust enrichir pour toute ma vie: mais je l'aborre tellement, que mesme si je ly par fois les oeuvres d'un autre, ce n'est que pour m'empescher de me rencontrer avec luy en ses conceptions, et y suis si religieux que quand j'en pourrois faire couler quelques-unes parmy les miennes, sans qu'on s'en peust appercevoir, il m'est advis que ma conscience me le reprochant secretement, me feroit rougir lors que je viendrois à les reciter, ou que les loüanges qu'on m'en donneroit me seroient autant d'accusations de mon crime.

(*Oeuvres* I, 22-23)

And finally, the notion that Saint-Amant was ignorant originates both in the persona of a *goinfre,* for whom the tavern is the only study, and in a passage of the 1629 *Avertissement* in which the poet declares: ". . .Dieu mercy, ny mon Grec, ny mon Latin ne me feront jamais passer pour Pedant: Que si vous en voyez deux ou trois mots en quelques endroits de ce Livre, je vous puis bien asseurer que ce n'est pas de celui de l'Université" (*Oeuvres* I, 21).

A poet's persona and apology, however, are not reliable grounds on which to form a critical assessment. The truth is that whether it is based on a willful distortion of facts (as was probably the case with the Romantic polemicists), or simply on a somewhat naïve faith in the "sincerity" of poets (as seems too often to be the case with more recent critics), the modern image of Saint-Amant and his works is belied both by history and by some of the most salient characteristics of the works themselves. Against the view that he was a spontaneous and artless poet we have the rather troublesome observation that in matters of form and versification Saint-Amant, from his first poem to his last, was more faithful to the Malherbian reform than were either of Malherbe's principal disciples, Racan and Mainard.[7] Against the view that he was ignorant of classical literature and refused to imitate it, we find poems like *La Métamorphose de Lyrian et de Sylvie,* and especially *L'Andromède,* large portions of which are translated directly from Book IV of Ovid's *Metamorphoses,* as the poet himself is forced to admit in his *Avertissement* ("Il me semble desja que je vous oy dire que je ne laisse pas pourtant d'imiter, et qu'Ovide a traitté devant moy des Fables que j'ay escrites apres luy; Je le confesse. . .," *Oeuvres* I, 23). As for Saint-Amant's alleged ignorance of Greek and Latin, assertions to this effect are in fact directly contradicted by the very passage of the *Avertissement* on which they are based: "Dieu mercy, ny mon Grec, ny mon Latin ne me feront jamais passer pour Pedant: Que si vous en voyez deux ou trois mots en quelques endroits de ce Livre, je vous puis bien asseurer que ce n'est pas de celui de l'Université." It is a strange violence against language that allows critics to read this coy excuse for "*mon* Grec" and "*mon* Latin" so litotically as to mean "I know no Greek or Latin at all." We have no reason to believe that Saint-Amant does not mean precisely what he says here—that he is not a Humanist or a philologist, and that his command of classical languages is not comparable to that of Doctors of Theology ("celui de l'Université"), but merely equivalent to that which all men of letters have attained.

This point is a crucial one. The modern understanding of Saint-Amant's "confession of ignorance" is based not only on a misreading, but on anachronism as well. It fails to take into account a fundamental historical reality: the fact that *all* literate men in the early seventeenth century began their lives with a solid classical education firmly grounded in good Latinity. Their teachers were the students and beneficiaries of the Renaissance Humanists, and their curricula were the creation of the great pedagogical reformers of the preceding century—Erasmus, Vives, Loyola, Platter, Sturm, Ramus. The ideal of *pietas litterata* was beginning to subordinate the pure Humanism of the 1530's and 40's to practical religious training, but whether educated in a Protestant college or (to a slightly lesser degree) according to the Jesuits' *Ratio Studiorum* (1586 and 1599), every schoolboy who learned to read and write at the turn of the century still learned Latin and Latin literature if nothing else, and most learned some Greek as well. No literate male could arrive at the age of 18 without having spent several hours every day, six days a week for anywhere from eight to twelve full years studying Cicero's letters and orations, imitating Ciceronian style, studying and reciting the histories of Caesar and Sallust, and reading, parsing, scanning, commenting and memorizing long passages of the canonized Latin poets, of whom the most modest curriculum was likely to include Vergil (the *Georgics* and *Eclogues* as well as the *Aeneid*), Horace (the *Odes* as well as the

Epistles) and Ovid (both the *Fasti* and the *Metamorphoses*).[8] We know almost nothing about Saint-Amant's youth and education. But whether he had been a student of the Jesuits at the Collège de la Marche or a student of the Huguenots at a college in Normandy,[9] the author of *La Solitude* and *Le Fromage* could not possibly have been the unlettered original we picture him to be.[10] In the absence of concrete and positive evidence we are entirely unjustified in interpreting his disparaging remarks concerning his own learning by the standards of our own century. Saint-Amant would have been a strange anomaly indeed if at the age of 18 he had not learned by heart ("ad unguem," as a school boy in 1600 would have said) more Latin poetry in the original Latin text than most modern graduate students of literature have even *read* in English.

What little biographical information we do possess concerning the real Saint-Amant actually suggests that even by contemporary standards his literary culture was exceptional for a non-professional scholar. Among his acquaintances, correspondents and admirers were some of the most erudite Humanists of the day—Piat Maucors, Samuel Bochart, Christophe Dupuy, Claude Ménétrier, Claude Peiresc—and among his personal friends some of the most important literary figures—Chevreau, Chapelain, Balzac, Vaugelas, Marolles, the brothers Dupuy.[11] Nor may we assume that it was by a mere fluke that Saint-Amant was elected to the Académie Française in its first year of existence. Balzac's words concerning the poet in a letter to Vaugelas dated October 10, 1625, are telling: "Advouëz-moy que nous avons deux amis qui sont deux grands ouvrages de la nature, et que [Racan] et Monsieur de Saint-Amant ont autant d'avantage sur les Docteurs que les vaillans sont au-dessus des maistres d'escrime."[12]

Of even greater significance are these words written by the severe Chevreau: "Il entendoit. . .fort bien la Fable."[13] This judgment, like the disclaimers of Saint-Amant's *Avertissement*, must be read in its historical context. To be distinguished for one's knowledge of mythology in the generations following the Pléiade, especially in the first decades of the seventeenth century when dictionaries of mythology were on the shelves of every private library and the *Metamorphoses* had become the common thesaurus of every poetaster, and furthermore to be so judged by one of the most erudite engineers of the classical doctrine, is a distinction of considerable importance. It marks Saint-Amant as an expert, a recognized specialist in the stuff and substance of seventeenth-century poetry. Such expertise as this required knowing Ovid nearly by heart—not in Renouard's popular but approximative prose translation, but in the original Latin text. It required a thorough knowledge of the Renaissance mythographers who had digested and classified vast quantities of information on mythology—particularly of Natalis Comes' *Mythologiae* which was published repeatedly in J. de Montlyard's French translation during Saint-Amant's youth (1604, 1607, 1611, 1612 and 1627).[14] Expertise in mythology also required a solid knowledge of Greek literature. Even if Saint-Amant's Greek ("mon Grec") might not have been adequate to extended reading in original Greek texts, he had access to all the most important texts through both Latin and French translations. The *Iliad* had been available in the Salel-Jamyn translation since 1580, the *Odyssey* in Salomon Certon's translation since 1604. Certon's translation of the complete works of Homer, including the Homeric Hymns and the *Batrachomyomachia*, was published in 1615. Other important Greek sources were also readily available: the *Bibliotheca* of Apollodorus (published in Jean Passerat's French translation in 1605), the complete works of Lucian (translated by Saint-Amant's intimate friend Jean Baudoin and first published in 1613), the *Imagines* of Philostratus (translated by Blaise de Vigenère and published in 1578, 1597, 1614, 1615, etc.), and Plutarch, whose *Oeuvres morales et philosophiques* in Amyot's translation had been published ten times in Paris alone before Saint-Amant wrote *La Solitude* (1572, 1574, 1575, 1579, 1587, 1603, 1604, 1606, 1616, 1618). The frequency with which Plutarch and Philostratus were published indicates that they were widely read and extremely popular. The recentness of the first French editions of the *Odyssey*, Apollodorus and Lucian suggests that during Saint-Amant's youth the general reading public shared an avid interest in the original sources of Greek mythology. A poet judged by Chevreau to be distinguished for his knowledge of "Fable" would have to have had far more than a casual familiarity with all of these.

From what we know of early seventeenth-century education and reading habits, and from what we know of Saint-Amant himself, it is easy to infer that by contemporary standards, Saint-

Amant's classical literary culture was at least adequate. By the standards of the modern literary critic, it was enormous.

Why, then, did Saint-Amant cultivate the pose of spontaneity, originality and ignorance which proved to be so useful to the Romantics, and has proven to be so misleading to modern critics? In order to answer this question we must make an effort to reconstruct the historical and literary context in which Saint-Amant grew up and began to write. In reading Saint-Amant's early work it is essential never to lose sight of the fact that the lettered community of the 1620's had no sense of living at the dawn of a "Grand Siècle," and certainly no sense of living in an autonomous and independent period called the "Baroque." To their eyes, the period in which they were living was—for better or for worse—a prolonged moment of shadows and twilight following that glorious effulgence which we now call the "Renaissance." The young Saint-Amant, it must constantly be remembered, is a late *Renaissance* poet.[15] It must also be remembered that the most prestigious and most emulated poet at the beginning of Saint-Amant's career was not Desportes, nor d'Aubigné, nor Régnier, nor even Malherbe . . .but Ronsard. The "Prince des Poètes" continued to have a strong and direct influence on the poetic production of the early seventeenth century, and Ronsard himself was still more widely read than any other poet.[16] His complete works were published at fairly regular six-year intervals in successive editions from the first posthumous edition until the end of the third decade of the following century: 1587, 1592, 1597, 1604, 1609, 1617, 1623, 1629-30. Only if we keep clearly in mind this lasting presence and stature of Ronsard is Saint-Amant's stance entirely comprehensible.

The 1629 *Avertissement au Lecteur*—the ultimate source of all our misunderstandings concerning Saint-Amant—is in fact a straight-forward and unabashed piece of polemic directed against the prestige of the Pléiade. In its first sentence it claims to be motivated by the poet's indignation at being plagiarized by rhymesters ("Le juste despit que j'ay de voir quantité de petits

Poëtes se parer impudemment des larcins qu'ils ont faits dans les ouvrages qu'on a desja veus de moy. . .," *Oeuvres* I, 19). In the lines that follow, however, the long and militant condemnation of imitation of any kind is clearly not aimed at the petty thefts of Saint-Amant's contemporary rivals, but rather at a general conception of poetry—one which no reader could fail to recognize as the most fundamental principle of Pléiade poetics. Saint-Amant's remarks concerning his Greek and Latin and his neglected studies simply serve to focus the object of his polemic. If he claims that neither his Greek nor his Latin will make him out to be a pedant ("ne me feront jamais passer pour Pedant"), it is because Ronsard's Greek and Latin had won him precisely that reputation. If he assures his readers that they will not find any more than an occasional word of Greek or Latin in his poetry, it is because Ronsard had made such a show of erudition in his odes and sonnets, and had even boasted of his *Franciade* that:

> Les François qui ces vers liront,
> S'ils ne sont et Grecs, et Romains,
> En lieu de mon livre ils n'auront
> Qu'un pesant faix entre les mains.[17]

If he adopts a conventional argument used for more than a century by Italian Modernists against the Ancients—that Homer, the greatest of all poets, knew no language other than the one his nurse taught him—it is in order to force Ronsard, the Hellenophile who had sought to become the modern-day Homer of France, into the camp of those who "ne jugeront pas qu'un bon esprit ne puisse rien faire d'admirable sans l'ayde des langues estrangeres." Similarly, if Saint-Amant claims in his first preface that his "voyages. . .ont bien valu un estude" it is by no means because he never studied, but because Ronsard had made precisely the opposite claim in his first preface: "Bien que la jeunesse soit tousjours elongnée de toute studieuse occupation pour les plaisirs voluntaires qui la maistrisent: si est ce que des mon enfance j'ai tousjours estimé l'estude des bonnes lettres, l'heureuse felicité de la vie, et sans laquelle on doit desesperer ne pouvoir jamais attaindre au comble du parfait contentement."[18]

Lest we miss the point of all these barbs, Saint-Amant

identifies his adversaries in clear and unambiguous terms:

> Je dy cecy pour *certaines gens à la vieille mode,* qui lors que la
> verité les contraint d'approuver ce que je fay, n'ont rien à dire
> sinon, C'est dommage qu'il n'ayt point estudié! Je le dy encore
> pour ceux qui au lieu d'essayer à faire quelque chose d'eux-mesmes
> s'amusent non seulement à imiter, mais à prendre laschement tout
> ce qu'on void dans les autres Autheurs.
>
> (*Oeuvres* I, 22)

If we understand the polemical purpose of Saint-Amant's
first critical preface, we will have no difficulty in coming to
terms with his persona. Just as the *Avertissement au Lecteur* is
an *Anti Deffense et Illustration de la Langue Françoyse* in which
Ronsard's critical prefaces are echoed and overturned, so the
spontaneous, original and ignorant "bon Gros Saint-Amant"
which we have incautiously received from the hands of the militant Romantics is originally a literary mask whose negative
counterpart is clearly delineated in the first three command-
ments of the *Abbregé de l'Art Poëtique François* (1565): "Sur
toutes choses tu auras les Muses en reverence, voire en singuliere
veneration. . . . Apres tu seras studieux de la lecture des bons
poëtes, et les apprendras par coeur autant que tu pourras. Tu
seras laborieux à corriger et limer tes vers."[19]   The modern
error has been to read the *Avertissement* not as a polemical
"warning" addressed to contemporary readers, but as a sincere
and candid confession addressed to posterity. We have been as
mistaken in doing this as we have been in reading Théophile
Gautier's *Les Grotesques* as serious literary scholarship. Gautier
was not writing about Saint-Amant in *Les Grotesques;* he was
writing against Boileau and Classicism.   Saint-Amant was not
writing his autobiography in the *Avertissement,* he was writing
against Ronsard and the High Renaissance.

Preconceptions influence the way we read more profoundly
than we would like to think. Despite our efforts to read only
"what is in the text," a poem written by a disciple of Dorat and a
reverent student of Pindar, Homer and Anacreon tends to have a

very different meaning for us than a similar poem written by a *bon vivant* who never studied and rarely read. Studies of Saint-Amant's poetry almost always reflect, to one degree or another, the Romantic image of "le bon Gros." Since Saint-Amant is presumably spontaneous and undisciplined, anthologists and critics have felt free to exerpt and dissect his poems, selecting "characteristic" passages here and there without any concern for the integrity of the works themselves. Until fairly recently, scholars have not even bothered to look for a logical or esthetic unity in works where they have assumed that none is to be found.[20] And since Saint-Amant's genius is presumably self-sufficient and his descriptions are drawn either directly from reality or from his own creative imagination, few scholars have bothered to consider how his poems might be reworkings of earlier texts, much less to look for ironic or parodistic imitations in either the content or the form of his poems.[21] And finally, since Saint-Amant presumably knew no Greek or Latin, no one has bothered to determine Saint-Amant's use of classical commonplaces or of specific *loci* from classical authors. The poet's reputation of ignorance is taken as licence to put the classics entirely out of mind when reading his poetry.[22]

If our Romantic image of Saint-Amant is indeed a fictitious and erroneous one, then our reading of his poetry has been, and remains, largely misguided. What would we discover in Saint-Amant's poems if we were to read them not with the idea of ignorant spontaneity and originality in mind but with the suspicion that, despite superficial appearances, they are the work of an expert in classical mythology, a voracious reader, a friend of Humanists, a conscious artist and careful craftsman? The following essays have their origin in precisely this question: each is an attempt to read one of Saint-Amant's poems as a serious work of art.

The orientation of such a project of critical re-reading is necessarily double. First of all, it must be *extrinsic*. If we begin by admitting the possibility that Saint-Amant is neither ignorant nor uncompromisingly "original," then we must be prepared to find in his poems reminiscences drawn from other works. If it is true that Saint-Amant was an expert in classical mythology, then his poetry may well contain allusions and echoes drawn from specific classical sources which his contemporary readers would have recognized automatically, but which our own twentieth-century education has not prepared us to discern. His poetry may also contain implicit references to the literary-historical context in which it was written. The 1629 *Avertissement au Lecteur,* as we have seen, is largely predicated on a reaction to the lasting presence of Ronsard. We must be prepared to find in his poems, too, a polemical stance with respect to the conventions and traditions of modern French poetry. In short, an indispensible part of our effort in reading Saint-Amant must be to bring to his poems the literary culture, experience and reflexes which all seventeenth-century readers, by virtue of the mere fact that they were literate and living in the seventeenth century, necessarily possessed.

At the same time, however, our reading must be *intrinsic.* If we also admit the possibility that Saint-Amant is not an undisciplined or careless extemporizer of rhymes, but rather the craftsman that his versification reveals him to be, then we must be prepared to read each poem as an integral, self-consistent and premeditated work of art. We must search for the coherence, the internal logic and ordering principles of works which modern criticism has conditioned us to perceive as open-ended and formless.

The chief difficulty involved in the kind of "contextual reading" proposed here is that its extrinsic and intrinsic aspects cannot legitimately be separated. It would be of little help simply to juxtapose two critical approaches to a poem by appending a formalistic analysis to an investigation into sources and influences. Classical borrowings and reminiscences are never particularly important or interesting in and of themselves; they are only worthy of our attention if they are used *functionally* in a poem, as semantic or formal elements in a structured pattern of meaning. When this is the case, recognition of their relation to an original context or of their place in a tradition external to the poem itself is necessary to and inseparable from the perception of their new function within the adoptive poem. A good reading, then, must deal not simply with borrowings and reminiscences themselves—with "sources," as they would then be called—but with the resulting patterns of allusiveness and the connotative *meaning* these patterns generate. Similarly, the formal structure of a poem may also have a correlative outside the poem, not only in a convention of composition, but in a specific work as well. Any correlation of this kind is necessarily *significant:* it generates a meaning of its own which in turn must inform our reading of the "content" of the poem. Here again, the extrinsic and intrinsic aspects of a good reading are inseparable.

These essays, then, are an attempt to reconstruct readings which will be as adequate as possible to both the formal and the historical realities of Saint-Amant's poems. Their principal focus must be the dialectic between internal and external literary reference, between text and context, poesis and tradition.

I have chosen to limit these essays in contextual reading to four of Saint-Amant's earliest poems. Saint-Amant began his career at a time when there were nearly as many versifiers as literate men, but which had failed, even in its own estimation, to produce a single poet of distinction in two generations. Sponde and d'Aubigné were generally ignored, and Malherbe was regarded even by his contemporaries primarily as a *chef d'école.* This was the age of the *recueil,* and of formulaic and circumstantial verse. French poetry had reached one of the lowest ebbs in the entire history of the vernacular. Saint-Amant was no Rimbaldian adolescent when he began his career. He was probably 24 or 25 when he wrote his earliest surviving work, and 29 when he published his first poem. His first major publication—the volume of his collected *Oeuvres* in 1629—did not appear until he was 34 years old, well into the canonical age of responsibility ("Que toutes mes hontes j'eus beues," as Villon had said), when any weakness in his bid for a place in literature could no longer be attributed to greenness. This late entry into an exhausted poetic tradition required something extraordinary, both a return to the great tradition from which poetry had fallen and a departure in a new direction. Such being the circumstances of a début which we know to have been spectacularly successful, Saint-Amant's very first literary efforts merit our special attention. The first three essays are consequently devoted to the first three significant[23] poems written by this unknown Norman: *La Solitude* (composed before 1620), *Le Fromage* (1621-1622)

and *L'Arion* (1622-1623).[24]

To these earliest pieces, all of which were published in the *Oeuvres* of 1629, I have chosen to add a fourth, composed at a slightly later date and published in the *Suitte des Oeuvres* in 1631. Because of the immediate and enormous success of the poet's first major publication, this sequel followed after an interval of only two years. Whereas the *Oeuvres* are the work of an unknown provincial, the *Suitte* is an encore by a popular modern celebrity. Its poems, understandably, pursue many of the same directions so successfully undertaken in the first collection. But at the same time they reflect a more mature and independent stance vis-à-vis the poetic tradition, and point the way toward a new and (to modern readers) more familiar kind of writing. From the *Suitte*, then, I have selected the most popular work, *Le Melon*. Since this is one of the most *read* of Saint-Amant's early poems, it is also one of the most *mis*-read, and seemed to be for that reason alone an ideal work with which to end a study whose chief purpose is to approach important texts without interference from the preconceptions through which they are traditionally viewed, strip them of misreadings which have accrued over the 130 years since their rehabilitation by the Romantics, and to reconstruct more accurate readings based as much as possible on the knowledge, experience and expectations of their first readers.

CHAPTER I:
LA SOLITUDE

. . .Si qua manent sceleris vestigia nostri,
Inrita perpetua solvent formidine terras.

· ·

Pauca tamen suberunt priscae vestigia fraudis,
Quae temptare Thetin ratibus, quae cingere muris
Oppida, quae iubeant telluri infindere sulcos.
—Vergil

La Solitude is Saint-Amant's earliest known work,[1] as well as his most famous. Its popularity was immediate and immense, if we can judge by the fact that it was both borrowed and pirated before its first authorized publication in 1629,[2] and subsequently underwent three separate translations into Latin.[3] Saint-Amant's contemporaries, even the most erudite among them, speak of the work as a masterpiece of the age,[4] and when Théophile Gautier rediscovered Saint-Amant two hundred years after the poet's death, this was the work he singled out as the most brilliant. Today, too, every poetic anthology in which Saint-Amant is represented invariably includes *La Solitude.*

Ever since the rehabilitation of the poem by the Romantics, its "originality" and its "feeling for nature" have been so frequently stressed that modern readers tend to lose sight of what is fundamentally and overwhelmingly conventional about the work. Much of the landscape in *La Solitude* is clearly an elaboration of the pastoral *locus amoenus* which had been transmitted, virtually unchanged, from Theocritus and Vergil through Ariosto and Guarini to d'Urfé and Racan, and which had been grafted onto the lyric tradition by the time of Guillaume de Lorris to be transmitted, in an equally conservative manner, through nearly every poetic generation from Petrarch to the Pléiade and beyond. It is precisely this lyric use of the topos that Saint-Amant exploits in his poem.

La Solitude in fact begins in a rut worn down by countless plodding poetasters who had followed in the footsteps of Petrarch. Saint-Amant's speaker seeks solitude in places "esloignez du monde" as solace for his "inquietude":

O que j'ayme la Solitude!
Que ces lieux sacrez à la Nuit,
Esloignez du monde et du bruit,
Plaisent à mon inquietude!

Petrarch had blazed this trail nearly three centuries earlier:

Solo et pensoso i più deserti campi
Vo mesurando a passi tardi et lenti
E gli occhi porto per fuggire intenti
Ove vestigio human l'arena stampi.
    Altro schermo non trovo che mi scampi
Dal manifesto accorger de le genti,
Perché negli atti d'alegrezza spenti
Di fuor si legge com'io dentro avampi:
    Sì ch'io mi credo omai che *monti* et *piagge*
Et *fiumi* et *selve* sappian de che tempre
Sia la mia vita, ch'è celata altrui.
                                    (*Il Canzoniere*, 35)

By the time of Ronsard the trail had become a three-lane high-way:

Le plus touffu d'un *solitaire bois,*
Le plus aigu d'une *roche* sauvage,
Le plus desert d'un separé *rivage,*
Et la frayeur des *antres* les plus cois,
    Soulagent tant mes soupirs et ma vois
Qu'au seul escart d'un plus secret ombrage,
Je sens guarir ceste amoureuse rage.[5]

    Seul et pensif aux *rochers* plus segrets,
D'un coeur muet je conte mes regrets,
Et par les *bois* je vay celant ma playe.[6]

Pensif je voy la fuite vagabonde
Du Loir qui traine en la mer son tribut.

Ores un *antre,* ores un *bois* sauvage,
Ores me plaist le secret d'un *rivage,*
Pour essayer de tromper mon ennuy.[7]

And although Ronsard had worked the theme nearly to death,
his epigones continued to develop it, turning "seul et pensif"
and "les antres et les bois" into the flat formulae of a worn-out
tradition of love lyric.[8]

In the last three decades of the sixteenth century and the
first two decades of the seventeenth, the conventional *locus
amoenus* of lyric solitude underwent a minor mutation: the inevitable "horreur" of the solitary landscape was accentuated to
become more explicitly sinister, lugubrious or terrifying—without, however, losing any of its former attraction for the unrequited lover. The same old disconsolate lovers began to seek
solace and lament their fates in landscapes like these:

Milles oiseaux de nuit, mille chansons mortelles
M'environnent, vollans par ordre sur mon front:
Que l'air en contrepoix fasché de mes querelles
Soit noircy de hiboux et de corbeaux en ront.[9]

Dessoubs le silence des nuicts
J'erre, je cours, je vagabonde,
Pour eschaper à mes ennuys
Ie me veux sequestrer du monde,
Afin de desrober au jour
Mon infortune et mon Amour.
   Ces champs de l'horreur habitez,
Retraicte de la solitude,
Ces bois tout par tout desertez
Fors que de mon inquietude,
Tristes objects de ma douleur,
Me representent mon mal-heur.
   Ces houx d'espines herissez,
Plancher de ces forests obscures,
Ces rocs de mousse tapissez,
Simulachre de sepultures,
Sinistres augures de mort,
Semblent refigurer mon sort.
   Ces antres reclus et relants,

Cachete de hybous, et d'horfraies,
Me sont pronostiques sanglants,
De morts, de meurtres et de plaies
De supplices et de tourments,
Malencontreux evenements.[10]

Obscur *valon, montagne* sourcilleuse
Qui vers Phebus tiens opposé le dos:
Nuict solitaire, hostesse du repos:
Démons voisins de l'onde Stygieuse.
   Rocher pierreux, et vous *caverne* hideuse
Où les Lyons et les Ours sont enclos:
Hibous, corbeaux, augures d'Atropos,
Le seul objet d'une ame malheureuse.
   Triste desert du monde abandonné,
Je suis esprit à grand tort condamné
Aux feux, aux cris d'un enfer ordinaire.
   Et viens à vous pour lamenter mon sort,
Flechir le Ciel, ou, s'il ne se peut faire
Mouvoir l'Enfer, les Parques, et la Mort.[11]

The similarity between the "baroque" landscapes near the center of *La Solitude* and the "cachete de hybous et d'horfraies" described above is so evident as to require no comment. What Saint-Amant does not borrow from the Renaissance version of the Petrarchan lament he has borrowed from the slightly modified baroque version. Gautier was obviously mistaken in reading *La Solitude* as "une très-belle chose et de la plus étrange nouveauté pour l'époque où elle parut," in which Nature "est étudiée immédiatement et non à travers les oeuvres des maîtres antérieurs."[12]   For the poem's first readers, on the contrary, the work was striking not for its "strange novelty," but for its overwhelming familiarity.   Every detail in the entire descriptive portion of Saint-Amant's "coup d'essay" can in fact be found in numerous "maîtres antérieurs."[13]

Such being the case, what can possibly account for the undisguised enthusiasm with which Saint-Amant's contemporaries all received his poem? There *is* something novel about *La Solitude,* and it is to this real novelty, not to the imagined novelty of a Romantic polemicist or an a-historical critic, that we must turn in order to understand the poem's meaning and value. First of all, we are struck by the fact that while Saint-Amant's land-scapes are all strictly conventional, they have been utterly stripped of their equally conventional *function*: these vignettes had served as a mere backdrop for centuries of elegiac outpour-ings by suffering lovers, and their appearance here, in conjunc-tion with the formulaic opening and the speaker's initial "in-quietude," lead us quite naturally, by a kind of over-determined Pavlovian response, to expect a lovelorn soliloquy. But our ex-pectations are disappointed: the "background" is elaborated at such length that the speaker appears to forget that he is even in love! After the requisite mention of his "inquietude" in the first strophe, his psychological turmoil is utterly forgotten.

Saint-Amant is not only playing with convention here, he is deliberately playing with his reader as well. Through the language of convention the poem initially promises to be some-thing which it subsequently fails to become. We wait for the lover to begin his lamentations, but he never does: we are thrown entirely off balance by bracing for a speech which is never de-livered. The force of convention is so great that the absence of the "lover" is almost tangible. And this is surely part of the ex-planation for the poem's title: not only is the lover's "solitude" —that is, the conventional "antres et bois"—promoted from background to principal subject in this poem, but that setting is at the same time depopulated even further by the radical elimina-tion of the persona which we inevitably expect to find there. What appears to us today to be pure description is in fact a Petrarchan love poem undone. In a far more dramatic and astonishing way than Du Bellay ever attempted, Saint-Amant says to his attentive readers: "J'ay oublié l'art de pétrarquizer."

La Solitude, then, is utterly conventional in its opening statement as well as in the kinds of scenes it describes, yet it is no more "plagiarized" than it is "pris sur le vif": the poem is a highly original form of literary play and literary criticism which uses the conventions of lyric to undercut conventional lyric. It is an ingenious blow to the heart of a long but dying tradition.

At the same time that it manipulates the conventions of Petrarchan-Ronsardian love poetry, *La Solitude* experiments even more boldly with the very basis of those conventions. The pastoral *locus amoenus,* which had come to occupy such a prominent place in love lyric, is an idealized, Utopian setting derived directly from the original lost Utopia of the Golden Age. Although the first seven strophes of *La Solitude* (which will henceforth be referred to as Part I) seem to conform strictly to the lyric *locus amoenus,* Saint-Amant has managed to restore to these their original force by means of unmistakable and direct allusions to standard descriptions of the Golden Age itself. From the very first strophes, these solitary places are described as literally primeval:

> . . .que mes yeux sont contens
> De voir ces Bois qui se trouverent
> A la *nativité du Temps,*
> Et que tous les Siecles reverent,
> Estre encore aussi beaux et vers,
> Qu'aux *premiers jours de l'Univers*!
> (11. 5-10)

The following strophe sustains the same idea by asserting that these trees, whose origin dates back to the separation of the four elements from pre-temporal Chaos ("les premiers jours de l'Univers"), are still in existence today because they were tall enough to survive the universal Deluge by which Jupiter destroyed the iniquitous race of Iron Age men.

Since they are primeval, these woods retain even today something of the pristine nature of the Golden Age. The primary function of strophes 6 and 7 is to recall, in the most unequivocal terms, the chief characteristics of that first Age. One of these is that there was no hunting and no killing, since all species lived in perfect harmony, and Mother Earth provided for all man's needs peaceably:

> Là, cent mille Oyseaux aquatiques
> Vivent, sans craindre en leur repos,
> Le Giboyeur fin, et dispos
> Avec ses mortelles practiques.
> . . . .

Jamais Chevreüil desesperé
N'y finit sa vie à la chasse;
Et jamais le traistre hameçon
N'en fit sortir aucun poisson.

(11. 51-54, 67-70)

These lines designate in a logical and sytematic way the entire animal kingdom, dividing it after the manner of classical antiquity into the groups which inhabit each of the three inhabitable elements; air, earth and water. In his nostalgic evocation of the universal concord of "vetus illa aetas, cui fecimus aurea nomen," Ovid's Pythagoras proceeds in exactly the same manner:

Tunc et *aves tutae* movere per aera pennas,
Et *lepus inpavidus* mediis erravit in arvis,
Nec sua crudelitas *piscem* suspenderat hamo:
Cuncta sine insidiis nullamque timentia fraudem
Plenaque pacis erant.

(*Metamorphoses* XV, 99-103)

Ovid's Pythagoras ends his long lesson by exhorting modern man to return to a Golden Age vegetarianism, and in so doing he recalls once again the ways in which Iron Age men are wont to delude and destroy the species of each of the three domains:

Retia cum pedicis laqueosque artesque dolosas
Tollite, nec *volucrem* viscata fallite virga
Nec formidatis *cervos* inludite pinnis
Nec celate cibis uncos fallacibus *hamos*.

(*Metamorphoses* XV, 473-476)

It is evident that Saint-Amant had passages such as these in mind in writing the descriptions of strophes 6 and 7. Indeed, similarities in both the general movement and the particular diction of these lines make it difficult to avoid the suspicion that Saint-Amant's lines may have been translated directly from Ovid's.

A second characteristic of the Golden Age which Saint-Amant has incorporated into the description of strophe 7 is another natural consequence of Mother Earth's original munificence: the absence of trade and commerce.

Jamais l'Esté, ny la froidure
N'ont veu passer dessus cette eau
Nulle charrette, ny batteau
Depuis que l'un et l'autre dure.
Jamais Voyageur alteré
N'y fit servir sa main de tasse.
            (11. 61-66)

To a modern reader these lines may appear to be little more than a platitudinous elaboration of the idea of "solitude": there are no carts, ships or travelers here because there are simply no human beings of any kind, not even passers by. But the seventeenth-century reader was very much aware that until Jupiter's revolt and the exile of Saturn there was no need to transport either goods or people, for the simple reason that there were no unfulfilled desires: everyone had everything he wanted, and in great abundance, without having to go elsewhere to find it:

Nondum caesa suis, peregrinum ut viseret orbem,
Montibus in liquidas pinus descenderat undas,
Nullaque mortales praeter sua litora norant.
        (*Metamorphoses* I, 94-96)

It was not until the Iron Age, the last and worst of all, that ships were first invented. Their invention, moreover, was a direct result of the new "amor sceleratus habendi":

Vela dabant ventis nec adhuc bene noverat illos
Navita, quaeque diu steterant in montibus altis,
Fluctibus ignotis insultavere carinae.
        (*Metamorphoses* I, 132-134)

For the first time men experienced wants that even agriculture (Silver Age) and war (Bronze Age) could not satisfy, and were forced by their greed to travel and trade. The implications of Saint-Amant's lines are unmistakable: if there has never been travel here, it is because these woods remain exactly as they were "aux premiers jours de l'Univers," under Saturn's reign.

The allusion to the Golden Age contained in these lines on travel is made even more explicit by the temporal indication they contain: "Depuis que l'un et l'autre dure" (1. 64). This line is not a *cheville;* it reminds us that there was once a time when neither carts nor ships existed, invites us to recall what time that was, and to realize that nothing has changed here since the Golden Age. Or perhaps "l'un et l'autre" refer not to the direct objects, but to the subjects of the sentence, "l'Esté" and "la froidure," in which case the temporal reference becomes even more precise still: ships and carts were first invented at the beginning of the Iron Age; summer and winter first came into being with the Silver Age. Under Saturn's reign the only season was spring:

> Ver erat aeternum, placidique tepentibus auris
> Mulcebant Zephyri natos sine semine flores.
> *(Metamorphoses* I, 107-108)

When Jupiter seized control of the universe, spring was reduced to a small quarter of the year:

> Postquam Saturno tenebrosa in Tartara misso
> Sub Iove mundus erat. . .
> . . . .
> Iuppiter antiqui contraxit tempora veris
> Perque hiemes aestusque et inaequalis autumnos
> Et breve ver spatiis exegit quattuor annum.
> *Tum primum* siccis *aer fervoribus ustus*
> Canduit, et ventis *glacies* adstricta pependit.
> *(Metamorphoses* I, 113-120)

If "l'un et l'autre" is read in this way, then the woods of *La Solitude* are not only as they were before the fourth and last age of man, but actually as they were in the very first age, under the reign of Saturn.

Regardless of how we choose to read "l'un et l'autre" in line 64, there is an unmistakable allusion to the perennial spring of the Golden Age to be found elsewhere in the poem. Strophe 2 develops the idea that the trees of these woods were already of considerable height when "Jupiter ouvrit les Cieux/Pour nous envoyer le Deluge." It begins with the following lines:

> Un gay *Zephire* les caresse
> D'un mouvement doux et flatteur.
> (11. 11-12)

The following strophe begins with a detail drawn from the same thesaurus:

> Que sur cette Espine fleurie,
> Dont le *Printemps* est amoureux. . .
> (11. 21-22)

Taken together, these four lines are a textual reminder of the *ver aeternum* in which

> . . .placidi. . .tepentibus auris
> Mulcebant Zephyri natos sine semine flores.
> (*Metamorphoses* I, 107-108)

Once again it is evident that these woods are not only ante-Diluvian, but actually Golden.

Throughout Part I of the poem we have found systematic reference to three of the most conspicuous characteristics of the Golden Age: absence of hunting and fishing, absence of travel and commerce, and perennial spring. Having begun as a love elegy on the "solo e pensoso" theme, *La Solitude* has continued to describe the *locus amoenus* at the expense of the lyric complaint which was to have been uttered here, and has done so in precisely such a way as to restore to those familiar "bois et antres" their original historical and moral significance.

But these first seven strophes are even more complex than this. At the same time that they create the image of a sacred forest of the Golden Age, these strophes also contain some curious intimations of a more recent and more violent past: there are, on second look, unmistakable vestiges of post-Diluvian iniquity in this ostensibly pristine setting. These are camouflaged to blend in with the idyllic surroundings, and will escape us if we read the conventional diction of the poem as *only* conventional. The third strophe of the poem, for example, begins by evoking the languorous song of a nightingale by means of the tritest of metonymies:

> Que sur cette Espine fleurie,
> Dont le Printemps est amoureux,
> Philomele au chant langoureux,

Entretient bien ma réverie!
(11. 21-24)

Latent in the name "Philomele," however, is a reminiscence of one of the most abominable crimes in classical legend: the story of Procne, Tereus and Philomela. The story is so familiar that we tend to forget its forcefulness. The Thracian king Tereus rapes Philomela, the sister of his Athenian wife Procne, and prevents her from revealing his crime by amputating her tongue and sequestering her in "stabula alta. . .*silvis* obscura *vetustis*." The prisoner communicates her situation to her sister by means of a message woven into a tapestry. Procne frees Philomela during the course of a feigned Bacchic rampage, and takes revenge on Tereus by slaughtering their five-year-old son Itys, dismembering him and serving his parts—some boiled, others sizzling hot *en brochette*—to her husband for supper. She then exults in the revelation of her revenge by producing Philomela, still drenched in blood from the slaughter, and throwing the gory head of Itys into her husband's face. Tereus is about to take counter-revenge by murdering his wife and his sister-in-law in cold blood, when all three are metamorphosed into birds. Of the two sisters, one takes up residence under the eaves of houses, the other in forests. The latter is tongueless Philomela, the nightingale. Such is the series of violent and atrocious crimes which accounts for the presence of the nightingale in these woods, and which is inevitably recalled by the name "Philomele." The same detail which serves to contribute yet another idyllic touch to the description of a Golden Age forest simultaneously suggests one of the most horrible crimes of the Iron Age.

A number of images and allusions in this and the following two strophes seem to have a similar function. The first of these is to be found in the remaining six lines of the Philomela strophe:

Que je prens de plaisir à voir
Ces Monts pendans en precipices,
Qui pour les coups du desespoir
Sont aux malheureux si propices,
Quand la cruauté de leur sort
Les force à rechercher la mort!
(11. 25-30)

This is one of the passages most frequently cited in support of the idea that Saint-Amant is a Romantic poet of Nature and passion. Christian Wentzlaff-Eggebert comes much closer to the spirit of the poem by pointing out that such "Romantic" suicides are in fact common fare in the pastoral romances of the period, and by reading these lines as a conventional topos drawn from *Le Sireine* of Honoré d'Urfé rather than as the vision of a precocious Werther. I would differ with this excellent reading only in suggesting that these lines are not inspired by the suicides in d'Urfé himself, but rather constitute a direct reference to one of the principal sources on which d'Urfé's and all such "Romantic" suicides are modeled: Ovid's *Metamorphoses*. Of the many desperate suicides in the *Metamorphoses,* the one to which these lines appear to allude is that of Daedalion, narrated in Book XI: Daedalion's beautiful daughter Chione was struck dead by Diana's arrow for having claimed that her own beauty surpassed that of the hunter-goddess herself. Driven mad by his daughter's death, Daedalion rages through the trackless wilds of Thessaly until he reaches Mount Parnassus, from the summit of which he hurls himself to death. Apollo takes pity on the wretched suicide however, and transforms him, in mid-air, into a hawk:

> Concita membra fugae mandat similisque iuvenco
> Spicula crabronum pressa cervice gerenti,
> Qua via nulla, ruit. . . .
> Effugit ergo omnes veloxque cupidine leti
> Vertice Parnasi potitur; miseratus Apollo,
> Cum se Daedalion saxo misisset ab alto,
> Fecit avem et subitis pendentem sustulit alis.
> (*Metamorphoses* XI, 334-336, 338-341)

Every detail of this account conforms to the circumstances evoked by Saint-Amant. Daedalion is indeed a "malheureux": his "patrius dolor" (1. 328) cannot be assuaged, and despite Ceyx's consolations he unremittingly laments his daughter's death ("natam delamentatur ademptam," 1. 331). His suicidal leap is the result of a "coup du desespoir," and his "sort" is indeed "cruel"—so much so that even Apollo, the brother of Chione's offended murderess, is moved to pity. And Daedalion consciously "recherche la mort," "velox cupidine leti." Not only does Ovid's story conform in all its details to Saint-Amant's six lines on the "Monts pendans en precipices;" it also conforms to the entire setting described in the course of the first seven strophes of the poem. Like the "I" of *La Solitude,* Daedalion has come to a place where there are no human beings, and through which no humans have ever passed: "qua via nulla ruit . . . . Effugit ergo omnes." If Saint-Amant had an Ovidian precedent in mind in writing these six lines, it is undoubtedly the story of Daedalion's metamorphosis.[14]

It should perhaps be observed here that Saint-Amant nowhere suggests that the desperate suicides of strophe 3 are necessarily *lovers,* as is presupposed by the suggestion that this passage of *La Solitude* is inspired by the numerous suicides of pastoral romances. In fact, the context of these lines has nothing whatsoever to do with the subject of love or lovers, either explicitly or implicitly, whereas the tension between Golden Age purity and Iron Age crime and sacrilege will continue to be developed throughout the poem. It may also be significant to note here that Saint-Amant speaks only of the *propitiousness* of these mountains for those who seek death, but does not extend his otherwise rather detailed hypothetical scenario to include the slightest indication concerning the *issue* of these searches for death. Daedalion does not die, but is only forced by the "cruauté de [son] sort" to "*rechercher* la mort."

To readers as steeped in Ovid as were those of the early seventeenth century, the parallels between the *Metamorphoses* and lines 25-30 of *La Solitude* were undoubtedly quite striking. To the modern reader, whose experience with Ovid tends to be less than quotidian, and whose literary memory is crowded with bits and pieces drawn from a much wider variety of readings, such echoes may appear remote and dubious. One argument to be made in this particular case is that every other strophe in the entire poem possesses a strict unity and compelling internal cohesiveness of its own. Only this one would appear to have a double subject, since lines 21-24 are concerned with a nightingale singing on a flowering briar, and lines 25-30 are concerned with steep mountains whose sheer cliffs offer a means to the end for the desperate and the star-crossed. But these two distinct parts of the same strophe *can* be perceived as closely interrelated if we recognize their respective Ovidian reminiscences. The nightingale and the sheer cliffs are both evoked in such a way as to recall similar metamorphoses. In both cases a human being is transformed into a bird: Philomela into a nightingale and Daedalion into a hawk. Both transformations take place at the last possible moment before certain death: Philomela at the very moment she is to die by Tereus' avenging sword, Daedalion mid-way between the peak and the foot of a "mont pendant en précipices." And most significantly, both transformations are the result of a heinous crime: Philomela's is the last in a long series of crimes and retributions from rape and mutilation to murder, by way of genocide and cannibalism. Daedalion's transformation is the ultimate effect of a sin against the gods: his daughter's *hubris* in placing her own beauty above Diana's. The unity of the strophe, then, is guaranteed by the common theme of a metamorphosis at the moment of imminent death: one metamorphsis is suggested by the *result* of the transformation, the other by its *occasion* and *setting*. We will discover yet another way in which this ostensibly double strophe functions as an integral whole when we come to discuss a parallel strophe in Part III. For the moment, the most crucial point is that both parts of this strophe serve to recall the horrors of Iron Age iniquity, while at the same time they appear to blend into the paradisiacal decor of *La Solitude.*

A third Ovidian reminiscence which functions in precisely the same way as those of strophe 3 is to be found in the marsh scene of strophe 5. Once again, Wentzlaff-Eggebert has provided an invaluable corrective to the Romantic reading accepted by earlier critics: he has demonstrated that many of the most "life-like" details in this peaceful swamp are not at all described "sur le vif," but are in fact purely conventional touches which can be found in Renaissance pastoral literature from Montemayor's *Diana* to d'Urfé's *Le Sireine.* But here again, Saint-Amant's poem seems not to derive from Renaissance works themselves, but to refer pointedly to the original sources of all such topoi in Renaissance literature and to manipulate these sources for its own ends. The strophe in question is the following:

> Que j'ayme ce Marests paisible!
> Il est tout bordé d'aliziers,
> D'aulnes, de saules, et d'oziers,
> A qui le fer n'est point nuisible!
> Les Nymphes y cherchans le frais,

S'y viennent fournir de quenoüilles,
De pipeaux, de joncs, et de glais,
Où l'on voit sauter les grenoüilles,
Qui de frayeur s'y vont cacher
Si tost qu'on veut s'en approcher.
                    (11. 41-50)

In his critical edition of the *Oeuvres* of 1629, Jacques Bailbé rightly points out that the flora of this description is more directly inspired by Ovid than by later pastoral literature, and he refers in his commentary to a scene described in the story of Dryope's metamorphosis into a "water lotus":

Est lacus, adclivis devexo margine formam
Litoris efficiens, summum myrteta coronant.
Venerat huc Dryope. . .
          . . .nymphis latura coronas.
· ·
Haut procul a *stagno* Tyrios imitata colores
In spem bacarum florebat *aquatica lotos.*
          (*Metamorphoses* IX, 334-337, 340-341)

There are numerous passages in the *Metamorphoses* which resemble Saint-Amant's lines much more closely than this one, however. One is the description of the forest in which the Calydonian boar hunt takes place:

Silva frequens trabibus, quam nulla ceciderat aetas,
Incipit a plano devexaque prospicit arva.
· ·
Concava vallis erat, quo se demittere rivi
Adsuerant pluvialis aquae; tenet ima lacunae
Lenta salix ulvaeque leves iuncique palustres
Viminaque et longa parvae sub harundine cannae.
          (*Metamorphoses* VIII, 329-330, 334-337)

The thick forest "quam nulla ceciderat aetas" (1. 329) would seem to have provided the model for Saint-Amant's "Bois. . . que tous les Siecles reverent" (11. 6-8), as well as for the swamp trees in the fifth strophe "à qui le fer n'est point nuisible" (1. 44).[15] Even more striking is the similarity between the specific trees and plants named in Ovid's catalog and those which appear in Saint-Amant's marsh: "lenta salix"/"saules"; "iunci palustres"/"joncs"; "vimina"/"oziers"; "longa harundo"/"roseaux"; "parvae cannae"/"pipeaux". The "Marests" of *La Solitude* bears a striking resemblance indeed to Ovid's Aetolian "lacuna."

If this is a functional and significant resemblance, then we should recall that it was to this very place that Diana, outraged because she alone had been overlooked by the Calydonian king Oeneus in his harvest libations to all the gods, sent the wild boar which disembowled so many of Greece's greatest heroes. The intimations of sacrilege and punishment here would thus be very similar to those of strophe 3. But even though the plant life of Saint-Amant's "Marests" and Ovid's Calydonian "lacus" are identical, Wentzlaff-Eggebert's work has shown that the flora of marshes had become so conventional as to make recognition of any specific reminiscence extremely unlikely, and it would be difficult to maintain that the allusion could have been a functional one, even in the seventeenth century.

There *is* a functional allusion in this strophe, however, and an unmistakable one, thanks to the very frogs which Théophile Gautier and Jean Lagny undoubtedly thought to have been observed first-hand by the poet during the course of his strolls through the Breton countryside. These frogs are actually transposed directly from the *Metamorphoses,* from the etiological story of the Lycian peasants. Shortly after the clandestine birth of Apollo and Diana on Delos, Latona, still pursued by the jealous and spiteful Juno, flees with her infant twins to Asia Minor. When she reaches Lycia the sun is blazing hot, and she is weak from thirst and fatigue:

> . . .cum sol gravis ureret arva,
> Finibus in Lyciae longo dea fessa labore
> Sidereo siccata sitim collegit ab aestu,
> Uberaque ebiberant avidi lactantia nati.
> (*Metamorphoses* VI, 339-342)

She happens upon a cool pond to which peasants have come to gather osier, rushes and sedge, and stops to slake her thirst:

> Forte lacum mediocris aquae prospexit in imis

Vallibus; agrestes illic fruticosa legebant
Vimina cum iuncis gratamque paludibus ulvam;
Accessit positoque genu Titania terram
Pressit, ut hauriret gelidos potura liquores.
(*Metamorphoses* VI, 343-347)

But the mean-spirited peasants approach and forbid her to drink from their pond. Without revealing her divinity, the goddess humbly begs them to allow her to enjoy that which nature has provided as *publica munera* for the common enjoyment of all alike. The impious peasants are moved neither by Latona's reasoning, nor by the supplicating gestures of her infants. They threaten her, heap insults upon her, and out of sheer malice they make the water unpotable by stirring up mud from the bottom of the pond. Unable to restrain her anger any longer, the outraged goddess cries "Aeternum stagno. . .vivatis in isto," and transforms this vile lot of men into equally vile amphibians:

Eveniunt optata deae: iuvat esse sub undis
Et modo tota cava submergere membra palude,
Nunc proferre caput, summo modo gurgite nare,
Saepe super ripam stagni consistere, saepe
In gelidos resilire lacus. . . .
. . . .
Limosoque novae saliunt in gurgite ranae.
(*Metamorphoses* VI, 370-374, 381)

Saint-Amant's "Marests,"

Où l'on voit sauter les grenoüilles,
Qui de frayeur s'y vont cacher
Si tost qu'on veut s'en approcher,

is obviously none other than Ovid's Lycian *stagnum*. The timorous frogs in our peaceful *Solitude* are described exactly after the manner of Ovid's metamorphosed peasants who "saliunt in gurgite" and whom "saepe/In gelidos resilire lacus [iuvat]." For readers of the early seventeenth century, the mere mention of frogs in a marsh would undoubtedly have been sufficient to recall the story of their origin. But Saint-Amant further helps his reader to recognize the source of this passage by deliberately choosing each and every detail in his description to recall an important moment in the original Ovidian narrative itself. The nymphs who come to this marsh "y cherchans le frais" are a direct transposition of Ovid's Latona who had come, thirsty from the dry heat, "gelidos potura liquores." And the activity of these nymphs, whose express purpose is to "se fournir de quenoüilles,/ De *pipeaux*, de *joncs*, et de *glais*," is directly transposed from the activity of Ovid's Lycian peasants who "fruticosa legebant/ *Vimina* cum *iuncis* gratamque paludibus *ulvam*." It should be observed here that the word "glais" is a troublesome one which Jacques Bailbé identifies as another form of *glaïeuls*, "gladioli" (even though Richelet and Furetière attest only this more familiar form of the word), claiming at the same time that Saint-Amant's real meaning in this context is not "gladioli" strictly speaking, but rather *iris d'eau*. But the really crucial point is that the word was already archaic in the early seventeenth century, and its meaning already obscure. The reason for this deliberate archaism would appear to be simply that it translates Ovid's "ulva" just as "pipeaux" translates "vimina" and "joncs" translates "iunci." Since *ulva* was an unusual word which seems to have caused earlier translators of Ovid considerable difficulty,[16] Saint-Amant chose to render it with a correspondingly obscure word which nevertheless respects the original's meaning of "herbe marine, feulu de mer" (Robert Estienne). Saint-Amant's "pipeaux" line is actually a word-for-word translation of the corresponding line in Ovid's fable of the Lycian peasants.

The marsh scene of *La Solitude*, then, not only recalls a corresponding scene in the *Metamorphoses*, but actually transposes and incorporates *narrative* elements from the same Ovidian passage into its very description, "describing" them "in sequence," as it were. I am tempted to think that this rather astonishing technique of implicit or "descriptive" narrative is precisely what Saint-Amant is referring to later in the poem when he calls these descriptions a "peinture vivante." Be that as it may, the allusion in Saint-Amant's marsh strophe to Ovid's story of the Lycian peasants is undeniable. And like the similar allusions in strophe 3 to Ovid's Philomela and Daedalion stories, this is a *functional* allusion whose recognition is essential to a proper understanding of the poem. Philomela and Daedalion were both principal actors in notorious episodes of violence and sacrilege, and both have now been reintegrated into the serenity of an apparently crimeless and pristine Golden Age forest. The same is true of the wicked Lycian peasants: the marsh, like Daedalion's towering cliff, has regained its former serenity, and the violators themselves, like Philomela, Procne and Tereus, have been incorporated into this peaceful solitary setting. The hopping frogs, like the sweet-songed nightingale and the "Monts pendans en precipices," all contribute to the tranquillity of the conventional *locus amoenus,* while at the same time they are all presented in such a way as to recall, deliberately and unmistakably, a story of past wickedness and violence.

Through a brilliant use of literary allusiveness Saint-Amant has succeeded in sustaining an implicit but uninterrupted narrative line beneath an ostensibly "pure" and guileless description. By failing to perceive the narrative currents under the descriptive surface, modern readers, of whom Théophile Gautier was the first, have necessarily overlooked the real virtuosity of the poem, which consists not in describing nature "immédiatement et non pas à travers les oeuvres des maîtres antérieurs," but precisely in drawing *everything* from the "maîtres antérieurs" in such a way as to reconcile the timeless with the sequential, the descriptive with the narrative. The effect of this reconciliation, moreover, is a quintessentially literary and ironic one. Having restored to the conventional *locus amoenus* of the conventional Petrarchan solitude of lovers its original force of a Golden Age utopia, *La Solitude* has gone on to undercut the convention of the Golden Age as well, infusing it with unmistakable traces of Iron Age violence and sacrilege. Petrarchan love, the *locus amoenus,* the Golden Age. . .these are so many conventions of an exhausted literary tradition which Saint-Amant has adopted only in order to debunk them in what is surely one of the most witty and parodistic *tours de force* to be produced in the entire seventeenth century.

Part II of *La Solitude* (strophes 8-13) stands in striking contrast to Part I. The outdoor scenes of the first seven strophes—forests, mountains, rivers and marshes—are followed by six strophes describing interior scenes: a delapidated castle, a grotto and a cave. Unlike the first section, this one is filled with *concrete* vestiges of a human presence (architectural ruins, a hanging skeleton, inscriptions on marble and on tree trunks), and with reified forces which affect only human existence (demons, ominous birds, sleep). At the same time, the poem is marked by a radical shift from the apparently immutable and timeless to the visibly transient. Whereas the first part of the poem describes forest trees

> . . .qui se trouverent
> A *la nativité du Temps,*
> Et que *tous les Siecles reverent,*
> [qui sont] aussi beaux et vers,
> Qu'*aux premiers jours de l'Univers,*
> (11. 6-10)

as well as swamp trees "à qui le fer n'est point nuisible" (1. 44), the second part, in direct contrast, describes

> . . .la decadence
> De ces vieux Chasteaux ruinez,
> Contre qui *les Ans mutinez*
> Ont déployé leur insolence,
> (11. 71-74)

as well as "devises du *temps passé*" and "chiffres taillez sur les arbres" which "*l'âge* a presque éffacé" (11. 102-104). The articulation of the poem is predicated here on a clear shift from exterior to interior, from the natural to the homocentric, from the timeless and pristine to the transient and corrupt.

This shift in subject corresponds to an equally abrupt shift in "inspiration." Whereas the nature scenes of Part I can all be identified as belonging to the conventional Classical-Renaissance repertoire which was so abundantly illustrated by the poets of the Pléiade, the descriptions of Part II are inspired by the kind of "baroque" scenes of which the passages quoted at the beginning of this chapter from d'Aubigné, Du Mas and La Roque are representative samples. It is important to recall once again that these were no more novel or astonishing to Saint-Amant's first readers than were the Petrarchan-Ronsardian "bois et antres": such descriptions had already been in vogue for at least forty years by the time *La Solitude* was written. The poet has merely abandoned one familiar convention for another here; or to be more precise, he has pursued the same convention one step further, presenting the Golden Age topos now as it had been presented not through the reign of Henri II, but during the reign of the last of the Valois kings. The real originality of *La Solitude* is no more to be found in the "baroque" atmosphere of this central section than it is in the Renaissance *loci amoeni* of Part I: once again, the poem's importance is to be found in the *manipulation* of these familiar conventions for the production of new meaning.

As in Part I, many of the scenes in Part II derive directly from, and are in turn meant to recall, specific passages from the *Metamorphoses*. The most obvious of these is strophe 12, in which a vault below the castle ruins is described:

> Là dessous s'estend une voute
> Si sombre en un certain endroit,
> Que quand Phebus y descendroit,
> Je pense qu'il n'y verroit goute.
> Le Sommeil aux pesans sourcis
> Enchanté d'un morne silence,
> Y dort, bien loing de tous soucis,
> Dans les bras de la Nonchalence,
> Laschement couché sur le dos
> Dessus des gerbes de pavos.
> (11. 111-120)

This description of Sleep's cave is the most unmistakable of all the Ovidian reminiscences in the poem. It is in fact little more than a free translation from Book XI of the *Metamorphoses*. Lines 111-114 are slightly adapted from the following passage:

> Est prope Cimmerios longo spelunca recussu,
> Mons cavus, ignavi domus et penetralia Somni,
> Quo numquam radiis oriens mediusve cadensve
> Phoebus adire potest; nebulae caligine mixtae
> Exhalantur humo dubiaeque crepuscula lucis.
> (*Metamorphoses* XI, 592-596)

Even the ostensibly "Marinesque" *concetto* on Phoebus is copied directly from these lines of Ovid. Saint-Amant's "morne silence" of line 116 condenses the next six lines of Ovid's description:

> Non vigil ales ibi cristati cantibus oris
> Evocat Auroram, nec voce *silentia* rumpunt
> Sollicitive canes canibusve sagacior anser;
> Non fera, non pecudes, non moti flamine rami
> Humanaeve sonum reddunt convicia linguae.
> *Muta quies* habitat.
>   (*Metamorphoses* XI, 597-602)

Line 115, "Le Sommeil aux pesans sourcis," is translated from Ovid's lines in which Iris, with some difficulty, awakens Somnus: "tardaque deus gravitate iacentes/Vix oculos tollens" (11. 618-619). Line 117, "bien loing de tous soucis," was suggested to the poet by the beginning of Iris' exhortation to Sleep, whom she addresses as "*Somne,* quies rerum, placidissime, Somne, deorum,/Pax animi, *quem cura fugit*" (11. 623-624). Saint-Amant's last three lines are a conflation of two successive sentences in Ovid's description:

> Ante fores antri fecunda *papavera* florent
> Innumeraeque herbae, quarum de lacte soporem
> Nox legit et spargit per opacas umida terras. . .
> . . . .
> At medio torus est ebeno sublimis in antro,
> Plumeus, atricolor, pullo velamine tectus,
> *Quo cubat ipse deus membris languore solutis.*
>   (*Metamorphoses* XI, 605-607, 610-612)

Saint-Amant has simply substituted the poppies growing *outside* Sleep's cave for the feather bed *inside* the cave, and transformed *languor* (rendered as "nonchalence") into another allegorical figure by means of a capital "N."

Strophe 13 is also unmistakably Ovidian, despite the fact that "resonabilis Echo" frequently appears in both the lyric poetry and pastoral romances of the sixteenth and seventeenth centuries. Ovid is the earliest surviving author to relate the popular story of Echo, and it is his account that is recalled here. The beginning of this strophe appears at first to be determined only by the exigencies of a Petrarchistic "flame-ice" conceit, recalling the aquatic bird of strophe 6 who "allentit le feu d'Amour/Qui dans l'Eau mesme le consume" (11. 57-58):

> Au creux de cette grotte *fresche*
> Où l'Amour se pourroit *geler,*
> Echò ne cesse de *brusler*
> Pour son Amant *froid,* et revesche.
>   (11. 121-124)

But the palor of the conceit can be excused for its efficacy in recalling Ovid's narration. Echo's nascent passion is given an unusually long development in Book III of the *Metamorphoses,* and this development is constructed entirely around the notion of burning:

> Ergo ubi Narcissum per devia rura vagantem
> Vidit et *incaluit,* sequitur vestigia furtim,
> Quoque magis sequitur, *flamma* propiore *calescit,*
> Non aliter quam cum summis circumlita *taedis*
> Admotas rapiunt vivacia sulphura *flammas.*
>   (*Metamorphoses* III, 370-374)

The sylvan "grotte fresche" in which Echo continues to nourish her love also recalls Ovid's account: having tried in vain to win Narcissus' love, the nymph

> Spreta latet *silvis* pudibundaque frondibus ora
> Protegit et *solis* ex illo vivit *in antris;*
> Sed tamen haeret amor crescitque dolore repulsae.
>   (*Metamorphoses* III, 393-395)

The formula in the last line of the strophe, "la voix qui luy sert de corps" (1. 130), not only conforms to Ovid's insistence on the dissolution of Echo's body:

> Extenuant vigiles corpus miserabile curae
> Adducitque cutem macies et in aera sucus
> Corporis omnis abit,
>   (*Metamorphoses* III, 396-398)

but it also helps to recall the similar formulae with which Ovid frames his entire digression on Echo: "*Corpus* adhuc Echo, non *vox* erat" (1. 359). . ."*sonus* est, qui vivit in illa" (1. 401). As was the case with Nature's creatures like the nightingale and frogs earlier in the poem, the natural reverberation of sound in a grotto is described here in such a way as to recall an etiological narrative involving human passions.

If strophes 12 and 13 are among the most obviously Ovidian of all the descriptions in *La Solitude*, the single scene described at great length in strophes 8-11 is easily the least Ovidian. There are of course metamorphoses involving "Couleuvres" and "Hyboux," and witches and sorcery are common fare in the *Metamorphoses*, but nowhere does Ovid describe a scene like this one: ruins and hanging skeletons are nearly as foreign to Ovid's vigorous universe as anything can possibly be. This sequence on castle ruins is apparently unique in every respect: it is the only four-strophe description in the entire poem of one-strophe vignettes, it holds the narrator's attention far longer than any of the others, it is placed at the very center of the work, and it is the only scene in which there is a clear trace of "baroque horror." Is it also unique as the only non-Ovidian scene of the entire poem, and is its only literary analogue to be found in contemporary pastoral poetry?[17]

Before answering too hastily, we should recall that some of the most effective allusions of Part I described not the *setting*, but the *aftermath* of an Ovidian story: both Philomela-turned-nightingale and the Lycian peasants-turned-frogs are examples of this kind of entelechy-decor. With these precedents in mind, let us consider more carefully the un-Ovidian skeleton to which sixteen full lines of the poem are devoted. Of the many desperate suicides in the *Metamorphoses* there are three by hanging, and of these there is one whose specific details are curiously consistent with the desolate scene in which Saint-Amant describes the skeleton of his hanged lover: this is the story of Iphis and Anaxarete as it is related by Vertumnus to Pomona in Book XIV of the *Metamorphoses*. The entire drama of Iphis takes place at the threshold of Anaxarete's palace. It is at the threshold that the humble lover first comes to declare his love ("supplex *ad limine* venit," 1. 702), at the threshold that he weeps and sleeps:

> Interdum madidas lacrimarum rore coronas
> *Postibus* intendit posuitque *in limine* duro
> Molle latus tristisque serae convicia fecit,
>   (*Metamorphoses* XIV, 708-710)

at the threshold that he speaks his last words ("*ante fores* haec verba novissima dixit," 1. 717), at the threshold that he attaches his noose and hangs himself as a last lugubrious garland for Anaxarete's door post:

> . . .ad *postes* ornatos saepe coronis
> Umentes oculos et pallida bracchia tollens,
> Cum *foribus* laquei religaret vincula *summis,*
> «Haec tibi serta placent, crudelis et inpia!» dixit
> Inseruitque caput, sed tum quoque versus ad illam,
> Atque onus infelix elisa fauce pependit.
> (*Metamorphoses* XIV, 733-738)

The threshold is of course one of the privileged *loci* in Greek and Latin elegiac poetry (the *paraclausithyron*), as well as in pastoral and Marinistic verse (it is consequently one of the major pastoral topoi parodied in Sorel's *Le Berger extravagant*). But the relentless insistence on the "limen" and the "postes" in this passage of the *Metamorphoses* is unusual even for the genre. This peculiarity is perhaps significant. One of the very few concrete details provided in Saint-Amant's description of the swaying skeleton is that the poor lover has hanged himself from what is now a "chevron de bois maudit" in a ruined castle.

The actual details of the horrible account of Iphis' suicide are also curiously consonant with the tone of Saint-Amant's ghastly scene of the swaying skeleton: as Iphis hangs by his broken neck from Anaxarete's doorpost, his feet kick convulsively, striking against the door; the door is knocked open, producing a long groaning sound as it turns slowly on its hinges:

> Icta pedum motu trepidantum ut multa gementem
> Visa dedisse sonum est adapertaque ianua factum
> Prodidit. . . .
> (*Metamorphoses* XIV, 739-741)

There is a third and much more striking peculiarity in Ovid's story which Saint-Amant also seems to have incorporated into his own description. This is the particular importance given to sight and seeing in the narration. The episode begins with an act of seeing:

> *Viderat* a veteris generosam sanguine Teucri
> Iphis Anaxareten, humili de stirpe creatus,
> *Viderat* et totis perceperat ossibus aestum.
>   (*Metamorphoses* XIV, 698-700)

Iphis sees and loves Anaxarete, but Anaxarete spurns and mocks her suitor. The latter's only desire in hanging himself is *to be seen,* to become a *spectacle* for his lady's eyes:

> «Nec tibi fama mei ventura est nuntia leti:
> Ipse ego, ne dubites, adero praesensque *videbor,*
> Corpore ut exanimi *crudelia lumina pascas.»*
>   (*Metamorphoses* XIV, 726-728)

He dies with his eyes still turned in the direction of his lady (1. 737). Anaxarete, unaware of the entire incident, hears the wailing and the beating of breasts as Iphis' funeral procession marches past her palace, and the first word she utters, is "Videamus," "let's *see*," a word accentuated by its separation from the rest of the sentence as well as by its initial position. She climbs to her high chamber, *looks out,* and is unable to avert her *gaze* as she is turned into stone:

> Forte viae vicina domus, qua flebilis ibat
> Pompa, fuit, duraeque sonus plangoris ad aures
> Venit Anaxaretes, quam iam deus ultor agebat.
> Mota tamen «*Videamus»* ait «miserabile funus»
> Et patulis iniit tectum sublime fenestris
> Vixque bene inpositum lecto *prospexerat* Iphin:
> *Diriguere oculi...*
>   ...conata avertere *vultus,*
> Hoc quoque non potuit....
>   (*Metamorphoses* XIV, 748-757)

This accumulation of verbs of seeing, and this relentless insistence on eyes and sight prepares the unusual ending of the tale. The petrified Anaxarete is now a statue which admonishes ladies not to be heartless. It can be seen in Salamis, in a temple dedicated to "Outlooking Venus," *Venus Prospiciens* (11. 759-761).

Ovid's story lends a curious resonance to several lines of *La Solitude* which otherwise appear to be purely conventional or arbitrary. Saint-Amant's "pauvre Amant"

> . . .se pendit
> Pour une Bergere insensible,
> Qui d'*un seul regard* de pitié
> Ne daigna *voir* son amitié.
>
> (11. 87-90)

Both the *Bergere* and Anaxarete are punished for a lack of compassion expressed in terms of *not seeing*. Saint-Amant's *Bergere* is punished by "le Ciel Juge équitable" (1. 91), just as Ovid's Anaxarete is punished by a "deus ultor" (1. 750). Her punishment consists in *seeing*, moreover, living on as an eternal shade, "Ayant tousjours son crime *devant soy*" (11. 99-100), just as Anaxarete's punishment began, according to Iphis' last wish ("adero *praesensque videbor*"), when her gaze was made to fix immovably on Iphis, and was completed with her transformation into a statue dedicated to a "*seeing* Venus."

Is it possible, then, that these "vieux Chasteaux ruinez" are meant to be recognized as the remains of Anaxarete's palace,[18] that the "chevron de bois maudit" from which the skeleton swings is Anaxarete's *postis,* that the "vieux ossemens" themselves are all that remain of the "pauvre Amant" Iphis, that the "marbres" on which "devises du temps passé" can still be read are the "blandae tabellae" to which Iphis committed his messages to Anaxarete (1. 707), or fragments from the Temple of *Venus Prospiciens,* or even from the inscribed statue of Anaxarete itself, and that the "plancher du lieu le plus haut" which has now fallen into the cellar and is soiled by the slime of slugs and toads was once the floor of Anaxarete's "tectum sublime" from whose open windows she first *looked out* onto the funeral procession? A categorical assertion is obviously unwarranted, yet I find it difficult to dismiss the possibility altogether. The conventionality of such suicides as Iphis' in later literature argues against the significance, if not against the validity, of this *rapprochement.* So do several major points of divergence between the two texts: the lady of noble blood in Ovid is a "Bergere" in Saint-Amant;[19] Iphis' body is taken down and presumably incinerated, whereas the body of Saint-Amant's "Amant" is left hanging; Ovid makes no mention of Anaxarete's survival as an "Ombre aux peines condamnée," nor Saint-Amant of his shepherdess' metamorphosis into stone.

In favor of the *rapprochement,* however, is the cumulative effect of all the striking and sometimes very peculiar similarities I have discussed above, as well as the particular perspective adopted by Iphis himself in his last speech to Anaxarete:

> «Nec tibi fama mei ventura est nuntia leti:
> Ipse ego, ne dubites, *adero praesensque videbor,*
> Corpore ut exanimi *crudelia lumina pascas.*
> Si tamen, o superi, mortalia facta videtis,
> Este mei memores (nihil ultra lingua precari
> Sustinet) et longo facite ut narremur in aevo,
> Et, quae dempsistis vitae, date tempora famae!»
> *(Metamorphoses* XIV, 726-732)

If the scene described by Saint-Amant is the aftermath of the story of Iphis and Anaxarete, observed archeologically centuries later, it is not the actual aftermath narrated in Ovid, but rather the one specifically hoped for by Iphis just before his death, and Saint-Amant's 16-line description itself seems to fulfill the lover's prayer that his story, such as he perceives it, be "narrated" in the distant future.

Whether or not there is a real Ovidian reminiscence in these four strophes on castle ruins (and if so, whether or not Saint-Amant could count on his reader to recognize it), this scene clearly belongs with the two which follow it and which, as we have seen, are irrefutably Ovidian. All three center around various aspects of human existence: death (skeleton and shade), sleep (*Sommeil*) and love (Echo). And if the context of the specific Ovidian passages to which these last two strophes refer us is considered, then the three scenes are consistent in yet another way: all three are related to the tragedies of human love, both shared and unrequited. The poor lover (Iphis?) has committed suicide out of dispair and his heartless lady (Anaxarete?) is punished for her "rigueur" according to the terms of a "sentence épouventable" passed down by the gods; Sleep is described after an Ovidian passage in which the pious Ceyx has just died in a terrible sea storm, his faithful wife Alcyone is about to discover his body washed up on the shore, and both are to be transformed into sea birds whose conjugal fidelity had become exemplary in the Renaissance; Echo has dissolved into a mere voice by pining away for Narcissus who, as we know, also perished by dispair and inanition as punishment for heartlessness toward lovers.

The allusions contained within the interior "baroque" scenes of Part II now appear to be as consistent with each other as were the outdoor Renaissance scenes of Part I, while at the same time they are sharply differentiated from the latter, in respect to subject, setting and patterns of allusiveness, as well as to literary mode. The descriptions of Part II are characterized by the same kind of narrative undercurrent as those of Part I. But whereas Part I infused Golden Age *loci amoeni* with intimations of Iron Age crime, *hubris* and sacrilege, Part II infuses the no less conventional *loci horrendi* of more recent literature with echoes of exemplary human passion and tragic love.

The successive strophes of Parts I and II of *La Solitude* have been arranged in such a way as to trace a continuous descent: from the forest trees so tall they towered above the waters of the Deluge (strophe 1), we are led to sheer mountain cliffs (strophe 3), at the foot of which we find a valley and a rushing river whose torrents gradually become streams (strophe 4) and finally marshes (strophes 5-7). Part II prolongs this descent underground: we are transported to castle ruins, from the basement and fireplace of which (11. 106 and 109) we descend even farther to a vault directly beneath the ruins (strophe 12), and a grotto (strophe 13). As we have seen, this uninterrupted downward movement from mountain top to subterranean cave is articulated by an abrupt shift from outside to inside, from natural to human, from the Renaissance *locus amoenus* to its baroque avatar, and from intimations of sacrilege to intimations of passion.

Part III of *La Solitude* (strophes 14-17) contrasts with each of the preceding sections and with both together in that it is devoted not to landscapes but to seascapes. At the same time, this final section provides the poem with a strong sense of symmetry and closure. First of all, it marks an abrupt return from the interior depths of Part II to the outside, to the natural setting, and most noticeably, to the extreme heights of the beginning of Part I:

> Tantost, sortant de ces ruïnes,
> Je monte au haut de ce Rocher,
> Dont le sommet semble chercher
> En quel lieu se font les bruïnes.
> (11. 131-134)

From the summit of this sea cliff, the poem then retraces a downward movement exactly parallel to that of Parts I and II, descending to the base of the cliff (11. 135-140), whence the katabasis is transferred to the sea itself: violent storm waves are gradually calmed until the sea is perfectly flat in strophe 17. In the final line it appears that even the sun "s'est laissé tomber des Cieux" (1. 170). This curious solar image contained in the last line of Part III corresponds exactly to the poet's remark concerning the sun near the end of the first descent in Part II: that the underground vault is so dark that "quand Phebus y descendroit,/ Je pense qu'il n'y verroit goute" (11. 113-114). Part III, then, serves to close the frame around Part II by describing a symmetrical marine counterpart to the scenes of Part I, and at the same time it serves to close the poem as a whole by neatly recapitulating the entire downward movement of Parts I and II together. Even the articulation between Parts I and II is recapitulated in Part III. Strophes 14 and 15, like Part I, describe pristine nature, while strophe 16, like Part II, contains concrete vestiges of human existence, both cadavres and ruined artifacts. The rigorous symmetries created by Part III and their structural function as a recapitulatory and closural device will become even more evident as we discover that each of these four final strophes also functions semantically in precisely the same way that we have observed throughout the poem: by recourse to Ovidian allusions.

The high "Rocher" and "falaize escarpée" of strophe 14, which correspond both positionally and topographically to the "Monts pendans en precipices" of strophe 3, provide one of the clearest examples not only of the inadequacy and impertinence, but of the real harmfulness of biographical and realistic criticism.

> Tantost, sortant de ces ruïnes,
> Je monte au haut de ce Rocher,
> Dont le sommet semble chercher
> En quel lieu se font les bruïnes:
> Puis je descends tout à loisir,
> Sous une falaize escarpée,
> D'où je regarde avec plaisir
> L'onde, qui l'a presque sappée
> Jusqu'au siege de Palemon,
> Fait d'esponges, et de limon.
>
> (11. 131-140)

These are impressive and evocative lines. So much so that Gautier may perhaps be excused for claiming, in what is after all a polemical work, that "la nature y est étudiée immédiatement et non à travers les oeuvres des maîtres antérieurs." It is more difficult to excuse Françoise Gourier for claiming, in a strictly scholarly work, that "Saint-Amant peint avec sentiment et couleur le calme et la richesse de Belle-Isle. . . . Il décrit avec sensibilité les aspects divers et changeants de l'océan,"[20] and Jean Lagny for disagreeing with this identification and claiming on the basis of biographical data that in this strophe "nous avons devant les yeux ces falaises crayeuses du Pays de Caux, dont tous les ans les vagues font écrouler quelque pan."[21] The scene is actually neither Breton nor Norman, but Boeotian. It is in fact one of the most literal translations from Ovid to be found in the entire poem. The error of the Romantic reading appears even more serious when we note that the Ovidian lines Saint-Amant has chosen to incorporate into his poem at this point are precisely those which set the scene for the metamorphosis of Melicerta into the sea god Palaemon, who is mentioned by name at the end of this very strophe.

The story of Palaemon's metamorphosis is this: Juno is outraged because Bacchus, the illegitimate son of her faithless husband, has risen to such great power throughout the world, and in Thebes in particular. She can contain her wrath no longer when Semele's sister Ino boasts of her good fortune in having reared so great a god. Juno resolves to punish this *hubris* in a way reminiscent of the various punishments which Bacchus himself has inflicted on his victims. First, Ino's husband Athamas is seized by madness, and mistaking his wife and his infant son for a lioness and her cub, he snatches the smiling Learchus from his mother's arms, hurls him three times around his head like a sling, and dashes his head against a rock. Ino is in turn seized by a quasi-Bacchic frenzy, and just as her sister Agave was once made by Bacchus to destroy her miscreant son Pentheus, so she is now made by Juno to destroy her own innocent son Melicerta. But instead of lacerating and dismembering her son as Agave had done, Ino seizes the infant Melicerta in her arms and leaps with him from a high cliff into the Saronic Sea. Venus takes pity on them, and persuades Neptune to spare them both by transforming each into a new sea god. Ino becomes Leucothoë, and Melicerta becomes Palaemon.

Ovid interrupts his rapid narrative in mid-action in order to describe the cliff from which Ino is about to plunge. It is this description which Saint-Amant has translated, nearly word-for-word, in his first seascape:

> Inminet aequoribus scopulus: pars ima cavatur
> Fluctibus et tectas defendit ab imbribus undas,
> Summa riget frontemque in apertum porrigit aequor.
> (*Metamorphoses* IV, 525-527)

Saint-Amant's "Rocher" which is so high that it seems to "chercher/En quel lieu se font les bruïnes" is none other than Ovid's "scopulus" whose peak "tectas defendit ab imbribus undas." Saint-Amant's famous "falaize escarpée" which has been "presque sappée" by the sea is clearly none other than Ovid's, whose "pars ima cavatur/Fluctibus." And of course Saint-Amant's "siege de Palemon" is not merely a conventional metonymy for the sea, but like the Philomela of the corresponding strophe describing "Monts pendans en precipices" in Part I, it serves to recall for the literate reader a specific Ovidian narration by designating in explicit and unmistakable terms the story's *dénouement*.

The correlation between strophes 3 and 14 can now be appreciated in all its complexity. Both passages describe towering peaks. One of these is so high that it escaped the waters of the universal Deluge; the other is so high that its summit is to be found where the rains are made. There is a sheer drop from each summit: to the "precipices" of the first corresponds the "falaize escarpée" of the second.   Each is the site of a suicide leap: the first is described as inviting suicide, and would appear to be the peak from which Daedalion jumped when his daughter was slain for her *hubris* by Diana; the second is clearly the cliff from which Ino leaped when she was punished for her *hubris* by Juno.   To the metamorphosed Philomela-nightingale of strophe 3 corresponds the metamorphosed Melicerta-Palaemon of strophe 14.   These two metamorphoses are themselves very similar, and are narrated by Ovid in such a way as to recall one another: both are stories of marital infidelity, jealousy and genocide; the terms in which the innocent Learchus is described just before he is slaughtered by his father Athamas are nearly identical to those in which Itys is described just before he is murdered by his mother Procne; both Philomela and Melicerta are speechless victims, both are now inhabitants of nature's domain.   And finally, to the "Espine fleurie" on which Philomela is perched in strophe 3 correspond the "esponges" and "limon" which make up the "siege de Palemon" in strope 14.[22] The Ovidian borrowing in the first seascape strophe is obviously not an accidental or a surreptitious one.   The allusion serves to recall that of the corresponding strophe in Part I, and thereby to reinforce the poem's symmetry which has already been suggested by a striking similarity, on a literal level, between the topographical details of the two passages.

At the same time, the Ovidian reminiscence in this first seascape strophe functions in precisely the same way that all the preceding reminiscences have been observed to function.   Saint-Amant assumes that his reader's culture will be sufficient to allow him to recognize the traces of a cruel and violent narrative under the surface of what first appears to be a straight-forward and ingenuous description.   Once again Nature and solitude are made to recall past crimes of the human race, tranquillity to recall violence, and the descriptive mode in the present tense to suggest an implicit and simultaneous narrative in the past.

The following three strophes describe three different faces of the sea: the calming of the waves after a storm, the tireless pounding of breakers which wash flotsam up onto the shore, and dead calm.   The first of these (strophe 15) pictures the familiar process by which classical sea-storms are calmed:

> . . .les chevelus Tritons,
> Hauts sur les vagues secoüées,
> Frapent les Airs d'estranges tons
> Avec leurs trompes enroüées,
> Dont l'eclat rend respectueux
> Les vents les plus impetueux.
>
> (11. 145-150)

No one has ever claimed, as far as I know, that Saint-Amant actually observed Tritons blowing their conches off the coast of his native Normandy. But neither has anyone considered the possibility that these lines might refer to something more specific than a purely conventional archaicizing topos. To the reader who has Ovid well in mind, the allusion is more suggestive. These lines recall a famous storm which ends in the following way:

> Nec maris ira manet, positoque tricuspide telo
> Mulcet aquas rector pelagi supraque profundum
> Exstantem atque umeros innato murice tectum
> Caeruleum Tritona vocat conchaeque sonanti
> Inspirare iubet fluctusque et flumina signo
> Iam revocare dato: cava bucina sumitur illi,
> Tortilis in latum quae turbine crescit ab imo,
> Bucina, quae medio concepit ubi aera ponto,
> Litora voce replet sub utroque iacentia Phoebo;
> Tum quoque, ut ora dei madida rorantia barba
> Contigit et cecinit iussos inflata receptus,
> Omnibus audita est telluris et aequoris undis,
> Et quibus est undis audita, coercuit omnes.
>
> (*Metamorphoses* I, 330-342)

The storm in question here is of course that of the Deluge, by means of which Jupiter destroyed all but two members of the iniquitous race of Iron Age man. It can be no mere coincidence that this scene, in which the end of the Deluge is indirectly re-called, appears in a position corresponding to that of the direct allusion to the Deluge earlier in the poem. The second strophe of the landscape sequence (Part I) describes trees so high that they towered above the waters when "Jupiter ouvrit les Cieux/ Pour nous envoyer le Deluge" (11. 17-18). It is likewise in the second strophe of the seascape sequence (Part III) that we find the lines drawn from Ovid's description of the receding of the waters after that very same Deluge.

The last two strophes in the seascape sequence are less allusive. Strophe 16, in which drowned men, dead monsters, shattered ships, diamonds and ambergris are washed up on shore by an angry sea, may have been suggested by Ovid's story of Alcyone and Ceyx, where we read the longest (one hundred lines) and most impressive (as a direct challenge to *Aeneid* I) description of a sea-storm to be found in all the *Metamorphoses* and perhaps even in all classical literature. Alcyone tries to dissuade her husband from his proposed sea voyage to Claros by recalling vestiges of shipwrecks she has seen washed up on the Trachinian shore:

> Aequora me terrent et ponti tristis imago:
> Et laceras nuper tabulas in litore vidi
> Et saepe in tumulis sine corpore nomina legi.
> (*Metamorphoses* XI, 427-429)

And at the end of that story, following the terrible storm whose description is so gripping, she watches as her drowned husband's body, too, is washed ashore (11. 714-725).

But the allusiveness of this strophe seems to be more internal than Ovidian. Whereas the preceding strophe resembled those of the first section of the poem in which no concrete trace of human existence was anywhere to be seen, this strophe returns somewhat to the "baroque" inspiration of Part II: the shipwreck of this third seascape strophe corresponds positionally, thematically and in tone, to the ruined castle of the inland strophes; the drowned men here correspond to the hanging skeleton there; the diamonds correspond to the inscribed marble. Both passages describe vestiges of human existence and activity in an unmoved, unchanged natural setting, the first on land, the second at sea. Both suggest the transience and corruptibility of everything human in contrast to the immutability of everything natural. Whether on land or at sea, men become corpses and skeletons, the houses and ships they build to protect themselves against the elements are at length destroyed by those same elements, their treasures become *épaves*. The third strophe of Part III, in short, constitutes a virtual point-for-point transposition of the entire second section of the poem from the domain of the landscape to the domain of the seascape, both in regard to its detail and in regard to its broader implications.

While it functions as a kind of microcosm of Part II—and partly as a consequence of that fact—this third seascape strophe also functions as a negative counterpart to Part I, and to strophe 7 in particular. The latter, as we have seen, suggested a Golden Age setting by observing that "Nulle charrette, ny batteau" had ever passed over the waters of the "Marests paisible." But ships *have* passed over the angry waters of this post-Diluvian seascape, and traces of disaster are all that remain of those voyages. These few traces are nevertheless sufficient to indicate that the motive for travel here is identical to that which first drove Iron Age man to invent ships (that is, their *amor sceleratus habendi*), for among the flotsam of shattered ships and drowned sailors are found vestiges of the object of their voyages: diamonds and "mille autres choses de pris." It is clearly far less to the point to recognize in this strophe a description of Dieppe or Fécamp, as Saint-Amant's biographer is at pains to do, than it is to recognize the clear and meaningful contrast between this Iron Age wreckage on the one hand and the pristine and un-traveled waters of the Golden Age scene in strophe 7 on the other.

The following strophe (17) is the last of the seascape sec-tion, and the last of the poem properly speaking. Of the seven-teen descriptive strophes in *La Solitude,* this concluding one is surely one of those most apt to strike us as "modern":

> Tantost, la plus claire du monde,
> [l'onde] semble un miroir flottant,
> Et nous represente à l'instant
> Encore d'autres Cieux sous l'onde:
> Le Soleil s'y fait si bien voir,
> Y contemplant son beau visage,
> Qu'on est quelque temps à sçavoir
> Si c'est luy-mesme, ou son image,
> Et d'abord il semble à nos yeux
> Qu'il s'est laissé tomber des Cieux.
> (11. 161-170)

Images reflected in standing water, and the agreeable confusion resulting from the apparent identity between the object and its image, are indeed commonplace in early seventeenth-century literature. Cyrano de Bergerac, for example, devotes an entire *Lettre* to musings on "l'ombre que faisoient des arbres dans l'eau."[23] But Saint-Amant seems to have been one of the first writers in France, if not *the* first, to develop the possibilities for "baroque *engaño*" inherent in mirror reflections, and it is likely that this strophe strikes us today as "typical" of early seventeenth-century imagery precisely *because La Solitude* was so enormously and immediately successful, and *because* it inspired such numerous imitations. The familiar image of the sun in Tristan L'Hermite's *La Mer*, for example,

> Le Soleil à longs traits ardans
> Y donne encore de la grace,
> Et tasche à se mirer dedans
> Comme on feroit dans une glace,[24]

and a similar image in the same poet's *Le Miroir enchanté*,

> Tous les matins l'Astre du Monde
> Lors qu'il se leve en se mirant dans l'onde,
> Pense tout estonné voir un autre Soleil,[25]

are both clearly indebted to Saint-Amant's lines which preceded them by several years.

Even though the image of these lines of *La Solitude* may appear to *us* to be strictly "modern," and even though Saint-Amant may indeed have been the most influential popularizer, if not the actual inventor, of this sun and sea topos, the image nevertheless had a very Ovidian ring for the poem's first readers. The description of the sun and the sea itself cannot be found in the *Metamorphoses*, but the indulged confusion between an object and its reflection is quintessentially Ovidian: Saint-Amant invites us to observe the sun's reflection in exactly the same way that Ovid makes Narcissus observe his own. The sun of *La Solitude* "se fait voir" in the mirroring sea, "Y contemplant son beau visage," just as Ovid's Narcissus, as he is about to drink from the Boeotian pool, "visae correptus imagine formae,. . . Spectat inexpleto mendacem lumine formam" (*Metamorphoses* III, 416-439). When we first see the sun's reflection we are "quelque temps à sçavoir/Si c'est luy-mesme, ou son image," just as Narcissus at first "corpus putat esse quod umbra est," (1. 417) and "quid videat, nescit" (1. 430), persisting in his error (despite the narrator's attempts to disabuse his hero in a complaisant apostrophe: "Quod petis est nusquam. . . . Ista repercussae, quam cernis, imaginis umbra est," 11. 433-434) until some forty-seven lines later, when he suddenly cries: "Iste ego sum: sensi, nec me mea fallit imago" (1. 463). And just as we are first made to see "d'autres Cieux sous l'onde," and to believe that the sun "s'est laissé tomber des Cieux," so Narcissus at first believes that his lover is actually submerged in the pond:

> Inrita fallaci quotiens dedit oscula fonti,
> In mediis quotiens visum captantia collum
> Bracchia mersit aquis nec se deprendit in illis!
> (*Metamorphoses* III, 427-429)

Saint-Amant may have been the first to describe a calm sea in these terms, but the terms themselves, as well as their complaisant tone and the artificial paradox they elaborate, are all borrowed directly from the *Metamorphoses*.

The borrowing, moreover, is no more a theft, and no more arbitrary than are those of the preceding sixteen strophes. Like all the earlier Ovidian reminiscences, this one is functional and significant, and is meant to be recognized. We have seen how the preceding three strophes of Part III establish a strict pattern of symmetries and correspondences both in relation to the successive strophes of Part I and in relation to the combined movement of Parts I and II together, both on the level of literal content and on the level of related Ovidian allusions. This final strophe completes those patterns. Part II ends in Echo's grotto as the bodiless nymph repeats the notes of the poet's lute; Part III ends as Phoebus himself assumes the attitude of Echo's "Amant froid," contemplating his reflection in still water. This final image marks a last return from the intimations of sin and sacrilege of Part I to those of desperate love of Part II, and at the same time constitutes a perfect visual counterpart to the echoing lute music with which Part II ends.

The allusion to Narcissus in the very last lines of the descriptive portion of the poem has another purpose as well. Throughout the poem, the reader's familiarity with Ovid has been exploited in such a way as to allow this "fantasque tableau" to signify much more than merely the scenes it appears to describe. As I have frequently had occasion to observe, the allusions have thus far had two principal effects. The first is to accentuate the poem's explicit contrast between the domains of the natural and the human by means of multiple reminiscences of both Golden Age purity and Iron Age iniquity and passion. The ostensibly pristine nature of the *locus amoenus* has in fact been the scene of numberless acts of violence, sacrilege, passion and destruction, and this "solitude" is actually more populous than any urban cross-roads of the Ancien Régime. The second effect of the Ovidian allusions has been a corresponding tension on the level of poetic diction: every strophe, while it appears to be purely and absolutely descriptive, is subtended by an implicit but no less real narrative line. For the cultured seventeenth-century reader, each scene inevitably recalled an action-filled narration in the *Metamorphoses* for which it is either the obvious setting, or the no less obvious aftermath. This "peinture vivante" is virtually teaming with implicit action.

Yet all that remains of Iron Age violence and passion is this primeval forest and a few scattered ruins, and all that remains of Ovid's eventful narrations is a series of static scenes of which Saint-Amant's poem purports to be the "description." All humans have been metamorphosed and reintegrated into Nature while their concrete artifacts are subject to ruin and reassimilation into the natural landscape; and all narrations have culminated and been reabsorbed in a final moment of stasis. The last Ovidian allusion of *La Solitude* suggests this new perspective on the double tension which has run continuously throughout the poem. The descriptions end in a dead calm in which Nature itself is seen to take on the solitary, impassive and self-sufficient gaze of Narcissus. This final image thus provides an appropriate and satisfying end to the poem not only by completing the recapitulation and multiple symmetries of Part III, but by functioning emblematically to create an overwhelming impression of wholeness, completeness, stability and closure.

The highly literary nature of Saint-Amant's genius should now be apparent. *La Solitude* is a brilliant *tour de force* whose real subject is poetic convention.[26] The poem begins with all the conventional ear-marks of a Petrarchan love song but fails to become one. Instead, it follows the historical development of those ear-marks from the Renaissance *locus amoenus* to the baroque *locus horrendus* and back again. At the same time, it restores to the *locus amoenus* its original force of a Golden Age utopia, while simultaneously undercutting even this new restored value with clear intimations of Iron Age iniquity and passion. Pure description becomes virtual narrative; apparent randomness and open-endedness is organized into a highly ordered and closed structure. On every level the conventions of lyric are undercut in order to be infused with a vital and original force, which is in turn undercut, and so on, in what would appear to be an infinite process of lyric deconstruction.

The fundamental convention which serves as the point of departure for all this elaborate manipulation, as we have seen, is that of the solitary setting in which unrequited lovers seek solace from society and lament their fate in soliloquies. But in the *envoi* of the poem, the descriptions of the preceding seventeen strophes are retrospectively revalorized and placed in the context of a very different convention.[27] From this new perspective, nature's solitude is seen not as a refuge for lovers whose ladies refuse their favors, but is positively valorized as a place where the Muses grant their favors to poets:

> Je ne cherche que les deserts,
> Où rêvant tout seul, je m'amuse
> A des discours assez diserts
> De mon Genie avec la Muse
>   (11. 175-178)

The tradition behind this solitude of poets is as long and well-founded as that of the solitude of lovers. Horace, for example, invariably seeks nature's solitude in order to write his poetry:

Scriptorum chorus omnis amat *nemus* et fugit urbem.
(*Epistulae* II 2, 77)

Me doctarum hederae praemia frontium
Dis miscent superis, me *gelidum nemus*
Nympharumque leves cum Satyris chori
Secernunt populo.
(*Carmina* I 1, 29-32)

Vester, Camenae, vester in arduos
Tollor Sabinos, seu mihi frigidum
    Praeneste seu Tibur supinum
        Seu liquidae placuere Baiae.
Vestris amicum fontibus et choris
Non me Philippis versa acies retro
  . . .extinxit. . . .
(*Carmina* III 4, 21-27)

Following in the same tradition Du Bellay clearly states in the *Deffense et Illustration de la Langue Françoyse* that poetic *cogitatio* requires solitude:

Les uns ayment les fresches umbres des *forestz,* les clers *ruisselez* doucement murmurans parmy les *prez* ornez et tapissez de verdure. Les autres se delectent du secret des chambres et doctes estudes. Il faut s'accommoder à la saison et au lieu. Bien te veux-je avertir de *chercher la solitude et le silence amy des Muses.*[28]

Pontus de Tyard's "Solitaire" offers one of the clearest indications of the Renaissance valorization of solitude as the necessary condition for receiving a "fureur Poëtique." Ronsard, finally, most frequently opts for the first of Du Bellay's two kinds of poetic solitude. In a 1550 ode imitated from Horace, for example, he addresses Calliope in the following way:

C'est toy qui fais que j'aime les *fontaines*
Tout esloigné du vulgaire ignorant,
Tirant mes pas par les *roches* hautaines
Apres les tiens que je vais adorant.
. . . .
Dedans quel *Antre*, en que *desert* sauvage
Me guides-tu, et quel *ruisseau* sacré

> Fils d'un rocher, me sera doux breuvage
> Pour mieux chanter ta louange à mon gré?[29]

Another of Ronsard's odes develops the same Horatian theme in the same terms:

> En quel *bois* le plus separé
> Du populaire, et en quel *Antre*
> Prens-tu plaisir de me guider
> O Muse ma douce folie?
> . . . .
> Il me semble desja que j'erre
> Seul par les *Antres,* et qu'au fond
> D'une *solitaire vallée,*
> Je chante les divins honneurs. . .[30]

To his protectrice Marguerite de France, the poet observes that Apollo does not lead the dancing Muses through "les Citez presumptueuses," but rather

> . . .sur les *rives* reculées,
> Ou dessous l'abry des *vallées,*
> Ou dessous les *tertres* bossus,
> Ou entre les *forests* sauvages,
> Ou par le secret des *rivages,*
> Ou dans le *Antres* bien moussus.[31]

In the "Ode à Michel de L'Hospital," the Muses ask their father Jupiter to dub them

> . . .Princesses des *montagnes,*
> Des *antres,* des *eaux,* et des *bois,*
> Et que les *prez* et les *campagnes*
> Resonnent dessous nostre vois.[32]

The brief evocation of nature in these passages is identical to that of Ronsard's love poems quoted at the beginning of this chapter. But as their genealogy shows, these scenes had come to be perceived as belonging to a separate convention altogether. One convention comes down to the Pléiade from Greek lyric poets through Horace, while the other comes by way of a more continuous tradition through Theocritus, Vergil, Petrarch,

Ariosto and countless epigones. The solitude in which poets commune with the Nine Sisters and receive their *furor poeticus* (Du Bellay's solitude of *cogitatio*) may resemble in every external respect the solitude in which lovers exile themselves in order to seek solace and lament the cruelty of their ladies, but these solitudes are valorized by the poems in which they appear as two entirely different phenomena. No poet, and least of all a poet of the French Renaissance, ever confused the two.

In revalorizing the solitude described in the preceding strophes, the *envoi* of *La Solitude* plays on precisely this sameness within difference.[33] The new perspective on the preceding strophes indeed finds a rather curious corroboration within the descriptions themselves. We remember, for example, that in strophe 2 the trees were described as being so tall that they towered above the waters of the Deluge. Saint-Amant does not identify the precise location of this scene, but the Ovidian allusion allows his reader to do so. We know without being told that Deucalion and Pyrrha survived the flood in Phocis, between Boeotia and the fields of Mount Oeta, on a high mountain whose peaks reach the clouds:

> Separat Aonios Oetaeis Phocis ab arvis,
> . . . .
> Mons ibi verticibus petit arduus astra duobus,
> *Nomine Parnasos*, supcrantque cacumina nubes.
> Hic. . .Deucalion. . .
> Cum consorte tori parva rate vectus adhaesit.
> (*Metamorphoses* I, 313-319)

The second strophe of the poem, then, contains a clear hint that the scene described here is none other than the mountain home of the Muses. Recognition of Parnassus in this description should not escape even a modern reader, since the very first words to be read in the volume containing *La Solitude* are the following, addressed by the poet to the Duc de Retz:

> Monseigneur,
>
> Je me suis souvent estonné comme parmy tant de grands Esprits qui ont pris plaisir à tirer de l'ancienne Poësie, des preceptes pour enrichir la Philosophie Morale, pas-un n'ait remarqué ce qui se peut

> dire de l'aventure de Deucalion et de Pirrhe, lesquels se sauverent
> de l'inondation generale de toute la Terre sur le *mont Parnasse,*
> *qui seul fut respecté du Deluge.* Cela ne fait-il pas voir clairement,
> Monseigneur, que ceux qui ayment les Lettres ne perissent jamais?
> (*Oeuvres* I, 11)

The following strophe contains a similar allusion to Mount
Parnassus. I have suggested that a seventeenth-century reader
would be most likely to recognize the "Monts pendans en precipices" as the scene of Daedalion's suicidal leap and subsequent
metamorphosis into a hawk. That leap, according to Ovid, was
from the summit of Parnassus:

> Effugit ergo omnes veloxque cupidine leti
> *Vertice Parnasi* potitur; miseratus Apollo,
> Cum se Daedalion saxo misisset ab alto,
> Fecit avem. . .
> (*Metamorphoses* XI, 338-341)

La Solitude describes a solitude of poets in another way
too: not only by virtue of an implicit identification with Mount
Parnassus in the second and third strophes of the poem, but also
as a secondary consequence of the implicit identification of all
the scenes in Part I as descriptions of the Golden Age. The
Golden Age, as the poem itself reminds us, is the epoch of
Saturn's reign; Saturn, as two thousand years of scientific tradition tell us, governs the melancholic humor; and melancholy,
as an equally long literary tradition tells us, is the poet's humor.
References to the Golden Age, then, in addition to their primary
meaning I have discussed above, conspire to reinforce the valorization of what is now seen to be a "solitude of poets" as a place
of poetic melancholy.

But while the double nature of Saint-Amant's solitude is
everywhere implicit in the descriptions themselves, the two
perspectives on these "same" scenes are placed in striking contrast. When the very first line of strophe 1 is repeated textually
at the end of the *envoi,* it appears not so much to recapitulate,
frame and close the poem, as to mark a new beginning, a departure in another direction. While the solitude announced in
the first strophe was unequivocally a refuge for the love-lorn:

O que j'ayme la Solitude!
Que ces lieux sacrez à la Nuit,
Esloignez du monde et du bruit,
Plaisent à mon inquietude!
(11. 1-4)

the same solitude in the last strophe of the *envoi* is unequivocally
a place of poetic inspiration:

O que j'ayme la Solitude!
C'est l'Element des bons Esprits,
C'est par elle que j'ay compris
L'Art d'Apollon sans nulle estude.
(11. 191-194)

It is as if these very similar quatrains belonged to two utterly
different poems—one a Petrarchan elegy and the other an Horatian ode—even though they are both equally appropriate to the
scenes they frame.

The speaker, too, undergoes a correspondingly radical
change of identity in the *envoi*: he is no longer presented as the
Petrarchan lover he was in the first strophe of the poem ("solo e
pensoso"), but rather as Cesare Ripa's emblematic figure repre-
senting the humor "melancholy" and the element "earth"
("Malenconico par la Terra"):

> Huomo di color fosco, che. . .tenghi con la sinistra mano un
> libro aperto mostrando di studiare. . . . Il libro aperto, e
> l'attentione del studiare, dimostra il malenconico esser dedito alli
> studii, e in essi far progresso; fugendo l'altrui conversationi; onde
> Horatio nell' ultima Epistola del 2. lib. dice: «Scriptorum chorus
> omnis amat nemus et fugit Urbes.»[34]

Having observed the perfect ambivalence which Saint-
Amant has conferred upon his "solitude," we must consider
more closely the nature and meaning of this double valorization.
Since the scenes which were initially presented as a solitude of
lovers now appear to be a solitude of poets, then what we first
observed to be places *in* literature—both *loci amoeni* of Renaissance and baroque love lyric and, simultaneously, specific *loci*
from Ovid—must now be seen as places *of* literature: the settings

in which, according to convention, all such poetry is actually conceived. And consequently, the scenes which appeared in the first seventeen strophes to be the *subject* of the poem, now appear to be the *condition* of its very existence.

This observation calls for three remarks. First of all, the usual function of the *envoi* is to reinforce the closure of a poem by designating the now ended lyric portion of the work from outside the "poem" itself, as a complete and completed artifact. It frames, defines and concludes by means of a simple shift in frame of reference. But while the *envoi* of *La Solitude* appears to function in this way, refering back to the preceding descriptions as a "fantasque tableau/Fait d'une peinture vivante" (11. 173-174), its real effect is precisely the opposite. From the very first word of the *envoi*, nature's impassive solipsism, as well as that of the solitary describer and that of his descriptive mode of discourse, is dramatically shattered. From the final image of narcissistic stasis and solitude, the poem brings us abruptly back to the domain of the human, the societal, the temporal, the discursive: "Alcidon. . .Reçoy ce fantasque tableau." This intrusion of the world and its commerce into the still solitude of nature is violent and shocking. Far from reinforcing the closure of the preceding lines, the *envoi* brutally violates the tone, the content and the formal unity of everything that precedes it. We may now add the *envoi* to the growing list of literary conventions which are undercut in *La Solitude*.

And yet once this intrusion has been made, it brings with it its own internal justification, and is in fact manipulated in such a way as to provide the entire poem with an ending ultimately more stable and satisfying than the one which its very existence so brutally destroys. The three final strophes of the poem are devoted almost entirely to the familiar notion that solitude is the necessary condition for poetic creation:

> Je ne cherche que les deserts,
> Où révant tout seul, je m'amuse
> A des discours assez diserts
> De mon Genie avec la Muse.
> (11. 175-178)

O que j'ayme la Solitude!
C'est l'Element des bons Esprits,
C'est par elle que j'ay compris
L'Art d'Apollon sans nulle estude.
(11. 191-194)

But by addressing himself to another, and by making a gift of the lines which precede, the poet necessarily re-enters the world and its commerce which he had fled in line 3. In the very process of doing so, he obliterates his own solitude which, according to the terms of the *envoi* itself, is the condition *sine qua non* for poetic creation. The poem *must* end here, because it has effectively prevented its own continuation.

The last strophe of the *envoi* elaborates and illustrates the consequences of this interruption which are inherent in its very first word. The new context within which the first line of the poem is reproduced ("O que j'ayme la Solitude!") is a societal one in which the poet has already confessed that to "discours assez diserts/De [son] Genie avec la Muse" he prefers Alcidon's "entretien" (11. 177-180). His reasons for loving solitude have now been modified accordingly. It is no longer as "lieux. . .Esloignez du monde et du bruit" (11. 2-3) that solitude is sought by the speaker, but as the "Element des bons Esprits" (1. 192) of which Alcidon himself is one:

Je l'ayme pour l'amour de toy,
Connoissant que ton humeur l'ayme,
(11. 195-196)

The last four lines of the poem, in the guise of a palinode, serve merely to state in explicit terms the paradox of a shared solitude, and to resolve the tension between solitude and society in favor of the latter, at the expense of the poem itself:

Mais quand je pense bien à moy,
Je la hay pour la raison mesme;
Car elle pourroit me ravir
L'heur de te voir, et te servir.
(11. 197-200)

Readers too often overlook the fact that the poet of *La Solitude* ends by rejecting in no uncertain terms the very solitude whose praises he has been singing. Yet this is a most crucial point, for the poem ends by creating the fiction of being abandoned by its poet, who leaves solitude (and consequently his Daemon, and consequently his poem), to re-enter the *monde* and its *bruit*, in short, to "*servir.*" Poetry ends at the very point that the speaker returns to "real life." By creating this fiction, moreover, the poem functions as a perfectly self-destructive artifact: having destroyed its *subject* (solitude) with the introduction of the world and others, and having destroyed the necessary *condition* for its prolongation (solitude), the poem ends with the destruction of its own fictional *creator* (the solitary poet), by making him abandon his poetic solitude in order to become a courtier.

The second remark to be made concerning the re-evaluation of solitude in the *envoi* is that if the solitude of lovers and the solitude of poets is in fact one and the same, then the conventional claims regarding inspiration made in the *envoi* take on a very different meaning from the one usually attributed to them. The virtuosity of the entire poem has consisted in its manipulation of the *locus amoenus* as a strictly literary convention. Now, if the places *of* literature (the solitude of poetic inspiration) are actually nothing more than places *in* literature (the conventions and topoi of 2000 years of poetry), then this is as much as to say that the poet receives his inspiration not in the woods, but in poetry—not in *Nature* but in *Art,* whether Ovid's, Petrarch's, Ronsard's or any other. In appearing ingenuously and spontaneously to slip from one convention to another, then, Saint-Amant has in fact ingeniously and artfully undercut both. When poets claim to seek solitude for their poetic inspiration, the poem tells us, the solitude they mean is that which they find in poems written by others. The *furor poeticus,* in other words, is pure sham. One of the most delightful external ironies of *La Solitude* is that by providing the model for decades of such fervent imitation, it provides a perfect illustration of the very process it exposes. For how many poets was Saint-Amant the principal Daemon! And how many poets came to *La Solitude,* rather than to their own "solitude," for their inspiration!

The third and final point to be noted is that while the "solitude of poets" is a convention as old as the Western Tradition itself, the particular terms chosen by Saint-Amant for the elaboration of the topos of solitary inspiration are undoubtedly meant to have more specific associations as well. The ideas and the vocabulary of all but the last four lines of the *envoi* are those of the Pléiade. The "Genie," the "Muse," the "fureur," the "Demon qui m'a transporté," all recall a theory of poetry which Ronsard and Du Bellay had brought back into common use, and on which Ronsard in particular had built his reputation. Even expressions like "une peinture vivante," which we now tend to perceive as particularly characteristic of Saint-Amant, were for Saint-Amant's first readers immediately recognizable as borrowings from the Pléiade. Poets, we read in Ronsard, "cognoissent la peinture/De ce grand Monde;" they are "Vrais peintres de la Nature."[35] Du Bellay, too, contrasts his humbler role in the *Regrets* to the higher inspiration of other poets, whom he addresses as "Vous autres . . . peintres de la nature."[36] And though we may think of lines like "j'ay compris/L'Art d'Apollon sans nulle estude" as typical of Saint-Amant and his *libertin* friends, contemporaries were bound to read them as imitations of Ronsard, in whose poetry abound passages like the following:

> Un *Démon* les accompaigne
> Par-sur tous le mieux instruit,
> Qui en songes toute la nuit
> *Sans nul travail les enseigne.*[37]

> «Elle [la fureur] de toutes vertus pleine,
> De mes secrets vous remplira,
> Et en vous les accomplira
> *Sans art, sans sueur* ne *sans peine.*»
> . . . .
> Vindrent les Poëtes divins:
> Divins, d'autant que la nature
> *Sans art* librement exprimoient,
> *Sans art* leur naïve escriture
> *Par la fureur* ils animoyent.[38]

In fact, the very passage of *La Solitude* which makes the most uncompromising claims to complete freedom of inspiration are those which are most clearly copied right out of the work of Du Bellay. The following lines have invariably been read by modern critics as a "sincere" profession of poetic freedom:

> Tantost chagrin, tantost joyeux,
> Selon que la fureur m'enflame,
> Et que l'objet s'offre à mes yeux,
> Les propos me naissent en l'ame.

They are actually an unmistakable transposition of a quatrain in two sonnets by France's greatest champion of imitation:

> Je ne peins mes tableaux de si riche peinture,
> Et si hauts argumens ne recherche à mes vers,
> Mais suivant de ce lieu les accidents divers
> Soit de bien, soit de mal, j'escris à l'adventure.
> *(Les Regrets* 1, 11. 5-8)

> Si j'escry quelquefois, je n'escry point d'ardeur,
> J'escry naïvement tout ce qu'au coeur me touche,
> Soit de bien, soit de mal, comme il vient à la bouche,
> En un stile aussi lent, que lente est ma froideur.[39]
> *(Les Regrets* 21, 11. 5-8)

By imitating from the champion of imitation a claim to spontaneous composition which itself was merely imitated convention, Saint-Amant extends his irony to yet another victim. The "theory" of poesis exposed at the end of *La Solitude* is clearly not to be taken at face value, but is to be understood on the contrary as a mocking jibe directed against all those who have adopted it in earnest, and most especially against that group of poets most responsible for the abuse of this and of all the other conventions undone throughout the poem: the Pléiade.

By leaving solitude and nature at the end of *La Solitude,* and by returning to "l'altrui conversationi," as Ripa puts it, the poet turns his back not only on the poem itself and on an age-old conception of literary creation, but on a consistent and conventional poetic *persona* as well. As the poem ends, an entire tradition whose culmination in France was the work of Ronsard, is left to consume itself in an elaborate act of self-destruction, while the figure of the poet himself leaves behind him these places *in* literature (Renaissance and baroque *loci amoeni* and Ovidian *loci*), places *of* literature (the solitude of poets, Parnassus and Saturn's reign), Petrarchan love, the Horatian ode, and the Classical-Renaissance mask of the *malenconico* poet. The work ends, in effect, with the rejection and destruction of all the conventions of which it is composed.

This astonishing poem, in which the lyric tradition is manipulated in such a way as to make it consume itself together with the manipulating poem itself, is Saint-Amant's first—his "noble coup d'essay" as he himself was later to call it. Where was the poet to go from here? The virtuoso performance of *La Solitude,* by its very nature, could not be repeated: the next poem either had to mark a palinodic return to the worn old conventions which the poet, then in his mid-twenties, had so completely mastered and utterly debunked, or to continue the impetus of the first work by inventing a new poetic mode to replace the rejected one.

The chronology of Saint-Amant's early works cannot be determined with complete certainty. It is generally accepted that the next poem to be written was *La Jouyssance,* and that works like *La Naissance de Pantagruel, Le Fromage, La Berne, Chanson à boire* and *La Desbauche* followed in rapid succession during the years between 1620 and 1623. In many of these poems we can observe the elaboration of a poetic mode entirely different from that of *La Solitude,* and of the singularly un-Romantic persona for which Saint-Amant has become famous: that of the spontaneous, sociable and tipsy libertine, "le bon Gros Saint-Amant." A typical example of this new poetic mode will be considered in detail in the next chapter. It should simply be observed here that the gradual elaboration of this new poetic persona is entirely consistent with—and perhaps in part a result of—the stance adopted in *La Solitude.* As modern readers, we readily perceive the relation between the final rejection of solitude and re-entry into society with which the first poem ends, and the convivial tavern poetry of "le bon Gros." Saint-Amant's readers saw a much more compelling relation. For the perfectly conventional *melancholia* rejected in *La Solitude* was substituted an equally conventional humor in the following poems. In Cesare Ripa's emblematic representation of the "Sanguigno per l'Aria" we recognize the description, accurate to the smallest detail, of the mask which Saint-Amant was to adopt in his later poems:

> Un giovane allegro, ridente, con una ghirlanda di varii fiori in capo, di corpo carnoso, e oltre i capelli biondi haverà il color della faccia rubicondo misto con bianco, e che sonando un leuto dia signo con rivolgere gl'occhi al Cielo, che gli piaccia il suono, e il canto, da una parte d'essa figura vi sarà un montone, tenendo in bocca un grappo d'uva e da l'altra banda vi sarà un libro di musica aperto. . . .

> Il montone con il grappo d'uva, significa il sanguigno esser dedito à Venere, e à Bacco.[40]

Saint-Amant's familiar trademark is for modern readers an effect of autobiographical candor in a poet without craft. For Saint-Amant's contemporaries it was one more element in a perfectly coherent, highly literary—and thoroughly Jovial—opposition to the Saturnine poetry and poetics of the Pléiade.

CHAPTER II:
LE FROMAGE

Fecundi calices quem non fecere disertum?
—Horace

Ars casum simulat
—Ovid

With the dubious advantage of hindsight, we tend to think of Saint-Amant first and foremost as "le bon Gros" whose most "characteristic" works are about food and wine. But this perspective is completely skewed. Bacchic and culinary poems are indeed numerous in the poet's works, but the dates and manner of their publication indicate that the real importance of such poems in Saint-Amant's *oeuvre* is very different from the one popularly imagined. *Le Fromage* (1621-1622), *La Desbauche* (1623-1624), *Les Cabarets* (1626), *Chanson à boire* (1626-1627), *La Vigne* (1627), and *La Naissance de Pantagruel* (?) were all published in the *Oeuvres* of 1629, but grouped together at the back of the volume with "realistic" and invective poems under the heading *Raillerie à Part*, as if to disassociate them from the more "serious" and elevated works whose inspiration is lyric (*La Solitude, Le Contemplateur*, etc.), heroic (*L'Arion, L'Andromède*, etc.), satiric (*Les Visions*) or gallant (*La Nuict, Elégie à Damon, La Jouyssance*, etc.), all of these poems being more elevated in style and "classical" in spirit. The *Suitte des Oeuvres*, published two years later in 1631, consists almost entirely[1] of works written in the vein of those pieces apologetically relegated to the back of the first volume. Almost all of these new poems are about eating and drinking: *Les Goinfres* (1628), *La Crevaille* (1630), *Le Melon* (?) and *Orgye* (?). The *Seconde Partie des Oeuvres* did not appear until 12 years after the *Suitte*, in 1643. This is the first collection to integrate all of Saint-Amant's poetic registers from gallant to invective. But of the 31 pieces included, only *four* are gastronomic: *Le Cantal* (1635), *Le Cidre* (1635),

Les Pourveus bachiques (1641) and *L'Epistre à Monsieur le Baron de Melay* (1642). The *Troisiesme Partie des Oeuvres* (1649) and the *Dernier Recueil* (1658) contain no such works at all; nor is a single one published separately in the years from 1644 to 1661.

The content and organization of the successive volumes of collected works published in 1629, 1631 and 1643 suggest the following conclusions: (1) Saint-Amant initially thought that he could make a name for himself as a "serious" poet, and published his poems of debauchery only in a rather tentative way, carefully separating them from what he considered to be his most important work. (2) The success of these half-condemned poems was so overwhelming that the poet was led to publish a second volume, only two years after the appearance of the first, consisting almost entirely of just such works. (3) Having nearly exhausted the poetic possibilities of the genre, having fully exploited it for the notoriety it could win him, and perhaps fearing that his poetic reputation would become exclusively associated with what he considered to be a minor vein of his own inspiration (and here it must be recalled that his first published work was *L'Arion,* and that he had already formed the project for an epic poem entitled *Les Travaux de Sanson* and a second epic which he thought would be his masterpiece, *Le Moÿse Sauvé*), Saint-Amant included only four gastronomic poems in the larger collection published twelve years later in 1643. Gastronomic and Bacchic poetry appears almost to have been an accident in Saint-Amant's poetic career, an unpremeditated formula for success which was intensely exploited during the mere six years between 1626 and 1631, and quickly abandoned thereafter.

Nor did Saint-Amant begin his poetic career as "le bon Gros." He developed his persona gradually and *became* "le bon Gros" only through the poems themselves. The historical anecdote behind this famous epithet is related in the *Historiettes* of Tallemant des Réaux. The Count of Harcourt, Tallemant reports, "avoit fait une confrerie de Monosyllabes, c'est ainsy qu'ils l'appelloient, où chascun avoit une epithete, comme luy s'appelloit *le Rond* (il est gros et court), Faret *le Vieux,* c'est pourquoy Saint-Amant l'appelle tousjours ainsy; pour luy, il se nommoit *le Gros.*"[2]   The epithet does not actually appear in

Saint-Amant's poetry until the *Chanson à boire,* written in 1626 or 1627 (*Oeuvres* I, 278), and can be found in only one other poem of the entire 1629 collection, that being the famous sonnet which begins "Me voyant plus frisé qu'un gros Comte Allemant" (*Oeuvres* I, 283).   What is more astonishing still is that the epithet is used only *once* in all the gastronomic poems of the *Suitte des Oeuvres* published two years later: in the last line of *Le Melon* the poet refers to himself as the "bon gros Saint-Amant" (*Oeuvres* II, 31).[3]   It is not until the *Seconde Partie des Oeuvres* (1643), from which poems on food and wine have all but disappeared, that we find the epithet used with any frequency or consistency at all.   The first poem in which the poet's nickname seems to have become a functional literary trademark is *Le Passage de Gibraltar* (1636-1638).   Here the poet retrospectively predicts the outcome of a naval skirmish "comme un bon gros Tirésie" (*Oeuvres* II, 183).   In the *Epistre au Baron de Melay* (1642) Saint-Amant actually refers to the epithet as his "titre" (*Oeuvres* II, 249), indicating once again that "le bon Gros" has by now become a universally recognizable trademark.   Similar uses of Saint-Amant's "title" are to be found in the *Epistre héroï-comique* (1644), where he retains his epithet even as an epic poet—"ton gros Virgile" (*Oeuvres* III, 94)—in the *Epistre au Baron de Villarnoul* (1646; *Oeuvres* III, 133), and in the *Epistre diversifiée* (1647), where he represents himself at the court of Queen Louise-Marie of Poland as "le gros Saint-Amant-sky" (*Oeuvres* III, 203).

Two rather astonishing conclusions must be drawn from Saint-Amant's use of his "title."   One is that outside a small circle of friends whose center was the Confrérie des Monosyllabes, Saint-Amant was not known as "le bon Gros" until 1636 at the earliest—that is, until well after the publication of almost all of his gastronomic poems.   Clearly, he does not write poems about food and wine *as* "le bon Gros;" on the contrary, he is able to adopt the epithet as a functional literary trademark *because* he has already become famous for his gastronomic poetry.   Secondly, we must observe that the trademark was most frequently used not in gastronomic poems, which Saint-Amant had long since abandoned, but primarily in his *caprices* and *épistres héroï-comiques* on political subjects, written between 1644 and 1647.

The author of *Le Fromage,* then, must not be thought of as "le bon gros Saint-Amant," or as the libertine poet of debauchery and gluttony we picture him to be on the basis of his later works. He is still the twenty-seven-year-old virtuoso who has proved his mastery of the tradition and the craft of poetry in *La Solitude,* who has just written or is about to write the elegant and erotic *Jouyssance,* the earnest and admiring ode "A Théophile," the brilliant and ironic *Arion,* and the Ovidian heroic poems *L'Andromède* and *La Métamorphose de Lyrian et de Sylvie.* These circumstances lead us to wonder why such an ironic and refined young poet, all of whose earliest work was written in an elevated or middle style, suddenly chose to write a poem whose inspiration is Bacchic and Epicurean, whose style is unabashedly low, and whose control is ostensibly nil. Was *Le Fromage* simply dashed off during a vacation from the intense labor required to compose complex little masterpieces like *La Solitude* and *L'Arion?* Or was this an experiment in an entirely new kind of poetry?

We must take care not to overestimate the originality of a poem like *Le Fromage,* at least as far as its external characteristics are concerned. Saint-Amant was by no means the first poet to write a hyperbolic poem in praise of food. In Italy, Berni had written a poem about peaches, and the Bernesque poet Lasca had written two about melons.[4] The gastronomic panegyric had already been imported to France by Annibal de Lortigue, who in 1617 published a similar poem in praise of cheese, "L'Hymne du fromage."[5] The Bacchic inspiration of Saint-Amant's poem of course has an even longer history. The tone of the work owes more to Rabelais than to the Bernesque poets, and it is perhaps significant that the dipsodic value of old cheese can be traced directly to the Pantegrueline books themselves. As for the idea of a vinous dramatic monologue, which might first strike us as particularly manneristic or libertine, the device can be traced back at least as far as Tibullus (III 6).

As for the apparent disorder of the poem, we must be equally cautious. It is true that the speaker wanders wildly from subject to subject in his drunken tirade, interrupts himself twice, and even loses sight of his subject altogether at one point. Yet several patterns and symmetries quickly emerge from this apparent disorder, which even a superficial reading cannot fail to note:

1.   Near the beginning of his harangue, the speaker addresses the following apostrophe to his cheese:

> O doux Cottignac de Baccus,
> Fromage, que tu vaux d'escus!
> Je veux que ta seule memoire
> Me provoque à jamais à boire.
>   (11. 13-16)

These same words appear again at the very end of the poem (11. 121-124).

2.   A long and rambling mythological digression on Apollo and Mercury is broken off by a four-line apostrophe at the exact center of the poem (11. 61-64 of the 124-line poem). The second half of the work ends with a shorter but parallel mythological digression on Jupiter and Io.

3.   The oration proper begins with the following exhortation:

> A genoux Enfans desbauchez,
> Chers confidents de mes pechez,
> Sus! qu'à plein gosier on s'escrie
> Beny soit le terroir de Brie.
>   (11. 17-20)

The second half of the speech begins with a very similar exhortation, two lines of which are actually identical to those of the first beginning:

> Encore un coup, donc Compagnons,
> Du bon Denys les vrais mignons,
> Sus! qu'à plein gosier on s'escrie
> Beny soit le terroir de Brie.
>   (11. 65-68)

The strictly symmetrical arrangement of these parallel passages and literal repetitions is sufficient to warn us, even after a hasty first reading, that if the speaker of the poem has lost control of his speech, Saint-Amant has by no means lost control of his poem. As was the case in *La Solitude*, the impression of random disorder in *Le Fromage* is generated from a basic structure whose logic and clarity are, if anything, excessively schematic.

These symmetrical patterns in the poem are extremely puzzling. In neither wine nor dialectic is there to be found an intrinsic ordering principle which could possibly serve as a substitute for *dispositio*, and the combination of wine and dialectic in fact allows for utter anarchy, the *Symposium* notwithstanding. How, then, is it possible for the extemporized monologue of a drunk, in which the speaker himself loses his subject, and which is interrupted by external interventions over which the speaker has absolutely no control whatsoever, to fall into a pattern whose order and logic are so rigorous? The speaker's perspective is resolutely pro-spective and anti-teleological: he reels from one thought to the next without any clear idea of where he is going or how he will end. The order and symmetry of the poem itself, on the other hand, betray a retro-spective and teleological view, an arrangement of parts from the perspective of the end. The tension between disorder and order, between the fiction of the poem's process and the reality of its form, is enormous. Having cursorily observed the poem's symmetry as a static quality of its final form, let us now consider in more detail the manner of its gradual unfolding in the dynamic process of the speech.

The setting for this dramatic monologue is established in the first five lines of the poem:

> Assis sur le bord d'un chantier
> Avec des gens de mon mestier,
> C'est à dire avec une trouppe
> Qui ne jure que par la Couppe,
> Je m'escrie en laschant un rot. . .

These lines serve as a "frame" for the rest; they narrate the circumstances and the context of the quoted speech which follows. Beginning with line 6, the poetic voice is that of the tippler speaking out loud to his drinking companions. The presence of an audience is maintained indirectly by the speaker's use of the vocative and the second person imperative:

> A genoux Enfans desbauchez,
> Chers confidents de mes pechez,
> Sus!
>
> (11. 17-19)

and the events of the dramatic situation are no longer narrated, but implicit in the speaker's reactions as they are expressed in the speech itself. We know, for example, that the speaker has first bitten into the cheese when in line 9 he breaks out into ecstatic ejaculations about its flavor:

> O Dieu! quel manger precieux!
> Quel goust rare et delicieux!
> Qu'au prix de luy ma fantaisie
> Incague la saincte Ambroisie!
>
> (11. 9-12)

From the very beginning of *Le Fromage*, then, two levels of discourse are clearly established: one on which written words are addressed to absent readers, and a second—reported from within the first—on which spoken words are addressed to present listeners. This perfectly ordinary way of introducing direct discourse in a narrative setting is so clear and unambiguous that the reader is not in the least confused by the absence of quotation marks which one might expect to find setting off the speech from its frame.

Less clear and unambiguous, however, is the introduction, from within the quoted speech itself, of yet a third level of discourse, one on which the present listeners are asked to join the speaker in a chorus of respectful praise:

> A genoux Enfans desbauchez,
> Chers confidents de mes pechez,
> Sus! qu'à plein gosier on s'escrie
> Beny soit le terroir de Brie,
> Beny soit son plaisant aspect,

Qu'on n'en parle qu'avec respect,
Que ses fertiles pasturages
Soient à jamais exempts d'orages. . .
(11. 17-24)

There are several curious things about the implied quotation-within-a-quotation of this passage. One is that the new, third level of discourse is introduced by an exhortation which closely echoes the "frame's" introduction to the speech:

Je m'escrie en laschant un rot (1. 5)
. . .qu'à plein gosier on s'escrie (1. 19)

Another is that the choral chant itself begins by echoing the direct discourse of the speech which contains it:

Beny soit l'excellent Bilot (1. 6)
Beny soit le terroir de Brie (1. 20)

Near the beginning of the actual *speech,* then, we find an exact replica of the movement, and a very close approximation of the diction, of the beginning of the *poem.* The three levels of discourse, in other words, seem to form a series of quotations *en abîme:*

1. Poem
Assis sur le bord d'un chantier   (first level)
Avec des gens de mon mestier,

. . . .
Je m'escrie en laschant un rot:
    «*Beny soit* l'excellent Bilot. . .   (second level)

2. Speech
«A genoux Enfans desbauchez,
Chers confidents de mes pechez,
Sus! *qu'à plein gosier on s'escrie:*
    « «*Beny soit* le terroir de Brie. . .» »   (third level)
    (quotation marks and italics added)

While the three levels of discourse are adequately identified by the text itself, the numerous structural, semantic and phonic parallels between the poem (level 1) and the speech (level 2) are perhaps confusing enough to justify the use of quotation marks to help the reader maintain the distinction between two kinds of discourse which, despite their many resemblances, are radically different in status, one being written on a page, the other being declaimed amid the tumultuous din of a tavern.

But Saint-Amant does not offer this assistance to his readers. What is more, he makes the editorial addition of quotation marks utterly impossible by failing to provide a clear indication of the *end* of the choral chant:

> Sus! qu'à plein gosier on s'escrie:
> Beny soit le terroir de Brie,
> Beny soit son plaisant aspect,
> Qu'on n'en parle qu'avec respect,
> Que ses fertiles pasturages
> Soient à jamais exempts d'orages:
> Que Flore avec ses beaux atours. . .
> (11. 19-25)

Does this entire litany of territorial beatitudes belong to the quotation-within-a-quotation which is to be repeated by the assembled listeners? Or does the choral chant consist only of the two lines beginning with the word "Beny," in which case the line "Qu'on n'en parle qu'avec respect" would belong to the series of exhortations pronounced by the speaker alone· "Sus! qu'à plein gosier on s'escrie,. . .qu'on n'en parle qu'avec respect . . ." The predominant use of hortatory subjunctives on both the second ("Beny soit l'excellent Bilot") and third ("Beny soit le terroir de Brie") levels of discourse make it all the more difficult to determine the precise status of the hortatory subjunctives appearing throughout this passage. We know that the quotation is closed *somewhere,* for we eventually encounter a first-person singular pronoun ("Mais *je* veux l'encharger aussi," 1. 41). But it is impossible to determine precisely *where.* It would seem that Saint-Amant has deliberately blurred the distinction between two separate levels of his text—that of the speech (level 2) and that of the choral chant (level 3).

As the work progresses, a similar blurring occurs involving the first and second levels of discourse. Before he has abandoned his ambiguous hortatory subjunctives, the speaker launches into a long digression, occasioned by his desire to place the cows of Brie under the divine protection of Apollo, but during the course of which he becomes increasingly more interested in mythology—Apollo's role as cowherd for Admetus, and Mercury's theft of his cattle—until Apollo's "douce rêverie" has replaced cheese altogether as the subject of his speech. This mythological meandering is prolonged even further through a rather lusterless Marinistic *concetto* in which Apollo's obliviousness ("aveuglement") is contrasted with his traditional role as god of the sun ("lumiere"). But at last the speaker seems to realize that he has strayed from his true subject, and he brings his rambling to an abrupt end:

> Tout-beau, Muse, tu vas trop haut,
> Ce n'est pas là ce qu'il nous faut,
> Je veux que ton stile se change
> Pour achever cette loüange.
> (11. 61-64)

This violent interruption in mid-*élan* brings the poem's apparently aimless discourse abruptly back to its point of departure. But to which point of departure: that of the speech, or that of the poem? In terms of the actual *speech*, the speaker's Muse "va trop haut" in several different respects. First of all, in speaking of Apollo, Mercury and Admetus, the Muse has "risen" to the nobler realm of mythology, whereas her proper subject in this speech is the pastures of Brie and the taverns of Paris. But she has risen too high topographically as well, in speaking of Apollo as Phoebus, who drives the sun's chariot across the heavens and illuminates the world ("Celuy dont la vertu premiere/Ne consiste qu'en la lumiere"), rather than as the divine cowherd whom she has just pictured sitting under an elm tree playing the flute. She seems to have forgotten that Apollo left his "torche" behind with his "violon," and is no longer to be found in the high regions of Parnassus, Olympus or the fourth celestial sphere, but is himself down in the pastures where her subject should be. The speaker's Muse will search in vain for the Musagetes if she rises to the regions where Apollo's "vertu premiere" is light. Thirdly, there is the question of "stile": the Marinistic *pointe* of the preceding lines belongs to a more cultivated and "elevated" style which is entirely inappropriate either to the praise of cheese, or to drunken extemporizing in a tavern.

But this brings us to a more crucial point. Just as the subject has shifted from cheese to gods, and just as the style has risen from both pastoral and Dionysian to "Apollonian," so it seems that the mode of discourse has mysteriously shifted from oral to written. Furthermore, it is not the live voice of a drunken client in a tavern, but rather the voice of a poet speaking from within his poem, that invokes the *Muse* and speaks of his own "stile" (a word which, after all, literally means an instrument for writing). Perhaps it is the *poet's* Muse, addressed in this Pindaric palinode, that "va trop haut," and begins to sound too bookish for what is supposed to be a speech quoted within the confines of a written text. The reader is forced to wonder here if these words have not somehow slipped past the absent quotation marks within which these lines are ostensibly contained, and become part of the written "frame" of the first five lines. It would seem that the distinction between the *poem* (level 1) and the *speech* it reports (level 2) has become as blurred as the now-obliterated distinction between the speech (level 2) and the choral chant (level 3) quoted from within the speech. Twice now we have observed a frame to blend with its contents, and what first appeared to be three distinct levels of discourse *en abîme* is beginning to look more like one single level of discourse which mysteriously changes its status and drifts in and out of quotation marks, the same words being now quoted, now spoken, now written.

The lines following this interruption are at first glance reassuring, in that they seem to mark an unambiguous return to the direct discourse of the speaker, in order to "achever cette loüange," leaving mythology, high style and poetry behind:

> Encore un coup, donc Compagnons,
> Du bon Denys les vrais mignons,
> Sus! qu'à plein gosier on s'escrie
> Beny soit le terroir de Brie.
>
> (11. 65-68)

But on reflection these lines themselves are extremely disconcerting. On the one hand they do take up the thread which was begun in lines 17-20 (and which was lost during the course of the intervening digression) by paraphrasing two of those earlier lines and by reproducing word-for-word the next two, as though the speaker wished to start all over again on his speech and make a fresh start from the top. But at the same time this repetition has precisely the opposite effect. It transforms the ostensibly spontaneous cry "Sus! qu'à plein gosier on s'escrie/Beny soit le terroir de Brie!" into a *refrain*—that is, a consciously contrived repetition of verbal elements within a larger, premeditated pattern. By implication, the entire vinous speech is at the same time transformed into something resembling a *song* or a *ballad*, —that is, an artificial form of discourse composed according to a preconceived structure of repetitions. The questions of mode and level of discourse, then, are not resolved but compounded by this apparently innocent return to the beginning of the "speech." The speaker backs down from a digression which starts to sound too much like written poetry; but while he himself appears to renounce an inadvertently "poetic" style and to return to the style of spontaneous speech, lyric patterns begin to emerge from the totality of his haphazard discourse. We seem to be witnessing in yet another way the mysterious metamorphosis of spoken speech into written poetry, and the unwitting transformation of a Bacchic orator into the voice of an Apollonian verse form.

The perplexing confusion of levels of discourse caused by this apparently simple return to the beginning of the speech is compounded even further when we notice that the two lines which are repeated—"textually," as it were—are those same lines which first created the (still unresolved) ambiguity concerning the second and third levels of discourse. That ambiguity is of course reproduced here. Is the speaker speaking for himself, or for "on" when he continues:

> Sus! qu'à plein gosier on s'escrie
> Beny soit le terroir de Brie.
> Pont-l'Evesque arriere de nous,
> Auvergne et Milan cachez-vous,
> C'est luy seulement qui merite
> Qu'en or sa gloire soit escrite.
>   (11. 67-72)

As before, closing quotation marks could be placed either after the word "Brie," or further along in the speech: there is absolutely no way to determine *where*. The only certitude is that the quotation has been closed *somewhere* by the time the speaker comes to speak of himself in the first person singular ("*Je* dis en or avec raison," 1. 73).

At the same time that they pose once again the very problem we have already encountered earlier in the poem, these lines corroborate the conclusions to which that problem itself has been leading us. The speaker's exhortations are no longer for unanimous *oral* praise of the cheese, but for *written* praise: the line "Qu'on n'en *parle* qu'avec respect" of the "first try" (1. 22) has become "qu'en or sa gloire soit *escrite*" in the second (1. 72). While emerging patterns of formal repetitions begin to suggest the metamorphosis of live speech into an ordered and premeditated poem, the semantic variants within those repeated passages mark a shift from oral to written expression, and once again we are given the impression of a kind of inadvertent congealing of speech into poetry.

Lines 73-88 continue to follow the pattern set in the speaker's abortive "first try." In place of the earlier comparison of cheese with ambrosia (11. 9-12) we find a comparison between cheese and gold, and a brief elaboration on the medicinal value of the brie, both therapeutic (languor) and prophylactic (plague). The encomium is then interrupted by a four-line apostrophe which functions exactly like the four-line palinode addressed to the Muse earlier (11. 61-64). Like the earlier interruption to which it corresponds positionally, this one is impossible to assign with certainty to one of the three levels of discourse already established in the poem. When the speaker suddenly realizes that while he has been eulogizing the cheese his companions have been eating it, he appears to cry out:

> Mais cependant que je discours
> Ces Goinfres-cy briffent tousjours,
> Et voudroient qu'il me prist envie
> De babiller toute ma vie.
>
> (11. 89-92)

But while these lines may first appear to be a kind of rhetorical aside, they seem on reflection to function best as a return to the level of discourse of the "frame" (11. 1-5). They are not *spoken*, as part of an oral discourse to a live audience, but are *written*, as part of a poem destined for a reading audience. They, like the first five lines of the work, serve to narrate circumstantial details which we readers, unlike the speaker's live audience, cannot observe first-hand: "Je m'escrie en laschant un rot:. . . Mais cependant que je discours/Ces Goinfres-cy. . ." Here, as in the invocation to the Muse, the initially clear-cut distinction between poem and speech has all but disappeared: without quotation marks to indicate their status, the words of the speaker's rambling harangue appear paradoxically to drift upward to the level of written words on the printed page.

In line 93 the confusion of levels is once again left behind, and the speaker has regained undisputed control over his words. He addresses his companions directly in the second person, exactly as he did earlier following his first interruption addressed to the Muse ("Encore un coup, donc Compagnons," 1. 65):

> Holà, Gourmands, attendez-moy:
> Pensez-vous qu'un manger de Roy
> Se doive traitter de la sorte
> Que vostre appetit vous emporte?
> Chaque morceau vaut un ducat,
> Voire six verres de muscat,
> Et vos dents n'auront point de honte
> D'en avoir fait si peu de conte?
> (11. 93-100)

These eight lines of direct address are followed by twelve lines of apostrophe to the absent donor of the cheese, during the course of which the speaker's style rises once again, if not to the heights of lyric poetry and Phoebus Apollo as it did in the "first try" (11. 33-60), at least to those of mock-Ciceronian oration and Diana:

> Pourquoy tousjours s'apetissant,
> De Lune devient-il Croissant?
> Et pourquoy si bas sous la nuë
> S'éclipse-t'il à nostre veuë?
> (11. 105-108)

But rather than straying hopelessly from his subject as he did in his first mythological digression, the speaker succeeds this time in subordinating myth to the praise of cheese. In place of the 28 lines on Apollo and Mercury in which the subject drifted from cheese to legendary love, the speaker now delivers eight modest lines in which he succinctly associates his cheese with the myth of Io, Jupiter and Juno. And whereas the first mythological development had to be cut short by an abrupt palinode and a return to the beginning of the eulogy, this one leads quite naturally to a satisfactory conclusion:

> O doux Cotignac de Bacchus,
> Fromage, que tu vaux d'escus!
> Je veux que ta seule memoire
> Me provoque à jamais A BOIRE.
> (11. 121-124)

And yet, the lines of this "satisfactory conclusion" are none other than those which preceded the speaker's first direct address to his listeners (1. 17). The peroration is nothing more than a mere repetition of the exordium, and this bizarre piece of demonstrative rhetoric has come full circle to its point of departure. Furthermore, the repetition in these concluding lines functions exactly like the repetition, encountered earlier in the poem, of the line: "Sus! qu'à plein gosier on s'escrie" (11. 19-20 and 67-68). More than a spontaneous cry or the conclusion to an actual *speech*, this last echo (11. 13-16 and 121-124) suggests the final refrain of a written *poem*. After several abortive attempts, then, the speaker has at last concluded his harangue. But his peroration is actually far less satisfactory as the conclusion of a speech than it is as the conclusion of a poem. The words of a live speech seem once again to have been transformed into those of a preconceived poetic structure.

The patterns which have emerged from this ostensibly aimless harangue in search of an ending can now be diagrammed in the following way:

> I. A.   Assis sur le bord d'un chantier
>   Avec des gens de mon mestier,
>   C'est à dire avec une trouppe
>   Qui ne jure que par la Couppe,

B.   Je m'escrie en laschant un rot:

    C.   «Beny soit l'excellent Bilot
           «Il nous a donné d'un fromage. . .

    D.   (Comparison with Ambrosia)

    E.   «O doux Cottignac de Baccus,
           «Fromage, que tu vaux d'escus!
           «Je veux que ta seule memoire
           «Me provoque à jamais à boire.

II.   A.   «A genoux Enfans desbauchez,
           «Chers confidents de mes pechez,

    B.   «Sus! qu'à plein gosier on s'escrie:

    C.   « «Beny soit le terroir de Brie. . .» »

    D.   (Apollo, Mercury and Admetus' herd)

> Tout-beau, Muse, tu vas trop haut,
> Ce n'est pas là ce qu'il nous faut,
> Je veux que ton stile se change
> Pour achever cette loüange.

III.   A.   «Encore un coup, donc Compagnons,
           «Du bon Denys les vrais mignons,

    B.   «Sus! qu'à plein gosier on s'escrie:

    C.   « «Beny soit le terroir de Brie. . .» »

    D.   (Comparison with gold and medicine)

IV.   A.   Mais cependant que je discours
            Ces Goinfres-cy briffent tousjours,
            Et voudroient qu'il me prist envie
            De babiller toute ma vie.

      C.   «Holà, Gourmands, attendez-moy. . .

      C.   «Bilot, qui m'en avois muny,
            «Hé! pourquoy n'est-il infiny. . .

      D.   (Comparison with moon)
            (Jupiter and Io)

      E.   «O doux Cotignac de Bacchus
            «Fromage, que tu vaux d'escus!
            «Je veux que ta seule memoire
            «Me provoque à jamais A BOIRE.»

At the arithmetic center of the poem is the invocation of ambiguous status addressed to the Muse. The entire poem is constructed symmetrically around this center: section III repeats the diction and movement of section II, as well as its blurring of the second and third levels of discourse; section IV repeats the diction and movement of section I, as well as its blurring of the first and second levels of discourse. At the same time, the entire second half of the poem (sections III and IV together) corresponds to the entire first half of the poem (sections I and II together) in that both culminate in a mythological glorification of the cheese.

As the speaker-poet's Muse begins to rise from the tavern to the twin peaks of Parnassus, these complex symmetries gradually unfold, suggesting on a formal level the transformation of live speech into written text, while at the same time the *mise en abîme* of its various levels of discourse begins to dissolve, suggesting in yet a third way that the reported speech is somehow being absorbed by its poetic "frame." Semantically, formally and structurally, *Le Fromage* seems to be a work about a bizarre transformation of life into art—a poem which is little more than the comical and paradoxical trace of its own genesis as a poem.

What makes *Le Fromage* a particularly interesting piece of self-conscious poetry is that the complex problems posed by various aspects of the text itself are also reflected in the images of its central digression on Apollo, Admetus and Mercury.[6] The digression, that is, contains a mythological model for the paradoxical genesis of the work in which it appears.

The ostensible purpose of this digression which takes its speaker so far afield is, as we have observed in passing, to contribute to the hyperbolic valorization of cheese by placing the cows from which it came under the divine protection of an Olympian god. The particular fable recalled here is actually not as unsuited to the subject of cheese as one might first be tempted to suppose. According to Tibullus, it was Apollo himself who, during his period of servitude as Admetus' cowherd, taught men how to make cheese from the milk of cows (II 3, 11. 11-16). But Saint-Amant's poem makes no mention of this pertinent detail of the legend. In fact, as the speaker pursues his thoughts he forgets about cheese altogether. He becomes more and more interested in the attendant circumstances and apparently irrelevant aspects of the episode, devoting a full eight lines to Mercury's theft of the cattle, and twelve lines to Apollo's obliviousness to the theft.

This disproportionate attention given to Mercury's role in the legend may be far from the speaker's purpose, but it is curiously relevant to his own circumstances. The cattle watched by Apollo are clearly associated at the beginning of the digression with the precious brie: the speaker would have Apollo be more attentive in guarding the cows from whose milk this ambrosial cheese was made than he once was as the "Vacher" of Admetus' herd. But as the speaker will soon discover, his brie itself is gradually disappearing into the mouths of his listeners who, like Mercury in the legend, are taking advantage of his own inattention to rob him of his prize. The situation described in the speaker's mythological vignette, then, corresponds point-for-point to the situation in which the speech itself is being delivered. To Apollo seated "sous un Ormeau" corresponds the speaker "assis sur le bord d'un chantier." To Apollo's idle improvisation on a *chalumeau* corresponds the speaker's extemporized eulogy. The correlation between the speaker and Apollo is further reinforced by Saint-Amant's familiar diction in describing Apollo's piping. While "fluster son soul d'un chalumeau" (1. 50) is an idiomatic way of saying "play the shepherd's pipe to one's heart's content," the figurative meanings of both "fluster" (which was a familiar equivalent for "drink") and "soul" (which had already come to mean "drunk")[7] appropriately suggest a punning metaphorical equivalence between Apollo's indolence and the speaker's present state of inebriation. To Mercury's theft of Apollo's cattle, meanwhile, corresponds the drinking companions' theft of the speaker's cheese. And like Apollo, the speaker is

> . . .si fort occupé
> Dans une douce rêverie
> Qu'il n'en vit point la tromperie.
> (11. 54-56)

In the very process of admonishing Apollo to be more attentive in guarding the cows of Brie than he once was in guarding those of Thessaly, the speaker himself commits Apollo's error. His digression, in effect, not only *allows*, but actually *describes*, through a mythological analogue, the pilfering of his cheese. Saint-Amant puts into the mouth of the speaker his own circumstances to which he himself is oblivious ("tragic" irony), while he puts into the mouths of the listeners the cheese whose praises they are hearing (circumstantial irony).[8]

But the ironic and emblematic functions of the speaker's mytholgoical digression are even more compelling than this: they reflect not only the speaker's own circumstances, but the enigmatic nature of his speech as well. Here it must be recalled that the theft of Apollo's herd is only one of the two related events which mark the first day of Mercury's existence. The other is the invention of the lyre, or *kithara*. According to the version of this legend which had greatest currency throughout the Renaissance,[9] the infant god, only hours old, escapes from his cradle and steals Apollo's cattle, two of which he sacrifices to the gods. With the entrails of the two slaughtered cattle, and with the shell of a tortoise, he devises the world's first *kithara*, the carapace serving as a sounding box, the entrails—

stretched and dried—as strings.[10]   Once discovered, the theft
is forgiven by Apollo in return for Hermes' marvelous new instrument.   Hermes, the new owner and tender of the cattle, in-
vents another instrument to help him while away the time: the
shepherd's pipe, or *syrinx*.   Apollo acquires this instrument too,
in exchange for a golden caduceus and the gift of prophecy.

Both of the musical instruments originating from Mercury's
theft of Apollo's cattle are recalled in Saint-Amant's allusion to
the theft.   Apollo in his pastoral role is of course seen to play
the shepherd's pipe: "*Fluster* son soul *d'un chalumeau.*" But of
even greater importance is a very similar expression used to
describe Mercury in the act of rustling the cattle.   The "Patron
des Mattois," says the speaker, "*Joüa* sur ses boeufs *de la harpe*"
(1. 48).   It is not likely that Saint-Amant invented this expression.   The phrase is attested in Antoine Oudin's *Curiositez françoises* (1640), which defines it as "desrober: parce qu'en joüant
de la harpe on a les mains crochuës," and a similar image is re-
corded in Cotgrave's *Dictionarie of the French and English
Tongues* (1611): "Il mania tresbien ses harpes.   He stirred his
fingers verie nimbly."   Saint-Amant has simply borrowed a
colorful expression already in current use, and adapted it here to
his own special purposes.   In the present context, "jouer de
la harpe" is not only a vivid metaphor for Mercury's furtive
sleight of hand; it also functions on a literal level as a pointed reminder that from these "boeufs" will come the strings of the
world's first *lyre*, the plucked stringed instrument whose first
cousin, and burlesque synonym, is the "harpe."

Saint-Amant's first readers could not possibly have missed
this comically syncopated allusion to the *dénouement* of the
speaker's story.   In this burlesque adumbration we are clearly
asked to recall that the theft we are witnessing will culminate in
the invention of an instrument which, from Pindar to Horace to
Ronsard and beyond, had been the universally recognized symbol
of lyric inspiration.[11]   But it is this same symbolic instrument,
designated by another burlesque synonym, that Apollo has left
behind, along with the symbol of his role as Phoebus, in order to
assume his duties as Admetus' cowherd:

> Que, comme autrefois, Apollon,
> Delaisse *torche et violon,*

> Et s'en vienne dans ces prairies,
> Dans ces grandes plaines fleuries,
> Garder en guise de Vacher
> Un troupeau qui nous est si cher. . .[12]
>
> (11. 33-38)

The god of Lyric Poetry, then, is pictured in Saint-Amant's mythological vignette, as having abandoned the elevated lyric mode (his *kithara*, or "violon") in favor of the humbler pastoral mode (the *syrinx*, or "chalumeau")[13] more suited to his new occupation and idyllic revery, while Mercury, the god of Rhetoric as well as the "Patron des Mattois," is described as committing his well-known larceny in terms that serve to recall the subsequent transformation of Apollo's cattle back into the abandoned instrument of lyric inspiration. While the implied chronology of this digression may be fanciful, its cluster of allusions to two antithetical kinds of poetic inspiration is entirely clear and consistent.

Furthermore, these allusions reflect exactly the transformation we have already observed in the speaker's panegyric itself. *Le Fromage* suggests in several places an inverse relation between Bilot's brie and the monologue itself. As words come out of the speaker's mouth, cheese disappears into the mouths of his audience; as the monologue waxes, the cheese wanes:

> Mais cependant que je discours
> Ces Goinfres-cy briffent tousjours,
> Et voudroient qu'il me prist envie
> De babiller toute ma vie.
>
> . . . .
> Hé! pourquoy n'est-il infiny
> Tout aussi bien en sa matiere
> Qu'il l'estoit en sa forme entiere?
> Pourquoy tousjours s'apetissant,
> De Lune devient-il Croissant?
> Et pourquoy si bas sous la nuë
> S'éclipse-t'il à nostre veuë?
>
> (11. 89-92, 102-108)

It would appear that at the end of the monologue the "poem" is complete and the cheese is gone: by the time the speaker's drunken harangue has been transformed into an Apollonian verse form, all that remains of the "doux Cotignac de Bacchus" is its "seule memoire," and all that remains of the cheese is *Le Fromage.*

This is precisely the metamorphosis that is reflected in Saint-Amant's image at the center. Just as Apollo has left the lyric mode to watch over Admetus' herd and "fluster son soul d'un chalumeau," so the besotted speaker has begun, with a burp, to eulogize a dairy product before an audience "qui ne jure que par la Couppe." Just as Apollo's stolen herd will be fashioned, through the good offices of the glib god of rhetoric, back into the instrument of lyric inspiration, so the speaker's pilfered cheese will be metamorphosed, in the course of the speech itself, into the poem entitled "Le Fromage." And just as Apollo Musagetes will come back into possession of the lyre he has momentarily abandoned so that he too will once again be able to "jouer sur ses boeufs de la harpe," so the voice of the orator's rambling lucubration will gradually and mysteriously be sublimated, in the multifarious ways we have already noted, into the poetic voice of a work whose refrains and rigorous symmetry are strictly lyric.

In the course of a digression so Dionysiac and aleatory that the speaker must break it off and begin his speech anew, Saint-Amant offers us a vignette emblematic of the process in which both the speaker and his speech are at that very moment engaged, premonitory of the Apollonian control and higher order which will become so evident from the perspective of the poem's final line.

At the end of *La Solitude,* the persona of an Apollonian poet rejects the melancholic solitude of poetry in order to re-enter the social world from which he had earlier fled. That final conversion in *La Solitude* would appear to be consummated in the sanguine conviviality and the Dionysian insouciance of *Le Fromage.* The much more limited—and more cavalier—use of literary allusiveness in the second poem can only corroborate this impression.

But on closer inspection, *Le Fromage* is every bit as "literary" as *La Solitude*. Its virtuosity, in fact, consists in accomplishing precisely the inverse of what we have observed in *La Solitude*. The first poem of course begins when the speaker has left society for solitude and ends as he leaves solitude for society, while the second begins with the speaker firmly established in a social setting with fellow "mignons du bon Denys," but ends when his apparently "real" speech has somehow been absorbed by its strictly poetic frame. The relation between the two works is far more significant than this, however. As we have seen, the real subject of *La Solitude* is poetry and poetic conventions. Before the speaker leaves solitude and his own poem, one convention after another has been assumed only in order to be undercut and debunked: Petrarchan elegiac love, the *locus amoenus* and its intimations of a vestigial Golden Age, mythological *topoi*, poetic melancholy and solitude, immediate inspiration, all have been used against one another in a breathtakingly ironic deconstruction of the classical *loci* and *loci communes* which had been for centuries the stuff and substance of Apollonian poetry. In *Le Fromage*, on the other hand, it is the aleatory randomness of the lower registers of Dionysian inspiration that is undermined in a process—precisely the inverse of that of *La Solitude*—of Apollonian *re*-construction. The drunken speaker reels from subject to subject, loses his train of thought and is even interrupted by his audience. Yet his uncontrolled discourse falls into patterns so regular, so symmetrical, so carefully punctuated by refrains which can only be called "lyric," that the poem's pretense of orgiastic abandon is utterly belied by its form. Having destroyed lyric from within by manipulating its own conventions in *La Solitude*, Saint-Amant now rebuilds lyric from without by manipulating conventions contrary and antagonistic to it.

This inverse correlation between the two poems is of course reflected in the symbolic representation of lyric composition which each of the works contains within it. The wanderer who, at the center of *La Solitude*, was seen to favor the sad passion of Echo "par la celeste harmonie/D'un doux Lut, aux charmes instruit," ends by putting his lute aside in order to serve Alcidon. At the center of *Le Fromage*, in direct contrast, we find a clear hint that the emblematic Apollo who has left behind his "violon" in order to "fluster son soul d'un chalumeau" will soon receive from the hands of Mercury the "harpe" which is his attribute as the god of lyric poetry. In *La Solitude* the Apollonian lyre is taken up only to be rejected; in *Le Fromage* it is abandoned only to be taken up again.

   Le Fromage, though less allusive to the conventions and *loci* of literature, is clearly no less concerned with literature itself than *La Solitude;* and the Saint-Amant whom Romantics from 1844 to the present have characterized as "le bon Gros" is no less a poetic alchemist than that other Saint-Amant whom the same Romantics have characterized as a Naturalist who only paints "sur le vif." These two early works complement each other in a witty but perfectly coherent project of rethinking the very foundations of the Western literary tradition.

CHAPTER III:
L'ARION

Orpheus in silvis, inter delphinas Arion
—Vergil

. . .ne forte pudori
Sit tibi Musa lyrae sollers et cantor Apollo
—Horace

In their self-conscious attempt to save poetry from "court-liness" in all senses of the word, and to restore the Poet to his former status of prophet, *vates* and thaumaturge, the humanistic poets of the Renaissance turned again and again to the examples of mythical and semi-legendary *kitharoidoi* of antiquity: Linus, Orpheus, Amphion, Musaeus. It is hardly surprising that Orpheus, the founder of the Orphic mysteries, whose song had the power to move wild beasts, trees, stones and Death itself, was more frequently celebrated than any of the others. It *is* surprising that Arion, who resembles Orpheus in so many ways, and who is credited with the invention of the dithyramb (and hence is the father of tragedy), received almost no attention at all. He is mentioned once by Sébillet in his *Art poétique fran-çoys*,[1] only once in the entire work of Ronsard,[2] occasionally by Du Bellay, and once by Baïf.[3] Of all of these, only Baïf's is anything more than a passing reference. The legend was developed fully by only two poets of the French Renaissance, neither of whom was associated in any way with the Brigade: Scève, whose *Arion* was published in 1536, and Du Bartas, who devoted ninety-two lines to the Arion myth in the fifth day of his *Création du monde, ou la Première Sepmaine* (1578).

But not even Scève and Du Bartas were concerned primarily with Arion himself. Nor for that matter were any of the classical authors who had treated the legend before them: in Herodotus (I, 23-24), the story is a marginally relevant digression on the

character of Periander, an ally of the Milesians in their war a-
gainst the Lydians; in Ovid (*Fasti* II, 83-118) it is an etiological
digression occasioned by the setting of the constellation Delphinus in what is principally a calendar of feast days; in Plutarch
(*The Feast of the Seven Sages*) it is a real-life incident that
interrupts a Platonic dialogue of feasting sages (including Periander) and provokes a conversation about miracles, providence
and grace;[4] for Scève the story provides little more than a circumstantial framework and a conceit (dolphin-Dauphin) in an
elegiac eclogue on the death of François I's eldest son; and for
Du Bartas it is a digression on the noblest of "fish" in the fifth
day of an heptameral creation epic.[5]   In all versions of the
Arion legend from Herodotus to Du Bartas, the fable is a mere
digression or pretext in a longer work on some other subject
altogether.   And in none of these earlier versions is Arion himself the protagonist: all are concerned primarily with either the
dolphin or Periander.

Arion, the legendary *kitharoidos* slighted by the ancients
and utterly neglected by the very French poets whose ideal he
so splendidly incarnated, was the subject of the very first poem
published by Saint-Amant.[6]   There is virtually no invention in
Saint-Amant's *Arion;* almost every detail of the narrative can be
traced directly to one of these earlier versions, as can a good deal
of the poem's actual diction.   What *is* new in the poem is its
dispositio.   The legend is treated here, for the first time ever,
not as a mere digression but as the unique subject of the poem;
and the figure of Arion himself is elevated, for the very first
time, above the dolphin and the king to the role of protagonist
and even hero.   The question usually raised concerning *L'Arion*
is why the poet was moved to write a work of 304 lines on a
rigidly determined fable which had attracted so few poets before
him.   Critics like to answer that Saint-Amant was a virtuoso
lutanist just as Arion was a *kitharoidos* whose art had earned
him universal fame; that Saint-Amant came to Paris to make his
fortune just as Arion had traveled to Ausonia to make his; that
Saint-Amant made several long sea-voyages and lost two brothers
at sea, just as Arion's adventure had taken place on the high
seas; and that Saint-Amant was a *compagnon de Bacchus* just as
Arion had been the inventor of the dithyramb; and so
forth.   But these similarities between the poet's life and
his subject are largely anachronistic, and in any case merely

anecdotal: they add nothing to our understanding of either the poem or the poet's reasons for writing it.

A more fruitful question to pose is why, having written the poem, Saint-Amant was moved to publish it before any of the others. It must be remembered that in 1623 he had already written several works worthy of publication, including *La Solitude*, *La Jouyssance* and *Le Fromage*. Yet the poet did not see fit to publish any of these until six years later when he consented ("malgré [sa] Raison," as he would have it in the fanciful *Elégie à Monseigneur le duc de Rets*) to the publication of his collected works. If it was *La Solitude* that was later to assure the poet's fame, it was nevertheless *L'Arion* with which he chose to launch his public career as a poet. One wonders why the poet himself put so much stock in *L'Arion*. The poem must have qualities that escape notice when *L'Arion* is read simply as the last poem of the "Ovidian" group (after *L'Andromède* and *La Métamorphose de Lyrian et de Sylvie*) in the collected *Oeuvres* of 1629.

We must of course take into consideration the fact that *L'Arion* is an encomiastic poem, dedicated to the Duc de Montmorency who in 1623 was the poet's "unique Mecene" (1.289, text of 1623). The early publication of the work can undoubtedly be explained, at least in part, by the strategy of a protégé who had calculated that praise in print is more likely to work the desired effect than a manuscript, no matter how eulogistic. The narrative portion of the poem is indeed neatly framed by two encomiastic passages whose hyperbole is as conventional as their symmetry is rigorous. The first wing of this triptych is the dedication:

> Grand Duc, grand Admiral, ornement de la France,
> De qui les hauts exploits surpassent l'esperance
> Qu'en tes plus tendres ans tout le monde eut de toy,
> Brave MONTMORENCY, de grace écoute moy,
> Ecoute ces accords qu'Arion te dedie,. . .
> (11. 9-13)

The third wing serves to frame the central narrative by echoing the dedication point for point:

> Invincible Heros, mon unique Mecene,
> Reçoy ces nouveaux fruits qui naissent de ma peine:
> Estime-les un peu, prens-y quelque plaisir,. . .
> (11. 289-291)

In accordance with the convention, moreover, the poem ends with the promise of a greater work whose praise will be more adequate to the dedicatee than is that of the present poem:

> Et cependant la Gloire ordonnant à ma plume
> De peindre tes vertus en un parfait volume,
> Portera ton renom, celebré dans mes vers,
> Plus haut que le flambeau qui dore l'Univers.
> (11. 293-296)

But this encomiastic aspect of *L'Arion* is not reinforced by the poem's new *dispositio:* while the subject of the poem would seem to be an appropriate one for dedication to the Admiral of France, Saint-Amant's unique version of the story—in which Periander, Arion's benefactor and the wise dispenser of marine justice, disappears from the poem altogether—is not. It is the *poet* who is exalted in Saint-Amant's poem, not the benefactor or the agent of salvation, and Saint-Amant's only major innovation is precisely this shift away from Periander and the dolphin to the poet-figure himself. Saint-Amant must have had some other purpose in mind in treating the subject as he did, and in choosing this work for his début as a published poet.

It is neither the subject of the poem (which is entirely determined by convention) nor Saint-Amant's biography (which in any case is sketchy at best for this early period) that will answer the question posed by the early publication of *L'Arion.* The text itself provides clear cues as to how we are to read and understand the poem. From the very first lines, our common literary experience is exploited and our expectations directed in the most straight-forward manner:

> Les sens pleins de merveille et saisis d'allegresse,
> J'entrepren de chanter ce beau Chantre de Grece,
> Qui malgré la rigueur des farouches Nochers,
> Dont les coeurs en la Mer sont autant de rochers,
> Passa sur un Daufin l'Empire de Neptune,

Fit de son avanture étonner la Fortune,
Et revit ondoyer par un decret fatal
La fumée à flots noirs sur son vieux toict natal.

These lines are modeled directly on the most famous opening passage in Western literature:

Arma virumque cano, Troiae qui primus ab oris
Italiam fato profugus Laviniaque venit
Litora—multum ille et terris iactatus et alto
Vi superum, saevae memorem Iunonis ob iram,
Multa quoque et bello passus, dum conderet urbem
Inferretque deos Latio; genus unde Latinum
Albanique patres atque altae moenia Romae.

Vergil's first seven lines are a one-sentence résumé of the entire poem which is to follow, sketched out from beginning to end in a series of subordinate clauses qualifying the "man" who is to be sung. Saint-Amant's first eight lines function in precisely the same way, both grammatically and in relation to the rest of the poem. To the Vergilian "arma virumque cano" corresponds the kernal of Saint-Amant's opening sentence: "J'entrepren de chanter ce beau Chantre de Grece." To Vergil's subordinate clause beginning with the relative adjective "qui. . ." (1. 1) corresponds Saint-Amant's subordinate clause beginning with the relative adjective "qui. . ." (1. 3). To Vergil's résumé of peripeteia ("multum iactatus. . .multa passus") corresponds the preview of Arion's tribulations ("malgré la rigueur. . ."). To the wrath of cruel Juno in Vergil's poem corresponds the "rigueur des farouches Nochers" in Saint-Amant's. And to the Roman *fatum* of Vergil's second line corresponds the classicizing French "decret fatal" of Saint-Amant's seventh line. Neither Aeneas nor Arion is mentioned by name in these periphrastic opening lines.

These parallels are so deliberate that they could not possibly have escaped the attention of contemporary readers, even if the first line—an adjectival clause qualifying the grammatical subject "je"—does tend to obscure the Vergilian echoes for twentieth-century readers. Literate people in the seventeenth-century had grown up with Vergil and knew great portions of the *Aeneid* by heart. Despite his apparent "modernism" and his iconoclastic pose, Saint-Amant was literate and he knew that his public was literate. He could be confident that in imitating a Vergilian passage his imitation would be recognized. There can be no question here of mere borrowing, or imitation for imitation's sake. Saint-Amant *uses* his public's previous experience as a resource for meaning in his own poem. Just as *La Solitude* begins by announcing in the most unmistakable terms the universe of the Petrarchan elegy ("solo e pensoso"), so *L'Arion*, by imitating the syntactical structure, vocabulary and general movement of seven of the most familiar lines in literature, begins by suggesting the vast context of the epic adventure. The opening lines of *L'Arion* are as explicit and unambiguous in their connotation as they are in their literal meaning. To the literate reader, these lines say: "this is an epic poem, Arion is an epic hero of the stature of Aeneas, and I am an epic poet of the stature of Vergil." One of Saint-Amant's projects in this poem, then, appears to have been to construct an "epic" poem, using as his subject the relatively uncommon legend of a poet-figure. The virtuosity of the poem, seen in this light, is evident: it consists in perceiving and developing the similar within the dissimilar—that is, epic elements in a legend which had never in Western literature been treated as anything more than a digressive anecdote.

The epic pretensions of Saint-Amant's prologue may seem puzzling at first, and strike the reader as arbitrary and formalistic panache, given the relative humbleness of the subject they propose and the tiny proportions of the poem. The manifestly Vergilian form of these lines leads us to expect a Vergilian subject. There are indeed some similarities and analogies linking the legends of Aeneas and Arion, which the prologue's form and diction force us to discover. Aeneas leaves Asia Minor for Italy, while Arion leaves Italy for Greece. The first adventure related in the *Aeneid* is a sea-storm so violent that the hero envies the fate of those who died defending Troy, while Arion's adventure— also a sea adventure—leads the poet to consider that his death is imminent and to sing a swan-song in order to "celebrer le terme de sa vie." But these parallels are distant and seem hardly sufficient to justify the implicit claims of the prologue. Considered as an epic voyage, Arion's adventure is actually much more Homeric than Vergilian. Arion is not the heroic agent of a *translatio imperii* as Aeneas is, setting out from a fallen Empire to establish an even greater one on foreign soil. He is a victorious competitor whose "epic" adventure is a return to the point of departure. The poem begins as he sets sail for home, laden with the spoils of victory won in poetic contests in a foreign land ("comblé de richesse et de gloire," 1. 21). The poem ends with his safe arrival in Greece, following a sea adventure during which he is stripped of all his earthly possessions. Arion, obviously, follows in the footsteps not of Aeneas, but of Odysseus.

The similarities between the adventures of Arion and Odysseus would be irrelevant to our reading of the poem if they were simply fortuitous and unexploited by the poem itself. But this is clearly not the case, as a rather curious echo in the last two lines of the prologue proves. Saint-Amant knew perfectly well from Herodotus and Ovid (and could also have learned from Lucian, Hyginus, Natalis Comes and Robert Estienne) that Arion was a Lesbian born in *Methymna,* and that Periander, who summons Arion "home," was the king of *Corinth.* Yet in a willful distortion of the details of the legend, Saint-Amant writes that by returning at Periander's command and landing safely "au pied du mont-*Tenare*" (1. 286)—which is a long way from either Lesbos or Corinth—Arion

> . . .revit ondoyer par un decret fatal
> La fumée à flots noirs sur son vieux *toict natal.*
> (11. 7-8)

These geographically and historically misleading lines constitute an echo which, thanks to Du Bellay, not even the modern reader can overlook:

> Heureux qui, *comme Ulysse,* a fait un beau voyage,
> Ou comme cestuy là qui conquit la toison,
> Et puis est retourné, plein d'usage et raison,
> Vivre entre ses parents le reste de son aage!
>   Quand revoiray-je, helas, de mon petit village
> Fumer la cheminee. . .[7]

It would perhaps be rash to attempt to prove a deliberate assimilation of Arion and Odysseus by referring to a single sonnet written more than sixty years earlier in which both Ulysses and the smoking chimneys of home are mentioned together, even though there can be no doubt concerning Saint-Amant's famil-

iarity with the works of Du Bellay. But Du Bellay was not himself an *auctor* in this regard. Smoking chimneys and Odysseus
were traditionally and proverbially linked in the Renaissance,
and Du Bellay, far from inventing a new image, merely incorporated a universally recognized topos into his Ulysses sonnet.
The same image can be found at the very beginning of the
Odyssey itself:

> Mais tout son desir et de revoir la fumee
> Qui sort à noirs replis de sa maison aymee.
> Ayme mieux voir la flamme allumer, et courir
> Sur sa douce patrie, et puis apres mourir
> Que de prendre d'un Dieu la semblance eternelle.[8]

Ovid took up the Homeric topos in the *Ex Ponto*:

> Non dubia est Ithaci prudentia, sed tamen optat
>   Fumum de patriis posse videre focis,
>   (I 3, 33-34)

Marot took it up in "A la Royne de Navarre":

> Ulixes sage (au moins estimé tel)
> Fit bien jadis refuz d'estre immortel
> Pour retourner en sa maison petite,
> Et du regret de mort se disoit quitte
> Si l'air eust pu de son pays humer,
> Et veu de loing son village fumer!

and Du Bellay took it up again in sonnet 130 of *Les Regrets*:

> Et je pensois aussi ce que pensoit Ulysse,
> Qu'il n'estoit rien plus doulx que voir encor' un jour
> Fumer sa cheminee, et apres long sejour
> Se retrouver au sein de sa terre nourrice,

and yet a third time in the Latin *Poemata*, where the allusion to
Odysseus is implicit but unambiguous:

> Foelix, qui mores multorum vidit et urbes,
>   Sedibus et potuit consenuisse suis.
> . . . .

> Quando erit, ut notae fumantia culmina villae,
> Et videam regni iugera parva mei?

It also appears in Ronsard's *Hymne de la mort:*

> Il ne faut pas humer de Circe les vaisseaux,
> De peur que transformez en Tigres ou Pourceaux,
> Nous ne puissions revoir d'Ithaque la fumée,
> Du Ciel nostre demeure à l'ame accoustumée,
> Où tous nous faut aller. . . .[9]

And in his *Adagia* Erasmus quotes the proverb "Patriae fumus, igni alieno luculentior," and remarks in his commentary that "apud Homerum, terrae natalis fumum Ulysses optat videre surgentem, unde et ductum proverbium."[10] In short, whether or not they recognized Saint-Amant's lines as a word-for-word translation of *Odyssey* I 57-59, contemporary readers could hardly have failed to recognize their allusion to Odysseus, and to have understood the implications of this allusion in its application to Arion.

Lest we forget the Arion-Odysseus assimilation, or overlook it as an isolated and fortuitous association, Saint-Amant reminds us again later in the poem of Odysseus and his return to Ithaca:

> Un naturel desir de revoir sa Patrie,
> Où l'on le reveroit avec idolatrie,
> Flattant ses sentimens en ce lointain sejour,
> Le vint solliciter d'y faire son retour.
> (11. 33-36)

Unless "Patrie" is taken to mean all of Greece, as opposed to the "rivage Latin" (cf. 11. 39-40), Saint-Amant has once again taken liberties with biographical and historical detail in order to transform Arion's return to Taenarum or Periander's court in Corinth into an Homeric homecoming.[11]

These two passages are sufficient to suggest Arion's resemblance to Odysseus: the implications of these lines could not possibly have escaped any of Saint-Amant's readers, and there was no need to belabor the Arion-Odysseus assimilation any further. Yet the suggestion is sustained in indirect ways well into the poem. When it comes time to describe the avarice of Arion's molesters, for example, the poet invokes his Muse for the first time, asking for assistance in portraying an act of treachery whose enormity seems to defy poetic description:

> Avec quelles couleurs, quels traits, et quels ombrages
> Representant au vif les plus mortels outrages,
> Muse, dépeindras-tu l'enorme trahison
> De ces maudits Nochers, infectez du poison
> D'une aspre convoitise en leur sein allumée. . . ?
> (11. 61-65)

As if in answer to the poet's rhetorical question, the Muse prompts him with a simile drawn from Ovid:

> Jamais Polymnestor, ce lasche Roy de Thrace,
> Qui de la triste Hecube accomplit la disgrace,
> Ne sembla si coupable aux Troyens malheureux,
> Lors qu'un injuste sort, trop acharné sur eux,
> O spectacle cruel, leur livra Polidore
> Couché mort sur la rive, et tout sanglant encore
> Des coups que ce Bourreau pour avoir ses tresors,
> En meurtrissant sa foy, luy donna dans le corps.
> (11. 73-80)

Not one of the earlier versions of the Arion legend had resorted to a simile in describing the crime against Arion, though all agree on the degree of its iniquity. The simile occurs in *L'Arion* by a conscious decision of the artist. Of the innumerable exempla of avarice in the Greco-Roman Judeo-Christian repertoire, why did Saint-Amant choose this one?

The most obvious reason is of course that the circumstances in which Arion and Polydorus find themselves are identical in so many respects. Both characters are defenseless and laden with treasures, and both travel to the court of a friendly king. Both Polymestor and the Corinthian sailors are doubly criminal in that their avarice moves them to an act of violence against an innocent victim whose safety and welfare have been specifically entrusted to them. The chief difference between the two stories is in their *dénouement*. The story of Polydorus ends in tragedy as the prince's throat is cut and he is thrown into the sea:

> . . .capit inpius ensem
> Rex Thracum iuguloque sui demisit alumni
> Et, tamquam tolli cum corpore crimina possent,
> Exanimem scopulo subiectas misit in undas.
> (*Metamorphoses* XIII, 435-438)

Arion, on the other hand, will plunge into the sea *before* his throat is cut: he "se precipite en l'onde" (1. 189) precisely in order to escape the sailors who attack him, "les glaives nuds au poing" (1. 169). While Polydorus is washed ashore as a mangled and bloody corpse, Arion rides to shore in triumph on the back of a dolphin. As a perfect negative counterpart to the Arion legend, Polydorus' fate, alluded to at the very moment of Arion's crisis, serves to heighten the tension of the narrative at this crucial moment.

There is another reason for the interpolation of the Polydorus simile, however, which is to be found in the larger context of the story itself. King Priam had sent his son Polydorus to Polymestor's court in Thrace in order to remove him from the perils of the Trojan war. The perfidious murder of Priam's son is made possible only by the fall of Troy—"ut cecidit fortuna Phrygum," as Ovid says (*Metamorphoses* XIII, 435)—that is, by the very event which occasioned two epic voyages, that of Aeneas and that of Odysseus. Saint-Amant is careful to remind us of the specific historical context of Polymestor's treachery in 1. 74: "de la triste Hecube" the Thracian king "accomplit la disgrace," that is, he contributed the last in a long series of catastrophes marking the Trojan queen's "fall from grace" with fate and the gods: the deaths of Hector, Paris and Priam, the destruction of Troy, most recently the sacrificial murder of Polyxena and the queen's own captivity as the slave of Odysseus himself,. . .and now the discovery of Polydorus' death.

The Ovidian passage from which Saint-Amant's simile is transposed is called to mind with the story itself, and a contemporary reader would not fail to recall that Ovid had framed the story of Polydorus' murder with vivid passages concerning both post-war hero-voyagers. The narration of Hecuba's discovery of her son's death is inserted into that of her capture at the hands of *Odysseus* and the latter's departure from Troy for home. The episode is followed by the narration of *Aeneas'* pilgrimage, which also begins with an allusion to Polydorus' death: Aeneas' first stop is in the land soaked with the blood of the young prince:

> Fertur ab Antandro scelerataque limina Thracum
> Et Polydoreo manantem sanguine terram
> Linquit. . . .
>
>   (*Metamorphoses* XIII, 628-630)

Saint-Amant has chosen his simile to fit not only the circumstances of the Arion legend, but to fit the chronology of Arion's Homeric counterpart. As the victorious Arion sets sail for "home" the narrator reminds us of an event which is chronologically, causally, and contextually linked with the beginning of two epic voyages, and particularly with the victorious homecoming of Odysseus. Saint-Amant's comparison thus helps to remind us that although Arion's present plight is similar to that of an unfortunate Trojan prince, his ultimate destiny is actually that of the victorious Greek hero.

  Once we have understood that the uniqueness of *L'Arion* lies not in its subject, or in Saint-Amant's resemblances to Arion, or even in the metaphoric language of the poem, but rather in the recasting of a legendary anecdote into epic form, we have no difficulty in understanding the reason for minor variants in the legend and small flourishes in the narrative which seem purely gratuitous when considered in themselves. One narrative problem in Saint-Amant's version of the story is the disappearance of Periander at the end of the poem. The problem ceases to exist when we realize the epic pretensions of the poem and the implicit identification of Arion with Odysseus. As the epic hero, Arion has simply usurped the kingly role of Periander. Or to be more precise, once the epic action has ended with the homecoming of the Odyssean hero, it is generically impossible to transfer the glory acquired by the hero to a character who is entirely dispensable to the adventure, and to allow this straw man *ex machina* to expel the suitors, as it were, by punishing the wicked sailors. The epic cannot end with the deeds of a character who is more powerful and more just than the epic hero himself. In a romance the returning hero must do obeissance to his king; in a classical epic such a *dénouement* is utterly impossible.

The generic necessity for Periander's disappearance becomes even more evident when we consider the way in which Arion's heroic identity is sustained near the end of the poem. As Arion rides safely to shore on the back of a dolphin he is described in terms which evoke not Odysseus, but rather a victorious military hero entering the city in a glorious triumphal procession:

> Tel que marche en triomphe aprés mainte conqueste,
> Quelque grand Capitaine un laurier sur la teste,
> Monté haut sur son Char, les trompettes devant,
> Accompagné de Peuple à longs cris le suivant,
> De toutes qualitez, de tout sexe, et tout âge,
> Qui devancent ses pas pour le voir davantage,
> Saute à l'entour de luy d'aise tout transporté,
> Admirant sa façon pleine de majesté,
> Tel estoit Arion sur sa vivante barque. . .
>
> (11. 201-209)

Not only is Arion described as a Caesar in this scene, but he takes on something of the grandeur of a god as well:

> Les Tritons à l'envy faisant bruire leurs trompes
> Comme devant Neptune en ses divines pompes,
> D'un rang bien ordonné devant luy cheminoient,
> Et de leurs tons aigus tous les Cieux étonnoient.
>
> (11. 213-216)

There is nothing in the legend of Arion, or even in Saint-Amant's retelling of the legend, that suggests that the *kitharoidos* possesses anything at all of the true essence of a conquering hero or a "grand Capitaine." The triumphal imagery finds its justification not in the *fabula* itself, but in the epic form into which the legend has been cast. It is quite evident that if the king of Corinth were suddenly to appear and to take charge of the legal aspects of the adventure after Arion's landing, not only the genre but the esthetic unity and coherence of the poem would be seriously violated. There is no room for a king because Arion, as an epic hero, is by definition regal.

Arion's twenty-four line strophic song is another innovation in Saint-Amant's version of the legend, and one which has always been more severely criticized than any other part of the poem. It is invariably judged to be trite, flaccid and unrelated to the narrative it interrupts. I will have occasion to examine it in some detail presently. The justification for its very presence in the poem, however, can already be perceived. Of all the classical and Renaissance Arion authors, not one includes the actual lyrics of Arion's miracle-working song. Saint-Amant does so because, unlike all of his predecessors, he is telling an *epic* tale, and classicizing epics must contain either a prayer to the gods or an interlude sung by a *kitharoidos:* Chryses prays to Apollo in the first book of the *Iliad;* Demodocus sings the events of the Trojan war and the adulterous love of Ares and Aphrodite in Book VIII of the *Odyssey;* Iopas sings of cosmology and Aeneas prays to Apollo in Books I and VI of the *Aeneid;* Helenus prays to Neptune in the first book of the *Franciade. L'Arion* merely follows the epic pattern by reporting a song which is both a prayer *and* a musical interlude.

The epic function of Arion's song justifies not only its *presence* in Saint-Amant's poem, but some of its own images as well. The poet-hero prays to Apollo for fair sailing weather, just as Ronsard's Helenus prays to Neptune for a calm sea. But he does so in such a way as to recall the two classical voyages on which *L'Arion* is patterned:

> Nous sommes bien certains qu'Eole te revere,
> Si ta faveur l'ordonne, au lieu d'estre severe,
> Il montrera pour nous autant d'affections
>   Que pour ses Alcions.
> Il calmera les flots que son sceptre gouverne,
> Enchaisnera Borée au fond de sa caverne,
> Et laissera courir Zephire seulement
>   Sur ce vaste Element.
>   (11. 137-144)

This eight-line development on Aeolus is indeed bathos if the

song is read out of context. Appearing as it does in a poem so
unambiguously identified as epic, however, it helps us to recall
two storms which were *not* averted in early epic voyages. One is
Homeric: just as Odysseus is about to arrive safely home in
Ithaca, his greedy crew opens the sack in which Aeolus has
obligingly imprisoned all contrary winds; the resulting storm
drives Odysseus' ship back to Aeolia, whence the Greeks must
travel to Lestrygonian shores and to Circe's island (*Odyssey* X).
The other is Vergilian: it is Aeolus himself who unleashes the
great storm that drives Aeneas' ship backward to Carthage and
Dido in the seventh year of his voyage (*Aeneid* I). Saint-Amant's
lines on Aeolus recall most directly the description by Vergil

> . . .Hic vasto rex Aeolus antro
> Luctantis ventos tempestatesque sonoras
> Imperio premit ac vinclis et carcere frenat.
> . . . .
> . . .Celsa sedet Aeolus arce
> Sceptra tenens, mollitque animos et temperat iras,
> > (*Aeneid* I, 52-57)

and those lines in which Ovid has Macareus recount Odysseus'
adventures:

> Aeolon ille refert Tusco regnare profundo,
> Aeolon Hippotaden, cohibentem carcere ventos;
> Quos bovis inclusos tergo, memorabile munus,
> Dulichium sumpsisse ducem flatuque secundo
> Lucibus isse novem et terram aspexisse petitam.
> > (*Metamorphoses* XIV, 223-227)

Even in the images of Arion's song, then, Saint-Amant has reinforced the characterization of his poem as an epic, and the
identity of his hero as a post-Trojan epic sea-voyager.

In regard to style and diction too, many aspects of the
poem can be explained only by their epic function. Since the
poem claims from the outset to be written in a "stile assez rare"
(1. 18), that is, in the elevated style of heroic verse, it is only
natural to find in it examples of epic periphrasis like "La Deesse
aux trois noms" for Diana (1. 217), affective interjections like
"ô chose bien estrange!" (1. 165) modeled on the Vergilian

"mirabile dictu" or "fide maius," and Homeric similes like the following:

> Comme on voit des roseaux la souple obeïssance
> Fleschir facilement sous la fiere puissance
> Des Aquilons émeus, soufflans de toutes pars,
> Qui pourroient ébranler les plus fermes rempars:
> Tout de mesme on voyoit Arion sur la Pouppe,
> Ceder à la fureur de cette avare trouppe. . .
>   (11. 177-182)

Readers who remain convinced that Saint-Amant was a naïve and spontaneous *moderne* for whom the "real world" of first-hand experience was a greater concern than the bookish world of Literature, will undoubtedly take a last refuge in the most famous passage of *L'Arion,* one which has been cited by critics for over a century as a prime example of the powers of observation and description of this "poète de la mer":

> On leve aussi tost l'ancre, on laisse choir les voilles,
> Un vent frais, et bruyant donne à plein dans ces toilles,
> On invocque Tethis, Neptune, et Palemon,
> Les Nochers font joüer les ressorts du Timon,
> La Nef seillone l'eau, qui fuyant sa carriere
> Court devant et tournoye à gros boüillons derriere.
>   (11. 49-54)

There can be no doubt concerning Saint-Amant's powers of description, and this passage is indeed one of the most evocative in the poet's works. Yet to explain the presence of this descriptive passage in mid-narrative by invoking acute first-hand observations, baroque myopia and *amplificatio,* or a personal gift for description which is indulged at any and every occasion without regard for the continuity of the narrative which it interrupts, is simply wrong. The passage occurs here for the simple reason that *L'Arion* purports to be an epic, and nearly every embarkation in classical epic narrative begins with just such a description. One appears when the Argonauts set out at the beginning of Catullus' *epyllion* on Peleus and Thetis, as the world's first ship

> . . .rostro ventosum proscidit aequor,
> Tortaque remigio spumis incanduit unda.
>   (64, 11. 12-13)

One appears when Aeneas and his Trojan crew leave Dido and Carthage:

> Idem omnis simul ardor habet; rapiuntque ruuntque;
> Litora deseruere; latet sub classibus aequor;
> Adnixi torquent spumas et caerula verrunt.
> *(Aeneid* IV, 581-583)

Though Saint-Amant's image is a beautiful one, it is not invented from scratch or suggested by a personal recollection. It is a description required by the conventions of epic narrative, and its detail consists almost entirely of elements collated from various epic embarkations.

Given the implicit Arion-Odysseus assimilation established early in the poem we might expect to find an even greater similarity in detail between Saint-Amant's famous description and lines from parallel passages in the *Iliad* and the *Odyssey*. And indeed we do. In Book I of the *Iliad* Odysseus returns by sea to the Greek camp, having successfully completed his mission to Apollo's priest Chryses. He and his men

> . . .reprirent la mer,
> Pour retourner au camp à force de ramer:
> Et Phoebus leur donna le vent fort favorable.
> Ils leverent adonc le mast avec le cable
> Et tendirent la voile, et le vent leur donnoit
> Par le milieu du voile, et le flot resonnoit
> Autour du vaisseau noir qui courroit dessus l'onde
> Et coupoit les sillons de la vague profonde.[12]
> *(Iliad* I, 478-483)

A similar description occurs in the *Odyssey* when Ulysses and his crew narrowly escape the Cyclops Polyphemus:

> Et de tout leur effort ouvrirent l'eau marine
> Haussans les avirons, et partissans la mer
> Qui bruyante escumoit à force de ramer.[13]
> *(Odyssey* IX, 563-564)

As the Greeks leave Circe's island off the Latin peninsula to continue their voyage in the direction of Greece (Arion's itinerary), the embarkation is described in the following terms:

> Ils entrent dans la nef, et tous selon leurs rans,
> Les Avirons en main, s'asseent sur les bans.
> Ils frappent les sillons des ondes blanchissantes.
> Les eaux vont resonnans sous les rames glissantes:
> Derriere nous avions les favorables vents
> Qui nos voiles enfloient nostre vaisseau suivans.
> . . . .
> . . .la nef à l'aise flotte
> Ayant pour gouverneurs le vent et le pilote.[14]
> (*Odyssey* XII, 146-152)

And as the sleeping Odysseus is rowed home to Ithaca from Alcinoos' court in Scheria, a similar description occurs:

> Ainsi dessus les mers le vaisseau se haussoit,
> Et la mer par derriere encontre luy poussoit,
> Et bouillonnante et noire. Il court de grand' vistesse
> Et de grand' fermeté et de grande allegresse.[15]
> (*Odyssey* XIII, 84-86)

Needless to say, similar embarkation scenes are also to be found in Ronsard's classicizing epic poem. At the end of Book I and the beginning of Book II of *La Franciade,* Francus' departure from the fatherland is described in these very terms not once, but three times:

> A-tant Francus s'embarque en son Navire,
> Les avirons à double ranc on tire:
> Le vent poupier qui droictement soufla
> Dedans la voile à plein ventre l'enfla,
> Faisant sifler antennes et cordage:
> La nef bien loin s'escarte du rivage!
> L'eau sous la poupe aboyant fait un bruit,
> Qu'un train d'escume en tournoyant poursuit.[16]

> L'eau se blanchist sous les coups d'avirons:
> L'onde tortue ondoye aux environs
> De la carene, et autour de la prouë
> Maint tourbillon en escumant se rouë:
> La terre fuit, seulement à leurs yeux
> Paroist la Mer et la voûte des Cieux.[17]

[the Olympian gods]
. . .contemploient la Troyenne jeunesse
Fendre la mer d'une prompte alegresse:
Flot dessus flot la Navire voloit,
Un trac d'escume à bouillons se rouloit
Sous l'aviron qui les vagues entame:
L'eau fait un bruit luitant contre la rame![18]

The inevitable conclusion imposed by all these Latin, Homeric and Ronsardian precedents is that the passage of *L'Arion* which modern readers take to be one of the most "natural" and unpremeditated in Saint-Amant's works, is in fact one of the most closely imitated and the most "literary."[19] The description is entirely consistent with the project of the poem as a whole because it is unmistakably epic, and because the epic hero it calls most clearly to mind is Odysseus. In failing to recognize this, modern readers have fallen woefully short of Saint-Amant's expectations. The intelligence of this most "literary" poem depends upon a considerable sophistication and culture which we neglect to bring to the work, allowing ourselves to be put off the track by the carefully cultivated pose of a gluttonous libertine who cannot be bothered with books.

Is Saint-Amant's epicization of an obscure anecdote sheer virtuosity, or does it serve some function? We must not forget that epic was the genre that the Pléiade had exalted as the highest form of literature. The life-long dream of Ronsard in particular had been to revive the Homeric-Vergilian tradition and to accomodate it to the French language. He had begun an epic poem, and had even published the first four books after what was perhaps the longest and most extravagant publicity campaign ever to be waged before the invention of cinema. But his long-awaited epic, as we know, was his most disastrous failure. Nor must we forget that Arion was precisely the kind of divinely inspired poet-*vates* in whose image the poets of the Pléiade had singled-mindedly sought to fashion themselves. Once again, it was Ronsard in particular who had claimed such a role for himself, in the early odes most especially. Yet Ronsard had failed

in his attempt to become a poet-*vates* as utterly as he had failed
in his attempt to produce an epic poem: at the end of his life
and in the eyes of posterity, Ronsard was cherished not as an
Orpheus, but as the Petrarchistic court poet of the *Sonets pour
Hélène.* Despite all his pretensions to Greco-Roman glory, his
renown was ultimately that of a latter-day Marot.

Keeping these things in mind, and remembering too that in
1623 Ronsard was still the undisputed prince of France's poets,
we may perhaps be justified in seeing in *L'Arion* the challenge
of a new young rival, an ironic pin-prick to the Ronsardian
afflatus. By publishing a small classicizing epic whose hero is
a Ronsardian poet in an age when "epic" had come to mean a
romance after the manner of Ariosto and Tasso, and "poet"
had come to mean a Malherbian artisan, a Priapic pornographer,
a Jesuitical polemicist, or a satirist in the manner of Régnier,
Saint-Amant seems to be drawing attention to the fact that he
is beginning his poetic career not in the abyss of early seventeenth-century versifying, but at the very point toward which
Ronsard's entire career had tended, and in fact on the very
ruins of Ronsard's disaster. Saint-Amant's anachronistic "epic"
is in fact an inversion of Ronsard's. The *Franciade* is self-con-
sciously Vergilian in subject, and was in fact intended to be the
French *Aeneid:* both Francus and Aeneas leave Troy as the walls
of Ilium lie in ruins, and both are destined by the gods to found
a new Empire—Aeneas to establish the race which will build the
"altae moenia Romae," Francus to "bastir les grans murs de
Paris" (*La Franciade* I, 12). But in matters of form Ronsard
followed Homer rather than Vergil whenever he was able. This
Hellenizing tendency is evident in the very first lines of the
Franciade, which are in fact little more than a didactic *amplificatio* of the Homeric Ἄνδρα μοι ἔννεπε Μοῦσα:

> *Muse,* entens moy des sommets de Parnasse,
> Guide ma langue, et *me chante la race*
> Des Rois François yssus de Francion
> Enfant d'Hector Troyen de nation.
> . . . .
> De ce Troyen *conte moy les travaux,*. . .[20]
> (ll. 1-7)

This is precisely the reverse of Saint-Amant's imitation: as we have seen, his more familiar Vergilian prologue announces a clearly defined Homeric subject. Ronsard, in short, borrows his invocation directly from the *Odyssey,* but his hero is an unimaginative copy of Aeneas; Saint-Amant models his opening lines after those of the *Aeneid,* while his hero is an Orphic poet cast in the role of everyone's favorite epic hero, Odysseus.

This inversion of Ronsard's models would not be especially significant if it were not for the fact that wherever the movement of Saint-Amant's "epic" departs from both the Homeric and the Vergilian models, it is modeled directly on the *Franciade* itself. The clearest instance of this is the dedicatory passage to the Duc de Montmorency—the same passage which led us earlier to consider the work to be composed according to a simple encomiastic structure, the narrative portion of the poem being little more than the meat of a eulogistic sandwich. Up to its first dedicatory passage *L'Arion* has been transposed point-for-point from the opening lines of the *Aeneid,* as we have seen. The next lines of the Vergilian model consist of an Homeric invocation to the Muse:

> Musa, mihi causas memora, quo numine laeso
> Quidve dolens regina deum tot volvere casus
> Insignem pietate virum, tot adire labores
> Impulerit. Tantaene animis caelestibus irae?
>
> (11. 8-11)

But Saint-Amant, instead of asking the Muse to aid his memory in recalling the divine motives behind the peripeteia of the story he is about to tell, asks his Maecenas simply to listen to the song he is about to sing, and to protect him, the new Arion, from any such violence at the hands of French sailors:

> Grand Duc, grand Admiral, ornement de la France,
> De qui les hauts exploits surpassent l'esperance
> Qu'en tes plus tendres ans tout le monde eut de toy,
> Brave Montmorency, de grace écoute moy,
> Ecoute ces accords qu'Arion te dedie,
> Contemple un peu son Lut, gouste sa melodie,
> Et regissant l'Estat de l'Ocean Gaulois
> Sous le joug glorieux de nos augustes lois,
> Empesche desormais qu'un dessein si barbare

> Qu'est celuy que j'exprime en ce stile assez rare,
> Ne naisse dans l'esprit d'aucun des matelots
> Que ta charge instituë au commerce des flots.
> (11. 9-20)

Despite appearances, this is not a creative adaptation of Vergil's classical topos to the social realities of modern France. That adaptation had already been made by Ronsard, who followed the twelve lines of his Homeric prologue with the following invocation not to the Muse, but to King Charles IX:

> Charles mon Prince enfle-moy le courage,
> Pour ton honneur j'entrepren cet ouvrage:
> Sers moy de phare, et garde d'abysmer
> Ma nef qui flotte en si profonde mer.
> (*La Franciade* I, 13-16)

Saint-Amant has merely copied the movement of *the* French epic by substituting his own benefactor for Ronsard's.

Saint-Amant's relation to Montmorency was very different from Ronsard's to King Charles IX, however, and the difference accounts for several changes in the detail of his dedication. Ronsard had been in search of a sponsor for his epic for years. Despite an unrelenting campaign which was launched with the *Ode de la Paix,* he had been unable to interest Henri II in the project. It was not until two reigns later that Henri's third son at last took a serious interest in both the poet and his proposed epic. This long-awaited favor was what finally allowed the poet to begin work on what he thought would be both his and France's greatest work. In a very literal way it was Charles to whom Ronsard owed the realization of his plan. The substitution of Charles for the Muse in Ronsard's second invocation is therefore quite appropriate. Though he did not inspire the poem as do the daughters of Mnemosyne, the king did encourage the poet to return to his project, and Ronsard plays on the etymology of "in-spiration" by calling on the king to "enfler" his courage. The punning assimilation of favor and poetic inspiration is prolonged in the second two lines of the dedication by means of another familiar topos. Like so many other poets from Pindar to Ovid and from Dante to Rimbaud, Ronsard uses the image of a ship as a metaphor for poesis.[21] Just as the Muses (as north star, beacon, pilot or favorable wind) traditionally guide the poem-poet over the uncharted waters of a new, profound and perilous subject to the safety of a secure harbor at the end of the poetic voyage, so Charles' protection is sought as a "phare" (in the first edition as a "guide"), as a direction-giver which can serve to avert a shipwreck at the moment when Ronsard is about to launch his new poem "en si profonde mer."

Saint-Amant's position with respect to his poem and to his patron was very different. *L'Arion* is one of the very first poems of his career, and was published shortly after his first arrival in Paris. Its composition was not deferred for years for want of royal subvention, and its existence was in no way dependent on Montmorency. On the contrary, it was more likely *because* he enjoyed the favor and friendship of the Admiral of the French fleet that Saint-Amant conceived the idea of the poem at all. This being the case, it was clearly impossible for the poet to make the same claims and requests in his dedication to Montmorency that Ronsard had made in the *Franciade*. Thus, while the very existence and placement of Saint-Amant's dedication depends on the example provided by Ronsard, several changes within the dedication itself are called for. Whereas Charles is projected into the role of a *Muse* who takes an active part in the making of the poem, encouraging and guiding the poet in his task, Montmorency is cast into the strictly passive role of *audience,* whose only responsibility in regard to the poem itself is to listen and to appreciate ("Ecoute ces accords. . .Contemple. . . gouste"). As a consequence of these changes this passage loses the superficial signs of its original Ronsardian function of a modified invocation to the Muse. Without these signs we tend to mistake the passage for nothing more than the first wing of a eulogistic triptych. A seventeenth-century reader, approaching the poem with literary experience and expectations different from our own, could not have made the same mistake. Recent literary history provided a perspective from which the epic function of this dedication was immediately discernible.

The actual biographical circumstances which necessitated these changes from the Ronsardian model are of course of little or no interest in considering the poem as a coherent work of art. The question is rather this: given the fact that his circumstances in writing *L'Arion* were not at all those of Ronsard in writing

La Franciade, why did Saint-Amant bother to follow the Ronsardian model at all?   Having begun the poem in a Vergilian mode, why did he not continue in the same vein and invoke his Muse here, incorporating his flattery of Montmorency into the body of the "epic" itself as Vergil had done with Augustus?

If we consider once again Ronsard's metaphor for poesis, Saint-Amant's purpose begins to reveal itself.   In asking for Charles' support Ronsard uses the conventional metaphor of a ship in need of a "phare" or a "guide."   Saint-Amant, it would seem, has simply adopted the same metaphor in order to reify it by applying it to the Admiral of France, who *literally and actually* guides and protects the *ships* of the French fleet.   And since Saint-Amant needs neither encouragement nor subsidy from Montmorency in order to write his poem, he applies the protection afforded by the reified metaphor not to himself as a poet or to his poetic project, but to the *subject* of the poem, Arion, who *literally and actually* makes a perilous voyage in a "nef qui flotte en si profonde mer."   The poet then uses those obvious similarities between himself and Arion, which have vainly arrested critics for so long, as a pretext for identifying himself with his hero ("Ecoute ces accords qu'*Arion* te dedie"). This identification in turn allows him to follow his Ronsardian model one step further by appearing to implore his patron for protection, even though neither he nor his poem has the slightest need of a "phare" in Ronsard's conventional metaphorical sense. On the one hand, then, the very action of Saint-Amant's poem becomes a mere projection of the literal sense of Ronsard's worn-out metaphor for poesis; and on the other hand the hero who performs the action of this literalized metaphor is himself a "Ronsardian" poet-hero.   The irony of Saint-Amant's borrowing is thus double-edged, and it allows him to mock Ronsard's lack of wit (in slavishly imitating a trite topos) while constituting in itself a supreme example of his own.[22]

We would be greatly mistaken in assuming that this Ronsardian imitation in the dedication to Montmorency is in any way a literary theft, or that it betrays a lack of imagination or self-confidence in an early work by an unpublished poet. Just as we are *meant* to recognize Vergil in the first eight lines of the poem, so we are *meant* to recognize Ronsard in the following twelve lines. By drawing on the reader's familiarity with Vergil the poem is able to connote much more about itself, its poet and its hero than could possibly have been contained in any eight denotative lines, no matter how dense. And by recalling Ronsard's epic through a purely formal device in the following lines, Saint-Amant invites us to compare the parallel passages and to discover his own brilliance at the expense of Ronsard's conventionality. And indeed we suddenly realize that the overwhelming virtuosity of *L'Arion* lies in its own ironic claims to grandeur and in its ironic comment on the great master in whose shadow a third generation of poets still remained obscure. As his very first published poem Saint-Amant has written a compact version of what the Pléiade considered to be the highest form of literary art; he has chosen as his hero the kind of legendary poet whose powers the Pléiade poets never ceased to claim for themselves, but one whom the Pléiade, curiously, had overlooked almost entirely; through a brilliant ordering of images, literary echoes and comparisons he has assimilated this Poet to the most engaging of Homeric Heroes, whereas the Hellenizing Ronsard had been forced by the exigencies of his proposed "national epic" to create a pale and lifeless reflection of pious Aeneas; in the dedicatory passage he has given an entirely new dimension to the Pindaric metaphor for poesis which Ronsard had slavishly and humorlessly transposed in his *Franciade,* and has done so by restoring to Ronsard's poetic "nef" its literal meaning and making it perfectly appropriate to the circumstances of his epic hero, to the circumstances of the dedicatee of his poem, and to the circumstances of the poet himself; and finally, by assimilating himself to the sea-going Poet who arrives safely at shore, Saint-Amant ironically predicts his own success while recalling the great disaster of Ronsard's poetic *nef* which sank "en si profonde mer."

Saint-Amant has chosen as his point of departure the culmination of Ronsard's long career, and inverted the entire project of the *prince des poètes.* If we are insensitive to the literary echoes and overtones of *L'Arion* we are bound to misread it as a "serious" work which contrasts with the joyful and humorous poetry of *Raillerie à Part.* Paradoxically, it is only if we read the poem "seriously," that is, with a degree of faith in the poet's powers of poetic suggestion and his awareness of the tradition in which he is writing, that we realize that *L'Arion* is in fact one of Saint-Amant's most ironic works. Given the extravagance of the claim it obliquely makes for itself, and the impudence of its implicit but relentless one-upmanship directed against the Pléiade in general and Ronsard in particular, *L'Arion* constitutes one of the most dazzling examples of Oedipal murder in the history of French literature.

Every detail of *L'Arion* cannot be considered to have an epic function or precedent, of course, and while Arion is assimilated to Odysseus in the ways and for the reasons I have discussed above, the essential aspects of his identity and his adventure are very unlike those of Homer's hero. He is first and foremost a singer-poet-musician—a *kitharoidos* in short—and the outcome of his adventure depends upon, and is inseparably linked to, his virtuosity in this most un-Ulyssean profession. But aspects of the story which cannot be made to fit the Homeric paradigm are not brought in simply as the unassimilable but necessary givens of the *fabula* which Saint-Amant has chosen as the content—indifferent in itself—of an ironic structure; they are integrated into a coherent pattern of their own, and create a meaning which is related not to the epic structure of the poem, but to the valorization of its lyric hero.

Arion is traditionally credited with the invention of the dithyramb. Readers who are aware of this attribution frequently express surprise that there is nothing dithyrambic about the poet's song in *L'Arion*.[23]   But the obvious reason for the non-dithyrambic tone of Arion's song is that the song is a hymn to Apollo, not a hymn to Bacchus. Furthermore, the poem is relentless and entirely unambiguous in establishing Apollo, not Bacchus, as Arion's tutelary god and unique source of inspiration: Arion is a virtuoso on the Apollonian *kithara* ("Lut"), not the Dionysian *aulos;* he is crowned with Apollo's "Laurier immortel" (1. 94), not with Dionysos' ivy; when "certains mouvemens" urge him to "prier Apollon" (11. 98-99) he is naturally transported by a "fureur poëtique" (1. 102), not by a Bacchic furor; and he is "tourné vers le Soleil" (1. 120) as he addresses his prayer to Phoebus, "Prince de la lumière" (1. 126). Arion is in fact so strongly identified with Apollo that shortly after the sun "se plonge en la mer Atlantique" (1. 146) the poet appears to imitate him as he too "se precipite en l'onde" (1. 189)—so much so that even the marine gods are subject to a momentary baroque *engaño*:

> Les Dieux qui font dans l'Eau leur mobile demeure,
> L'y regardans tomber et considerans l'heure,
> Creurent tous ébahis par un commun abus
> Que Thetis recevoit en son lict deux Phebus.
> (11. 197-200)

But while Arion is explicitly and repeatedly valorized as an Apollonian poet, there is a more specific and far more significant aspect of his identity to be considered as well. When Arion is first introduced in Saint-Amant's poem, he is described in terms which are unequivocal in recalling *Orpheus*:

> Ce fameux Arion. . .
> Qui par les tons mignars d'une amoureuse vois,
> Doucement alliez aux charmes de ses dois,
> Ostoit l'ame aux humains pour la donner aux marbres,
> Domtoit les animaux, faisoit marcher les arbres,
> Arrestoit le Soleil, precipitoit son cours,. . .
> (11. 22-27)

There is no classical authority for the attribution of these miracles to Arion, whereas classical antiquity is unanimous in attributing all of them to Orpheus. After Orpheus has drawn a forest of shade trees to Rhodope by the strains of his lyre, he is described by Ovid in the following lines which have clearly inspired those of Saint-Amant:

> Tale nemus vates attraxerat inque ferarum
> Concilio medius turba volucrumque sedebat.
> (*Metamorphoses* X, 143-144)

> Carmine dum tali silvas animosque ferarum
> Threicius vates et saxa sequentia ducit,
> Ecce nurus Ciconum. . .
>   . . .cernunt
> Orphea percussis sociantem carmina nervis.
> (*Metamorphoses* XI, 1-5)

Arion's tuning-up and preluding before his hymn to Apollo also recalls this passage from Ovid: Saint-Amant's Arion

> Accorde bien son Lut, en ajuste les touches,
> L'essaye avec sa voix, dont il émeut les souches;
> Puis montant sur la Poupe en superbe appareil,
> Profere ces propos. . .
>   (11. 117-120)

exactly as Ovid's Orpheus,

> Ut satis inpulsas temptavit pollice chordas
> Et sensit varios, quamvis diversa sonarent,
> Concordare modos, hoc vocem carmine movit. . .[24]
>   (*Metamorphoses* X, 145-147)

And when Arion has finished his hymn, the marvelous effects of the music are described in a passage which echoes the Orphic description of the opening, but transfers the miracles from the beasts of the forest to those of the sea:

> Soudain que ces accors sur les eaux s'estendirent,
> Mille et mille poissons en foule se rendirent
> Autour de ce vaisseau, mais sans bruit toutesfois,
> Pour gouster de plus prez une si belle vois:
> Là, pour l'entendre mieux l'effroyable Baleine
> Aussi bien que les vents retenoit son haleine:
> Là, ceux que la Nature a fait naistre ennemis,
> Et dont les sentimens furent lors endormis,
> Sans qu'aucune dispute y semast des alarmes,
> Se laissoient pesle-mesle attirer à ses charmes.
>   (11. 149-158)

It might be assumed that the Orphic aspect of Arion is simply an inevitable consequence of the obvious similarities between the two poets and the relative obscurity of Arion. But another of Saint-Amant's innovations leads us to a rather different conclusion. As Arion is carried to safety by the dolphin all the heavens seem to rejoice, but only two celestial bodies are singled out for specific mention. One is Phoebus-Apollo's sister Selene-Luna (11. 217-220), the other is the constellation Lyra:

> . . .entre tous on tient que la Lyre d'Orfée
> De l'amour de son Lut vivement échauffée,
> Ayant de ses rayons tout nüage écarté,
> Le réjoüit beaucoup avecques sa clarté.
> (11. 225-228)

The particular favor of Lyra seems at first to be nothing more than facile play with an affinity of lyres for lutes and poets for poets, perhaps suggested originally by the Ovidian source of the Arion legend in which Lyra and Delphinus are observed to set on consecutive nights. But the precise designation "Lyre d'*Orfée*," in conjunction with all the other oblique allusions to Orpheus in the poem, invites us to consider its mention more seriously.

Just as the moon and the other "planets" are real gods and goddesses in their celestial hypostases—and we have just been reminded of this fact in the preceding lines on Persephone-Artemis-Selene: "La Deesse aux trois noms l'*inconstante planette*"—so too the constellations of fixed stars are real people and objects which have been katasterized. Lyra is of course no exception, and the specific epithet "Lyre d'Orfée" recalls its pre-metamorphic reality as Orpheus' actual lyre, and invites us to recall the circumstances of its assumption into the heavens. That story in fact has considerable relevance to the question of Arion's inspiration. Ovid's version of Orpheus' death, in Books X and XI of the *Metamorphoses,* is in most respects standard: three years after Eurydice's second death Orpheus retires to the solitude of Rhodope and begins to sing. It is here that he draws shade trees by the sweetness of his music, and that mention is made of all the miracles that Saint-Amant attributes to Arion. As he sings he is attacked by a band of Ciconian women in a Bacchic frenzy. But the "vates Apollineus" (*Metamorphoses* XI, 8), is unharmed by the stones and thyrsis-blows of his attackers because these inanimate objects are all overcome by the sweetness of his music: "concentu victus vocisque lyraeque" (1. 11). It is only when the din of strident Bacchic instruments—the double-reed flutes and bronze cymbals—becomes so great as to drown out the sound of Orpheus' Apollonian lyre, that the deafened stones hurled by the Bacchae strike their target, killing the *kitharoidos:*

Cunctaque tela forent cantu mollita, sed ingens

Clamor et infracto Berecyntia *tibia* cornu
Tympanaque et plausus et *Bacchei ululatus*
Obstrepuere sono *citharae,* tum denique saxa
Non exauditi rubuerunt sanguine vatis.
(*Metamorphoses* XI, 15-19)

The Maenads then sever the poet's head and throw it with his
lyre into the Hebrus, whence both are carried downstream to the
sea, still singing and playing, and are eventually deposited on the
shores of Methymne in Lesbos. As a serpent is about to attack
the poet's head, Phoebus Apollo arrives in person to protect
these last vestiges of his son and consecrated poet. The Ovidian
narration ends here, but a most accessible tradition has it that it
was from the shores of Lesbos that the lyre was raised to the
heavens. Natalis Comes, for example, in his article on Orpheus
(VII, 14), relates the poet's end in the following terms: "Sa
teste jettee avec son luth dedans l'Hebre, fut par la violence de
la riviere emportee en Lesbos, et là ensevelie: sa lyre fut placee
entre les Astres, et embellie de neuf belles et claires estoilles,
dont chaque Muse bailla la sienne, pour avoir hautement chanté
leurs loüanges."

Two very striking points in the story of Orpheus' lyre will
not have escaped the reader's attention. The first is that in the
tension between Apollonian and Bacchic inspiration, Orpheus
is situated squarely in the former camp. Lyra shines in the
heavens *because* Orpheus was Apollo's poet, and *because* his
Apollonian lyre was beaten in a kind of decibel contest with the
Bacchic instruments of the Maenads. The motives for the murder
of Orpheus are significant as well. Ovid maintains that the
Maenads attack because Orpheus, after Eurydice's second death,
denied his attentions to all other women and introduced
pederasty into Thrace. A more common explanation is that
when the poet descended to Hades he sang the praises of all the
gods, and principally Apollo, but neglected to honor Dionysos
at all. The most accessible account of this legend is to be found
in Natalis Comes, who prefers this version to Ovid's: "On dit
qu'estant descendu aux Enfers il se prit à chanter les loüanges de
tous les Dieux, hormis de Bacchus, qu'il oublia par mesgarde:
dont malcontent il mit ses Bacchantes en furie, aprés qu'il fut
remonté, lesquelles le deschirerent en pieces vers la riviere
d'Hebre. . . . Il avoit fait merveilles en chantant sur tous autres

les loüanges d'Apollon" (*Mythologie,* VII, 14, "D'Orphée").
The special favor shown to Arion's lute by the "lyre d'Orfée"
is thus entirely consistent with the unwaveringly Apollonian
orientation attributed to Arion in Saint-Amant's poem.

But there is a far more striking resonance provided by the
story of Orpheus' lyre. Just before the katasterism of the lyre,
both it and Orpheus' severed head are carried across the Aegean
to Lesbos, and are washed up on the shore of the very town in
which Arion was born, Methymna.[25] The attribution of miracles
universally recognized as those of Orpheus to the poet-hero of
L'Arion has already suggested that Orpheus is in some way
Arion's prototype. But by inviting us to recall the manner and
place of Orpheus' end at the very moment that Arion, "triom-
phant de la Parque," is singing and playing his "luth" on dolphin-back, the poem seems to suggest further that the Lesbian
poet's homeward *croisière-concert* is actually a typological re-
enactment of the trans-Aegean peregrinations of Orpheus' singing head and playing lyre. In addition to being Orpheus' analogue, Arion also appears to be Orpheus' successor and heir. The
coincidence of Orpheus' terminus and Arion's birthplace suggests
a kind of *translatio poesis* by which the divine afflatus, born of
Calliope and Apollo himself, is carried in the person of Orpheus
from Thrace to Lesbos, and in the person of Arion (Musaeus,
Alcaeus and Sappho notwithstanding) from Lesbos to Greece
by way of Periander's Corinth. As the continuator of Orpheus'
"mission," Arion of course succeeds where his predecessor failed:
the mutilated Orpheus is washed ashore dead, while Arion arrives alive and triumphant. The role of Saint-Amant's allusion
to the Thracian bard with respect to Arion the lyric poet appears
to be exactly the same as that of his allusion to the Trojan
Polydorus with respect to Arion the Odyssean hero.

By repeating Orpheus' "voyage," by taking up where
Orpheus left off, Arion arrives at the very point at which his
prototype's adventure began. When Eurydice is bitten by a snake
and dies, the Thracian poet descends to Hades to fetch her back.
There is only one gate through which Greek heroes may descend
alive into Hades, and Orpheus is bound by tradition to take the
same route that Hercules and Theseus do: "Ad Styga *Taenaria*
est ausus descendere porta" (*Metamorphoses* X, 13), "*Taenarias*
etiam fauces, alta ostia Ditis. . .ingressus" (*Georgics* IV, 467-

469). It is to the same Taenarum that Arion is transported by his dolphin. Saint-Amant of course had little choice in this matter, since Herodotus, Aulus Gellius, Plutarch and Lucian all name Taenarum explicitly, and Du Bartas follows their authority by naming the region in which Taenarum is situated, "Laconie" (*La Premiere Sepmaine* V, 523). The poet either had to adopt Taenarum as the point of debarkation, or to follow Ovid in neglecting to specify the terminus at all. But the coincidence of Orpheus' point of departure and Arion's point of arrival is nevertheless made significant in *L'Arion* by a rather striking circumstance: of *all* the Arion authors, Saint-Amant is the *only* one to observe, directly or indirectly, that this Taenarum is the same one which serves as a gateway to the underworld. He does this, moreover, in the very last lines of his narrative at the moment of Arion's arrival:

> Ainsi par un secours si puissant et si rare
> Se voyant mettre à terre au pied du *mont-Tenare*,
> Aprés tant de plaisirs à son merite offers,
> Il trouva son salut *aux portes des Enfers*.
> (11. 285-288)

The general form of the *pointe* in the last line comes directly from Du Bartas, whose last word on the Arion legend is a résumé of the dolphin's role in this adventure: "La vie il luy redonne, où la vie il a prise" (*La Premiere Sepmaine* V, 528). But Saint-Amant's *concetto* has a much more important role in relation to the patterns of allusiveness which function throughout the entire poem. Just as the poem earlier recalled the coincidence of Orpheus' end and Arion's beginning (Methymna), it now recalls the coincidence of Orpheus' beginning and Arion's end (Taenarum). By echoing one last time Ovid's narration of the Orpheus legend, the ultimate line of Saint-Amant's narrative completes the circle, bringing Orpheus' analogue and heir back to his prototype's point of departure. And at the same time the reader is reminded once again in these final lines of Arion's *epic* prototypes who also had to pass through Hades in order to fulfill their destinies.[26] The lyric and epic circles are both neatly closed in the last line of Saint-Amant's narration.

The non-epic elements of Saint-Amant's poem all conspire to valorize Arion not only as a *vates* so dedicated to Apollo that dithyrambs are the last thing we would expect to fall from his lips, but as the analogue of a more illustrious Apollonian *vates* in poetic lore, Orpheus. As an epic hero, Saint-Amant's Arion *is*, typologically speaking, Odysseus; as a lyric poet he *is*, typologically speaking, Orpheus. Saint-Amant's little *epyllion*, then, fuses the epic and lyric modes not only by including a strophic ode within the alexandrines of an epic setting and by transforming a lyric poet into an epic hero, but by making of the poem's protagonist a typological fusion of *the* epic and lyric archetypes, Odysseus and Orpheus.

The precise nature of this epic-lyric fusion and the relevance of Arion's Apollonian identification to his epic adventure remain to be considered, and it is here that we must turn to the text itself of Arion's "cantique." The song which Saint-Amant alone of all the Arion authors includes in his narrative, and which he places at the very center of the poem, is a hymn to Apollo. It bears little resemblance to anything Horace or Ronsard ever wrote in honor of Apollo, but we would be mistaken to assume that it was written in ignorance, or that it is mere filler included solely to satisfy a baroque taste for dilation. We must not fail to realize how carefully the poem is composed, and how closely it conforms to the strictest definition of a "hymn." It is clearly divided by subject into two equal parts of three strophes each. The first half is an invocation in which Apollo's attributes and past deeds are magnified; the second consists of the prayer proper, a supplication for divine assistance in the present. In this respect, Arion's ode is a textbook example of the "Orphic" hymn:

> Le formulaire donc des hymnes estoit tel, que premierement ils chantoient en sacrifiant les loüanges des Dieux, leurs proüesses et vaillances, et les biens qu'ils avoient faits aux hommes, et de quelle affection et volonté ils avoient secouru et garanti les villes: de quelle benignité et clemence ils souloient favoriser les hommes. . . . Car Orphee a gardé cét ordre en ses hymnes, que premierement il raconte les vertus et la puissance des Dieux par laquelle ils peuvent bien faire aux hommes: puis apres il les prie de se montrer propices

et favorables.

(Mythologie I, 16, «Des hymnes des anciens»)

Though perfectly "regular," however, Arion's hymn to
Apollo is nevertheless quite different from Callimachus' *Hymn
to Apollo* which Comes proposes as a perfect model of the
Orphic hymn, and even from the original "Orphic" hymn to
Apollo which Joseph Scaliger had published in a Latin translation
only nine years before the publication of *L'Arion* (Paris, 1614).
One of the principal differences is the choice of attributes mentioned in Arion's invocation. The first strophe commemorates
the slaying of Python who terrorized the human race shortly
after the universal Deluge:

> O! le plus beau des Dieux, et le plus adorable,
> Toy qui par ta valeur aux Mortels favorable,
> Vainquis l'affreux Serpent indigne de tes coups,
>   Helas! pren soin de nous.

The second invokes Apollo in his role of Musagetes and divinity
of the sun:

> Phebus! que les neuf Soeurs reconnoissent pour Maistre,
> Prince de la lumière, à qui tout doit son estre;
> Grand et nompareil Astre aux flamboyans cheveux
>   Sois propice à nos voeux.

The third is addressed to the god of divination as he manifests
himself through the Pythia at Delphi. This third and final
strophe of the invocation ends with another appropriate reminder of Apollo's solar function, thanks to which he both measures
the days and years, and controls the weather:

> Supréme Deïté dont les sacrez Oracles
> Dans le Temple de Delphe annoncent des miracles,
> Seul arbitre du Temps qui sans toy ne peut rien,
>   Travaille à nostre bien.

All of these attributes indeed illustrate "les vertus et la puissance
par laquelle [Apollon peut] bien faire aux hommes" whose mention is required by the "Orphic" hymn. But why has Saint-
Amant chosen to mention in such detail Apollo's roles of

Python-slayer and of Oracle-giver instead of elaborating further
on the only Apollonian function which has any bearing at all
on the content of the prayer proper, that is, his solar function? The hymn is absolutely unwavering in its request for fair
sailing weather:

> Dissippe la fureur de ces noires tempestes,
> Que le malheur prepare à foudroyer nos testes;
> Et pour nous retirer de la nuict du tombeau,
>   Preste-nous ton flambeau.
> Nous sommes bien certains qu'Eole te revere,
> Si ta faveur l'ordonne, au lieu d'estre severe,
> Il montrera pour nous autant d'affections
>   Que pour ses Alcions.
> Il calmera les flots que son sceptre gouverne,
> Enchaisnera Borée au fond de sa caverne,
> Et laissera courir Zephire seulement
>   Sur ce vaste Element.

What then explains the presence of the non-solar attributes which
Saint-Amant has consciously chosen to develop in Arion's invocation?

These attributes are of course not arbitrarily chosen at all.
Nor are they unrelated. They appear to be so only if the hymn
is read in isolation from its literary lineage, and with a frag-
mented view of mythology. The work which establishes most
firmly the link between the parts of Arion's invocation is once
again Homeric, but whereas the matrix and model for the elaboration of Arion as epic hero was provided by the Homeric
epic, the authority for the necessary association of Apollo
Python-slayer and Apollo oracle-giver in Arion's hymn to Apollo
is provided by the Homeric *Hymn to Apollo.* It is the recognition of this model, moreover, that will reveal the absolute relevance of Arion's hymn to the outcome of his own adventure.
It is here, in other words, that we will find the last key to the
coherence of the entire poem.

The first 181 lines of the Homeric hymn concern Delian
Apollo—that is, the story of Leto and the birth of the god on
Delos. The remaining 365 lines are devoted exclusively to Pythic
Apollo: to the founding of the Oracle at Delphi. This narration

begins with Apollo's search for a suitable location for what is to be the first oracle in history. Many possible sites are considered and rejected, and construction is even begun near the Telphusa, but is abandoned at the hypocritical and selfish request of the local river goddess. It is finally at Crisa, later to be renamed Delphi, that Apollo resolves to build. As the foundations are laid, the narration is interrupted in order to recall an earlier event in the life of the god, one which took place close by this very spot: the battle between Apollo and Python, the monster to whom Hera had entrusted her own monstrous offspring, Typhaon. Following a long digression of 74 lines on Hera's rage over the motherless birth of Athena, the retaliatory birth of Typhaon and Apollo's battle with the latter's tutor-nurse Python, the hymn once again returns to its real subject. Apollo punishes Telphusa for her hypocrisy and completes the construction of his oracle at Crisa.

This is the story as it appears in the Greek text. The geographically motivated flashback linking Python and the Delphic Oracle in the Homeric hymn would appear to authorize and motivate the collation of the two episodes in the invocation of Arion's hymn, though the Homeric parallel seems far from irrefutable, and indeed is hardly interesting except as a possible "source" whose recognition adds nothing at all to the meaning of the poem.

Yet it is unlikely that Saint-Amant knew the Homeric hymns in the Greek text. Whether he did or not, he had access to them through the French translation published eight years before the publication of *L'Arion* (1615),[27] and it is unthinkable that a poet who "entendoit fort bien la fable" might not have been familiar with these translations which, for the very first time, made the complete works of the West's most venerable poet available to French readers. Now, the importance of this circumstance is that the French translation gives an entirely different impression of the relation between the slaying of Python and the institution of the Oracle at Delphi. Whether due to a faulty Greek text or to an error on the part of the translator, the French version of the *Hymn to Apollo* fails to distinguish the two temporal planes of the Homeric narrative. The result is that the battle with Python appears not as a flashback occasioned by the proximity of Crisa to Pytho, but as an event belonging to the same sequence of events, and which actually interrupts the building of the temple. At the same time, the translation fails to distinguish between Python and Typhaon, identifying the monstrous daughter of Hera with the monster killed by Apollo, calling the composite monster now by the name of the tutor, now by the name of the charge. Through the intermediary of Salomon Certon, then, "Homer" seems to state that the slaying of Python and the founding of the Oracle at Crisa are merely two moments in one and the same episode of Apollonian history, and that the epithet "Pythic" applies to Apollo as oracle-giver because the god slew Python in the same place, *and at the same time*, that he founded his Oracle at Pytho-Crisa-Delphi. If we adopt the view of a seventeenth-century French reader of "Homer"—that is, that the slaying of Python is in fact temporally and almost causally related to the institution of the Delphic Oracle—then we can perceive a powerful logic and coherence in an ordering of attributes in Arion's hymn which otherwise appears arbitrary and random: the invocation to Apollo as sun-god—the only role appropriate to the prayer itself—is symmetrically framed by a lyrical transposition of two consecutive events in Homer-Certon's hymn to Apollo.

The parallels between Arion's invocation to Apollo and Homer-Certon's *Hymn to Apollo* are even more compelling than this. Let us examine them one strophe at a time. Arion's first strophe treats the Python myth just as we find it treated in the Homeric Hymn. Unlike the Ovidian account of this battle, which is essentially etiological and culminates in the institution of the Pythian Games, the Homeric narration insists from the very beginning on the importance of the event as evidence of Apollo's favor to *mortals*. Arion's song, in conformity to the definition of a hymn, follows the Homeric example in this. The Homeric account is the following:

> . . .Là pres, une fontaine
> Jettoit ses belles eaux coulantes en la plaine,
> Où de son arc puissant le fils de Jupiter
> Mit à mort le serpent qui souloit molester
> Tous les circomvoisins: monstre grand et horrible,
> Qui faisoit *aux mortels* un dommage indicible,
> Et à tous leurs troupeaux: C'est le cruel Typhon
> Dommageable et sanglant qu'avoit produict Junon.

· ·
[Junon] enfanta Typhon, monstre horrible et sanglant,
La peste des *mortels,* à nul Dieu ressemblant,
Ny à homme qui fust: elle enfanta ce monstre
Malencontre *aux humains* portant sur malencontre,
Et personne n'estoit assez brave, assez fort
Pour l'oser accoster et luy donner la mort,
Paravant qu'Apollon avec sa forte fleche
Sur la beste eust ouvert une mortelle breche.
(11. 300-306, 351-358)

Upon killing the beast, Apollo addresses it in such a way as to make the significance of the deed perfectly evident:

«Demeure maintenant puante pourriture
Sur la terre qui donne aux hommes nourriture:
Tu n'affligeras plus et n'endommageras
Personne des *mortels* qui vivent icy bas,
*Les hommes desormais en devotion grande
Me viendront rendre icy hecatumbe et ofrande.»*
(11. 363-366)

This much of the Homeric hymn is condensed into the first strophe of Arion's invocation. The second strophe addressed to Phoebus Apollo is transposed from the next six lines of the Homeric hymn in which the names "Python" and "Pythian" are explained. Immediately following Apollo's apostrophe to the vanquished monster quoted above, the third-person narrative is resumed in the following manner:

Il dit, et le brouillas mortel alla frapant
Les yeux pleins de venim de l'horrible serpent,
Et du *Soleil* la force et la *lumiere belle*
Le corrompit soudain, dont *Python* on l'appelle,
Et *Phoebus Pythien* et luy on l'appella,
Pource que le *Soleil* brulant le pourrit là.
(11. 370-374)

The very next line takes us back to the story of the construction of Apollo's temple and the establishment of his Oracle at Crisa-Delphi. This is precisely the subject of Arion's third invocational strophe. To each of three successive events in the Homeric hymn, then, corresponds one strophe of Arion's hymn: Apollo and Python, Phoebus Apollo, Apollo and the Delphic Oracle.

Intriguing as this point-for-point correspondence between Arion's invocation and the Homeric hymn may be in itself, its true significance will not become apparent until we consider the *dénouement* of the Homeric model. When the temple at Crisa is at last completed Apollo, still a recent and relatively unknown god, has no one to cultivate his mysteries. He consequently sets out in search of mortals to serve as his priests. The first men he encounters are Cretan sailors en route to Pylos:

> . . .ce sont ceux que destine
> Pour faire son service, et de sa loy divine
> Anoncer les secrets, le Roy Phoebe Apollon,
> Son oracle rendant dans le sacré vallon
> De Parnasse hautain, son oracle authentique,
> Qu'il prononce du pied du laurier prophetique.
> Ces gens là navigeoient devers les Pyliens
> Pour negoce et trafique: et change de leurs biens
> A d'autres pour gaigner et faire leurs affaires.
> (11. 393-399)

In order to turn the sailors from their course and lead them to his new temple at Pytho, Apollo assumes the form—*mirabile dictu*—of a *dolphin:*

> Phoebus leur vint encontre et dans les ondes claires
> Saillit impetueux, la figure prenant
> D'un monstrueux Dauphin, puis tout incontinent
> Se mit tout de son long le monstre espouvantable,
> Gisant dans le vaisseau de façon admirable.
> (11. 399-401)

The ship no longer obeys the tiller or the sail, but is miraculously guided by the dolphin-god back to Crisa. It sails past Taenarum, where the crew hopes in vain to drop anchor, and when it has rounded Ithaca and turned eastward toward the "Soleil levant," Apollo guides it safely into port at Crisa, where he at last reveals his divinity and his purpose to the sailors. The latter are never to return home to Crete, but are to serve Apollo and tend his Oracle for the rest of their lives. It is at this point that Apollo changes

the name of his temple from Crisa to Delphi. His express purpose in the choice of the name "Delphi" is to commemorate the
form in which he first manifested himself to mortals and brought
them to his temple:

«Et comme cy devant vous me vistes en forme
D'un grand Dauffin saulter parmy vostre chiorme,
Ainsi reverez moy Dauffin, et d'un nom tel
Se nommera tousjours Delphien mon autel.»
(11. 493-496)

We are now in a better position to appreciate not only the
coherence of Arion's invocation, but its relevance both to the
rest of the hymn and to the entire poem. First of all, the three
principal attributes of Apollo which first appeared to be unrelated and arbitrarily chosen now appear to correspond directly
to three consecutive moments of the same episode in Apollonian
legend. Secondly and more importantly, whereas only the
second strophe and one line of the third strophe, in which Apollo
is invoked in his hypostasis as sun-god, at first seemed pertinent
to the nature of Arion's supplication, the entire invocation now
seems perfectly suited to the prayer. By recalling the Homeric
Hymn to Apollo and the complete story of the founding of the
Oracle at Delphi, the three strophes of the invocation work together to evoke the one and only episode in Apollonian legend
in which the god's favor was bestowed specifically and primarily
on *sailors*. Arion's prayer, as we have noted, is unwavering in its
purpose of imploring fair sailing weather and protection against
the dangers of the deep. Such a prayer might have seemed more
appropriately addressed to Neptune or to Jupiter. But in addressing it to Apollo, Arion invokes the god precisely by recalling
the one occasion in which he guided just such a ship safely to
port and honored its crew with the highest mark of his favor.
The prayer, in short, is for assistance in circumstances identical
to those in which the god is remembered in the invocation to
have shown his beneficence in the past.

Thirdly, in addition to guaranteeing the coherence of the
invocation and the logic of the entire hymn, the Homeric parallel
of the invocation establishes a profound link between the hymn
itself and the rest of the poem in which it is set. Arion's purpose
in singing the hymn (that is, to pray to Apollo for fair sailing

weather) and the effect it has on the outcome of his own adventure (that is, his own salvation by a dolphin) are, ostensibly, entirely unrelated. In Saint-Amant's as in all earlier versions of the story, it is the beauty of the poet's *music,* not the meaning of his *words,* that appears to attract the rescuing dolphin. But by "reproducing" the actual words of Arion's requisite prayer to Apollo in such a way as to recall the Homeric *Hymn to Apollo,* Saint-Amant succeeds in infusing into a gratuitous and essentially irrelevant detail of the legend a meaning utterly consonant with the rest of the work. By recalling that Apollo himself once assumed the form of a dolphin and guided those mortals he had elected for his own service to safe port and greater glory, Arion's song contains, as a precedent and a premonition, the model for his own dolphin-back ride to safety "en la grace des Dieux." Arion's little ode which critics invariably dismiss as bathos thus contains the key to the entire poem: it functions in precisely the same manner as the mythological digression on Apollo and Mercury at the center of *Le Fromage.*

Fourthly and finally, the Homeric parallel of Arion's invocation clinches the fusion of the lyric and the epic that we have already observed in *L'Arion.* Not only does the poem fuse the two modes by including a strophic ode in an epic poem, by transforming a lyric poet into an epic hero and by making of that hero a typological fusion of Odysseus and Orpheus; it does so in yet another way by infusing into the lyric poem the adumbration of the epic *dénouement,* or conversely, by appearing merely to elaborate in the epic narrative what is already implicit in the lyric song. The insistent identification of Arion as Apollo's *vates* thus finds its logical consequence in the outcome of his "epic" adventure: placed at the very center of the poem, the hymn reminds us that the dolphin is not simply Pliny's melomanic mammal, but Apollo himself, or at the very least the sea creature sacred to Apollo, in whose form Apollo guided his first priests to port at Crisa, and whose Apollonian function is commemorated in the very name Apollo gave to his Oracle at Delphi. Saint-Amant's elaboration of the idea of an heroic poet is as ingenious as his experiment with the limits of genres and the possibilities of generic intermixture is complex. If the poetic calling can ever be painted as an heroic one, Saint-Amant has done so in *L'Arion.*

Ronsard was too pious an admirer of antiquity to dare what Vergil and Dante and Ariosto had dared, and what Milton and Joyce have dared since—that is, to infuse old forms and myths with a new sense and a contemporary significance. His classicizing poems, for all their beauty and perfection, are frequently the work of a curator more than of a creator. The most convincing illustration of this weakness is precisely his most noble project, the single poem in which he placed his supreme bid for immortality, *La Franciade*. Saint-Amant was not a servile imitator of the Classics, and unlike Ronsard he succeeded, in his first published poem, in revitalizing a classical legend by accommodating it to his own ironic purposes. *L'Arion*, published approximately fifty years after the *Franciade*, mocks the *magnum opus* of the master by inverting its sources of inspiration, parodying its diction in such a way as to give a new and appropriate meaning to the tired nautical metaphor piously copied by Ronsard, choosing as its epic hero a lyric poet of precisely the Ronsardian kind but one whom the Pléiade had almost entirely overlooked, and finally by fusing recognizable lyric and epic elements of the classical tradition into a coherent whole which is authorized by an overriding unity of Homeric inspiration and a unity of Apollonian lore, as well as by an intrinsic unity resulting from the heroization of the lyric *vates* as a hybrid Odysseus-Orpheus figure.

When Saint-Amant comes to publish his larger and more ambitious epic poem exactly thirty years later, he will once again experiment with hybrid genres ("Idyle héroïque") and with a syncretic fusion of traditions (Christian epic); his subject once again will be the aquatic rescue of a helpless and innocent divine *vates* (the infant Moses). The poem will even begin by reproducing the precise movement of *L'Arion*'s satirical imitation of Vergil and Ronsard:

> Sur le luth eclatant de la noble Uranie
> Que me vient d'apporter mon fidelle genie,
> En joignant aux accords qui naissent de mes dois
> Les saints et graves tons de ma nombreuse vois,
> Je chante hautement la première avanture

D'un heros dont la gloire estonna la nature;
Je descris les hazards qu'il courut au berceau;
Je dy comment Moyse, en un fresle vaisseau
Exposé sur le Nil, et sans voile et sans rame,
Au lieu de voir couper sa jeune et chere trame,
Fut, selon le decret de l'arbitre eternel,
Rendu par une Nymphe au doux sein maternel.
　　Belle et divine reine, adorable exemplaire
Des hautes qualitez où l'âme se doit plaire,
Prodige de vertus, de qui le moindre rang
Est celuy que tu tiens et du trosne et du sang,
Louise, ma princesse, objet dont les merveilles
Font le seul desespoir des plus disertes veilles,
Daigne favoriser d'un rayon de tes yeux
Ce labeur que je t'offre au gré mesme des cieux;
Et, comme mon heros en sa nef vagabonde
Par une illustre dame eut victoire de l'onde,
Fay que de ton adveu son portrait ennobly,
Triomphe pour jamais du noir fleuve d'oubly.[28]

But the satirical edge will have disappeared with its object. Saint-Amant will himself have become a kind of Ronsard who after years of labor and set-backs has finally published, at the age of fifty-nine, the great work in which he in turn has placed all his hopes for immortality. A good share of the brilliance and virtuosity will have disappeared, along with the genius of allusiveness, the masterful manipulation of the tradition, the dazzling wit and the daring of the first brash gesture. Ironically, the *Moÿse sauvé* will do as great a disservice to its brilliant creator as *La Franciade* had done to the Prince of Poets. Saint-Amant's great masterpiece in the genre will remain his first.

CHAPTER IV:
LE MELON

Nec licet et longum est epulas narrare deorum
—Ovid

As Saint-Amant began to enjoy a solid literary reputation, he gradually abandoned the kind of specific allusiveness which is so remarkable in his earliest poems and which we have seen to play a particularly important role in *La Solitude* and *L'Arion*. As I suggested at the beginning of Chapter II, the *Suitte des Oeuvres* (1631) seems to be a direct response to the immense popularity of *Raillerie à Part*. Now a close examination of *Le Fromage* has indicated that the poems of this group, though often as allusive as the more "serious" poems of the 1629 collection, do not require the recognition of *specific* works or contexts in their allusions and reminiscences in order for their structuring patterns, and the meaning generated by those patterns, to be perceived.

Le Melon is typical of this more accessible kind of poetry in *La Suitte*.[1] As a burlesque poem—perhaps the first in France—it cannot afford to be indirect in its allusiveness. Burlesque, unlike more serious forms of parody, depends upon an immediate and untroubled recognition of the thing parodied. In this respect the following passage is typical of the entire "heroic" portion of *Le Melon:*

> Celle qui sur un Mont sa chasteté diffame,
> La Princesse des Fols, qui comme Sage-femme
> Assiste à ce travail où l'on pisse des os,
> Et dont elle delivre en disant certains mots;
> Diane au front cornu, de qui l'humeur sauvage
> Ne se plaist qu'aux Forests à faire du ravage. . .
>
> (11. 177-182)

The humor of this series of epithets would be lost if there were the slightest mystery concerning any of the attributes and functions to which allusion is made here: Diana as goddess of chastity, as goddess of the moon, the episode of Endymion, the moon's connection with insanity, Diana-Luna's assimilation to Lucina, maieutic incantations addressed to her in this capacity, Diana as goddess of the hunt. All the classical and mythological allusions of *Le Melon* are transparent, and refer to a common fund of general knowledge. The primary sources of this kind of knowledge in the seventeenth century were the *Metamorphoses* and Natalis Comes' *Mythologiae*, but the meaning of these more general allusions, unlike that of the reminiscences in *La Solitude*, is not dependent upon the recognition of a *particular* source and the *context* of that source. Locating specific passages in Ovid and Comes which establish the attributes of the gods parodied in *Le Melon*, in other words, would be of no use whatever in furthering our understanding of Saint-Amant's poem. It is sufficient simply to recognize the attributes parodied.

In many respecsts, *Le Melon* closely resembles *Le Fromage*. It is a humorous poem about food. It divinizes the food through outlandish hyperbole and recourse to mythology. It is a dramatic monologue addressed to drinking companions who are apostrophed directly by the speaker himself:

> Mais, que tandis, ô chere Troupe,
> Chacun laisse en repos la Coupe,
> Car ce que je vous vay chanter
> Vaut bien qu'on daigne l'escouter.
> (11. 113-116)

> Or pour venir au poinct que je vous veux déduire,
> Où je prie aux bons Dieux qu'ils me vueillent conduire,
> Vous sçaurez, Compagnons, que. . .
> (11. 249-251)

> Voilà, chers Auditeurs, l'effet de ma promesse. . .
> (11. 297)

The "action" of the poem is to be inferred only indirectly from what the speaker himself is saying:

Quelle odeur sens-je en cette Chambre?
(1. 1)

Qu'est-ce donc? Je l'ay descouvert
Dans ce panier remply de vert;
C'est un MELON. . .
(11. 19-21)

Baillez-le moy. . .
. . . .
Page, un cousteau, que je l'entame.
. . . .
C'en est fait, le voila coupé.
(11. 33-47)

Just as we knew from his ecstatic exclamations precisely when the speaker of *Le Fromage* first bit into Bilot's brie:

O Dieu! quel manger precieux!
Quel goust rare et delicieux!
Qu'au prix de luy ma fantaisie
Incague la saincte Ambroisie!
(*Le Fromage*, 9-12)

so we know that the speaker of *Le Melon* has had his first bite of melon when he cries out:

Ha! soustenez-moy, je me pâme,
Ce morceau me chatouille l'Ame;
Il rend une douce liqueur,
Qui me va confire le coeur,
Mon appetit se rassasie
De pure et nouvelle Ambroisie.
(*Le Melon*, 61-66)

If anything, *Le Melon* seems to be a simpler poem than *Le Fromage*. Not only does the speaker remain sober enough to stick to his subject when he begins to mythologize, but the words of the poem are restricted to one unequivocal level of discourse: there are no framing lines, no second degree quotations, no ambiguities concerning the proprietor and status of the words we read on the page. Lines 117-296 (the mythological digression) may be different from the rest in that they narrate an episode in the past, while lines 1-116 and 297-332 are spontaneous utterances that reflect the speaker's responses to his environment in the present; but there is never any doubt as to who is speaking, to whom he is speaking, where, when, how or why he is speaking.

And yet, though simpler in its allusiveness than the earliest poems, and simpler in its mode of discourse than its prototype *Le Fromage, Le Melon* is nevertheless equally complex in its experimentation with the limits and possibilities of genres and literary form. It, like all the poems I have discussed from the 1629 collection, is directly and principally concerned with the questions of the origin, nature and locus of poetry. The resources of meaning have become less oblique, but the "literariness" of its central preoccupations remains the same. Rather than generating its paradoxes through the manipulation of other texts and the elaborate patterning of specific reminiscences, or through a complex tension between form and formlessness, *Le Melon* does so through its equivocal metaphors and through the literal content of its mythological narration. Let us begin by examining its metaphors.

The first part of the poem—the dramatic monologue properly speaking—is a comic panegyric whose humor is an effect of the enormous disproportion between its lyrical style and diction on the one hand, and its homely object on the other. The incompatibility of form and subject is even greater here than it was in *Le Fromage,* since it is not justified by the drunkenness of the speaker. Nor is the hyperbole of the poem itself Dionysiac. Italian scholarship has shown that the movement of the first part of *Le Melon* is in fact most closely related to a late sixteenth-century description of religious ecstasy—and Protestant ecstasy at that![2] All aspects of the melon are praised as the fruit appeals successively to four of the five senses—olfactory:

> Quelle odeur sens-je en cette Chambre?
> Quel doux parfum de Musc et d'Ambre
> Me vient le Cerveau resjouïr
> Et tout le Coeur espanouïr?
> Ha bon Dieu! J'en tombe en extase!
> . . . .

A-t'on bruslé de la pastille?
N'est-ce point ce vin qui petille?
. . . .
O quelle odeur!. . .
                    (11. 1-5, 9-10, 35)

visual:

C'est un MELON, où la Nature
Par une admirable structure,
A voulu graver à l'entour
Mille plaisans chiffres d'Amour.
. . . .
O Dieux, que l'esclat qu'il me lance,
M'en confirme bien l'excellance!
Qui vit jamais un si beau teint?
                    (11. 21-24, 49-51)

tactile:

. . .qu'il est pesant!
Et qu'il me charme en le baisant!
                    (11. 35-36)

and finally, gustatory, to which the preceding three senses are all
reduced:

Ha! soustenez-moy, je me pâme,
Ce morceau me chatouille l'Ame;
Il rend une douce liqueur,
Qui me va confire le coeur,
Mon appetit se rassasie
De pure et nouvelle Ambroisie;
Et mes sens, par le goust seduits,
Au nombre d'un sont tous reduits.
                    (11. 61-68)

This entire development is then concluded with a long catalog of
rare and exotic fruits (including Manna!) listed in an anaphoric
sequence ("Ny. . .Ny. . .Ny. . ."), all of which

Ne sont qu'amertume et que fange
Au prix de ce MELON divin,
Honneur du Climat Angevin.
                    (11. 86-88)

Up to this point *Le Melon* has not departed in any significant way from the Bernesque tradition of gastronomic encomium. But here the poem takes a sudden palinodic turn which
ostensibly reinforces, but in fact displaces, all of the preceding
panegyric:

Que dis-je, d'Anjou? je m'abuse,
C'est un fruict du crû de ma Muse,
Un fruict en Parnasse eslevé,
De l'eau d'Hyppocrene abreuvé,
Mont, qui pour les Dieux seuls rapporte
D'excellents fruicts de cette sorte,
Pour estre proche du Soleil,
D'où leur vient ce goust nompareil:
Car il ne seroit pas croyable
Qu'un lieu commun, quoy qu'agreable,
Eust pû produire ainsi pour nous
Rien de si bon, ny de si dous.
                    (11. 89-100)

The object of praise here becomes perfectly ambiguous. If this
passage is read as a prolonged hyperbole, we understand that the
melon is being divinized in a way much like that of the first
mythological digression in *Le Fromage.* If, however, the metaphors of this passage are read on a more literal level, we realize
that the subject of these lines has become something altogether
different. A "fruict du crû de ma Muse" is not something to be
eaten, but a *poem,* which has been harvested from the fertile soil
of Mount Parnassus, and which has been irrigated by the Hippocrene whose waters, sacred to the Muses, are known to impart
poetic inspiration. The divinization of the melon, then, is at
the same time an even more startling metamorphosis, and that
which according to one reading is extravagant praise of a common melon, becomes through another reading a metaphorical,
yet very conventional, description of the poet's creative process.

The ambiguity concerning the subject of the poem's praise

is deliberately maintained throughout the quoted passage: the fruit's "goust nompareil" is at once the excellent flavor of the melon and the "excellent taste" of a poem; and the "lieu commun" which could not conceivably have produced anything "de si bon, ny de si dous" is at the same time any plot of land whose soil is less fertile than that of the celebrated Greek mountain, and a literary "commonplace" whose banality makes it unsuitable as the basis for a good poem. Even the verb "produire" lends itself equally well to the ideas of agricultural and literary production. The ambivalence of this passage becomes even more explicit in the following lines, where Phoebus Apollo is invoked as the "Dieu des *Fruicts*, et des *Vers*" (1. 104).

This deliberate confusion between food and poetry will become current practice in the later works of Saint-Amant. In the preface to the *Seconde Partie des Oeuvres* (1643), for example, the poet admits to his readers that some of the pieces he has included in this new collection were written several years earlier, and are "aussi flestries que ces vieilles Pommes de reinette qui se servent à la fin de la Saison." His advice to his reader, then, is the following: "si les Oeufs ne sont pas assez frais à ton gré, pour estre mangez en coque, fais-en des Aumelettes: Le Fromage et le Jambon avec quoy l'on en faict d'excellentes ne te manqueront point en ce lieu; et combien que ce soit en Caresme, tu en pourras manger sans dispense, si ce n'est qu'il en faille avoir pour les yeux et pour les oreilles à qui se destinent ces viandes-là" (*Oeuvres* II, 94-95). The poems of this collection are assimilated to eggs, and the entire collection to a potential omelette, complete with cheese (that of *Le Cantal*) and ham (that of the *Epistre au baron de Melay*). The poet concludes this preface by promising more poetry for the future, if you the reader "aymes les choses de haut goust, et as l'estomac capable de les digerer." Poetry and food are assimilated here even with respect to their manner of consumption.

In the preface to *Le Passage de Gibraltar* (1640) Saint-Amant defends the position that poetry's unique purpose is to entertain the reader ("plaire"), on the grounds that pleasure ("Joye") "contribuë le plus à l'entretien de la Santé." But, he adds, if Art is to have its proper salubrious effect it must be adequately seasoned ("assaisonné") with piquant wit: "Il faut sçavoir mettre le sel, le poivre et l'ail à propos en cette Sauce,

autrement au lieu de chatoüiller le goust et de faire espanoüyr
la ratte de bonne grace aux Honnestes-gens, on ne touchera, ny
on ne fera rire que les Crocheteurs" (*Oeuvres* II, 156).

In yet a third passage, in the *Epistre à Monsier le Baron de
Villarnoul,* Saint-Amant compares poetic conception to human
generation, speaking of his poems as "des Enfans comme fait ma
Cervelle," while at the same time using agricultural metaphors
to describe poetic production:

> Mais ces fruicts-là sont d'un autre Verger
> Que de celuy que la Nature humaine
> Plante et cultive avec plaisir et peine;
> La Chair perit; et l'Immortalité
> A l'Esprit seul donne sa qualité.
>
> (*Oeuvres* III, 144)

These passages in which food and poetry are in some way equat-
ed all date from the period in which Saint-Amant's nickname
"le bon Gros" had already become a "titre" and a consistent
literary trademark. As he developed the persona of a gluttonous
author of gastronomic poems, Saint-Amant also began to use
culinary metaphors in speaking of his own poems. Both the
epithet and the metaphor appear for the first time in *Le Melon.*

But while *Le Melon* is a first in this respect, it is also a
special case. The passage quoted above does not simply transfer
the poem's praise from fruit to poems, but from a particular
melon to a particular poem: the first being a gift from Apollo,
and the second the poem entitled *Le Melon* which we are now in
the very process of reading. The specific identification of the
melon-poem as *Le Melon* itself will be reinforced as the poem
progresses, but it has already been prepared and suggested in two
ways. One is that the word "melon" consistently appears in
capital letters throughout the poem, as if it were meant to be
read as the title of a literary work rather than as a common
noun. It was of course common practice during the Renaissance
to capitalize indiscriminately various substantives of a printed
text, and especially to print the title word of a poem in upper
case letters wherever it appears in the body of the text. Yet it is
a point worthy of note that Saint-Amant himself considered the
use of upper and lower case letters as a matter of utmost im-

portance, and became enraged when publishers or printers altered the desired case of a letter in his poems.[3] In this particular instance, the capitalization of "melon" seems deliberately to play on two printing conventions at once, accomodating the double meaning of the fruit announced by the title of the poem ("le melon"), and the poem itself (*LE MELON*).

The second indication that the poem described by pomonic metaphors might be *Le Melon* itself is to be found in the repeated use of the demonstrative article "ce" before the word "melon." Here again, a poetic tradition going back to Latin lyric accounts for this usage, descriptive poetry always having been concerned to make the object described as "present" as possible. But in this poem "ce MELON" sounds suspiciously like the expression "ces vers" by which so many of Saint-Amant's other poems are made to refer to themselves.

Once the possible meaning of "this poem" has been established for the words "ce MELON," we must re-read the first part of the poem and reinterpret its descriptions accordingly. As in so much of Saint-Amant's poetry we are given the uneasy, vertiginous feeling that we are reading a text which is not yet complete, and which is still being written as we are reading it. The object described here is the entire poem of which these are merely the opening lines, and which has not yet been realized as a finished, *describable* artifact. The description seems to precede the thing described, projecting its own virtuality before it, and at the same time filling out its project line by line. The description and its object (which is nothing more than the description itself) seem paradoxically to precede one another, to generate one another, and to undermine one another's reality.

Read as a work which is merely self-description, the poem first appears to praise itself for its elegant structure and its outer surface of metaphors, on which are engraved the letters of Love's writing:

> C'est un MELON, où la Nature,
> Par une admirable structure,
> A voulu graver à l'entour,
> Mille plaisans chiffres d'Amour,
> Pour claire marque à tout le monde,

Que d'une amitié sans seconde
Elle chérit ce doux manger.
(11. 21-27)

Before the cutting of the fruit, or exegesis of the poem, Pomona is invoked

Afin qu'au goust il se rencontre
Aussi bon qu'il a belle montre,
Et qu'on ne treuve point en luy
Le deffaut des gens d'aujourd'huy.
(11. 41-44)

Here the "taste" of the poem's real semantic content is contrasted with its external metaphorical appearance. Attracted by the poem's ostensible subject, we are not disappointed when we cut through its exterior surface to discover its real meaning: the poem itself. Nor does the poem offer much resistance to the exegetical scalpel, for "il est sec, son escorce est mince" (1. 57). Indeed, in the first reading we were able to penetrate it by the 100th line of the poem.

In lines 61-68 the poem, through its retroactive metaphor, begins to consume itself. The mouth which is speaking the poem into being tastes the melon (that is, its own medium without which it could not exist) and begins to faint: "Ha! soustenez-moy, je me pâme." Is this because the voice of the poem lacks any real sustenance, feeding as it does on its own elusive essence? In any case the poem's autophagy is evident, for in the process of narrating it, the poem's discourse momentarily designates itself specifically and locally ("*Ce morceau* me chatouille l'ame") and continues filling out its own existence with words:

Il rend une douce liqueur,
Qui *me* va confire le coeur
Mon appetit se rassasie
De pure et nouvelle Ambroisie.
(11. 63-66)

"Pure new ambrosia" is hardly an exaggeration, for there is certainly nothing organic in this insubstantial, self-digesting and self-alimenting "substance." In *Le Fromage* the speaker emits words instead of ingesting cheese, and as his speech grows, its objective correlative diminishes in size until the finished poem *Le Fromage* stands in the place of "le fromage" it sings. *Le Melon* is different in that the subject of the poem is metaphorically identified with the poem itself from the beginning, and in consuming the melon, the speaker is paradoxically producing *Le Melon.* Production *is* consumption, speaking *is* eating, and the "fruict du crû de [la] Muse" simultaneously diminishes and grows in size.

The first part of the poem ends with a passage which compounds its initial self-reference. The "poet" addresses Phoebus Apollo, "vive Source de lumiere" (both solar light and poetic illumination), "Dieu des Fruicts, et des Vers," thanking him for his generous gift, the melon-poem:

> Icy je te rends humbles graces
> D'un coeur d'ingratitude exent,
> De nous avoir fait ce Present:
> Et veux pour quelque recompense
> Dire en ce lieu ce que je pense,
> Et de ce MELON, et de toy
> Suivant les signes que j'en voy.
> (11. 106-112)

The gift is unequivocally designated as "ce MELON," that is, as the poem we have been reading: and "les signes que j'en voy" are, in terms of the extended metaphor, the scriptural traces which have already been materialized by the poem which is still in the process of writing itself out. This being the case, it is interesting to note that the way in which the grateful "poet" wishes to return the god's favor is to tell him what he thinks of the gift: "*Dire* en ce lieu ce que je pense,/Et de ce MELON, et de toy." The "Present," then, is what we have now read of the poem, and the "recompense" will be that part of the poem which is to follow. Apollo's gift and the poet's recompense will ultimately be included in the same poem in such a way that *Le Melon,* once completed, will constitute a self-contained and perfectly balanced system of exchange which cancels itself out to zero in the ledger books of Parnassus.

§

The second part of the poem, the "recompense" for the first, is a burlesque narration of a feast of the gods. Charles Sorel's charge of plagiarism in regard to this passage is well known. Saint-Amant being a far more engaging figure than Sorel, critics have a tendency to exaggerate the ridiculousness of this accusation. It is nevertheless extremely unlikely that *Le Melon* was directly inspired by *Le Banquet des Dieux*, the mock-heroic story which Montenor reads aloud in Book III of *Le Berger extravagant*.[4] The chief differences between the two pieces are not to be found in the details of the menu and the particular role assigned to each god, but rather in the tone and purpose of each. Sorel's satire is bitter and sarcastic. He develops the contradictions and absurdities of classical fables in what is first and foremost a relentless attack on the mythologizing trend in modern poetry. His *Banquet* ends with a terrible battle in which the entire pantheon is annihilated once and for all. There is no humor in this parody: it is the desperate and monomaniacal lucubration of a fanatic moralist who cannot tolerate the proliferation of pagan lies in modern poetry. *Le Melon* could hardly be more different. Nowhere is the reader confronted with the inherent contradictions and absurdities of mythology, and in no way does Fable come under attack: the immortal gods are simply deflated by means of diction which is ordinarily applied only to vulgar subjects. There is an evident love for Fable and fabulation in this humorous profanation, a fond indulgence in the literal falseness of myth, and a familiar *enjouement*. Sorel in his *Banquet* is a kind of Captain Ahab and a hater of poetry; Saint-Amant in *Le Melon* is an Arion *en belle humeur*.

There is another essential difference between these two burlesque feasts of the gods—a difference in actual content which is entirely consistent with that of their tone and purpose: Saint-Amant's long and detailed account of the dishes served at the feast is only a prelude to the real point of the narration, which is the invention of the lyre by Apollo. The burlesque portion of *Le Melon* culminates with the transcendence of music and poetry, and the glorification of the patron god of both. In *Le Banquet des Dieux,* on the contrary, Apollo is scarcely mentioned at all. At the end of Sorel's feast, the song of the Muses, the dance of the Tritons, and the mime of all the gods lead only to war and destruction. It is more than likely that Saint-Amant had read *Le Berger extravagant* before writing *Le Melon*, but there can be no question of any real filiation between the two feasts. The literary context of Saint-Amant's burlesque is to be found elsewhere.

For Saint-Amant's first readers, of course, *Le Melon* did not recall another burlesque as much as it recalled the classical topos which it parodies. It has become clear by now that Saint-Amant was not an imitating poet, but a manipulating poet. In the burlesque portion of *Le Melon*, as in *La Solitude*, *Le Fromage* and *L'Arion*, the appeal is to the reader's experience with familiar classical commonplaces. Now in the heroic literature of antiquity the gods are frequently seen feasting. There are many different occasions for these feasts. The primary ones are weddings (usually that of Peleus and Thetis, as in Catullus 64), the conclusion of a council (as in Book I of the *Iliad*), or a victory (usually that of the Olympians over the Titans or the Giants). Whatever the occasion, these feasts are invariably followed by a concert sung and played by Apollo himself. Apollo's lyre is so much a part of these occasions that the association became a commonplace in lyric as well as heroic poetry. Horace, for example, ends an invocation to his lyre by recalling its traditional place at divine banquets: "O decus Phoebi et dapibus supremi/ Grata testudo Iovis. . ." (*Carmina* I 32, 13-14).

Apollo's repertoire for such occasions is extremely limited. Tibullus has Apollo sing a victory hymn at the banquet celebrating the defeat of Cronos and the Titans by Zeus and the Olympians:

> . . .nunc indue vestem
> Sepositam, longas nunc bene pecte comas,
> Qualem te memorant Saturno rege fugato
> Victori laudes concinuisse Iovi.
> (II 5, 7-10)

This is also the paeon recalled by Natalis Comes in his article on Apollo (IV 11): "Il avoit le premier chanté sur sa harpe, habillé magnifiquement et bien gentiment frisé, les loüanges de Jupiter victorieux après qu'il eut chassé Saturne son pere hors de son royaume." In the poetry of the Renaissance the subject of Apollo's banquet song was most frequently a second theomachia, the revolt of the Giants (which the Renaissance usually confused with the battle of the Titans and the Olympians). Ronsard is typical in this regard:

> L'honneur est le seul prix que demandent les Dieux:
> Aussi l'homme mortel ne leur peut donner mieux.
> Et Jupiter apres la sanglante victoire
> Des Geans ne voulut recevoir autre gloire
> Sinon d'ouir sonner à son fils Apollon
> Comme son trait armé d'un flambant tourbillon,
> D'esclats, de bruit, de peur, de soulfre, et de tonnerre
> Avoit escarbouillé leurs cerveaux contre terre
> Par les champs Flegreans, et comme leurs grans corps
> Et leurs cent bras armez estoient renversez morts
> Sous les monts qu'ils portoient, et comme pour trophée
> De sa victoire Etna flamboye sur Typhée.[5]

> . . .là-haut aux Cieux
> Sous le chant d'Apollon se pasment tous les Dieux
> Quant il touche la Lyre, et chante le trophée
> Qu'esleva Jupiter des armes de Typhée.[6]

This is the tradition which serves as the basis for Saint-Amant's burlesque. Whereas Sorel's banquet is occasioned simply by Jupiter's desire not to be outdone by mortals in pigritude, that of *Le Melon* is a victory celebration following the revolt of the Giants:

> Aprés que Jupiter avecque son Tonnerre
> Eut fait la petarrade aux Enfans de la Terre,
> Et que les Dieux lassez revindrent du Combat,
> . . . .
> Aprés, dis-je, ce chocq, où l'Asne de Silene
> Aux plus mauvais Garçons fit enfin perdre haléne,
> . . . .
> On dit qu'il fut conclu qu'en signe de victoire,
> Tout le reste du jour se passeroit à boire,
> Et que chacun d'entr'eux fournissant au Banquet,
> Apporteroit son mets troussé comme un pacquet.
> (11. 117-119, 125-126, 129-132)

In accordance with the tradition, Saint-Amant's feast ends with a concert given by Apollo. The subject of Apollo's final number is also consistent with the convention: it is the victory of the gods in the battle they have just fought:

> Là maintes cordes d'Arc en grosseur differantes,
> Sous les doigts d'Apollon chanterent des courantes:
> Là mille traits hardis entremeslez d'esclats
> Firent caprioller les pintes et les plats;
> Le plus grave des Dieux en dansa de la teste,
> Et le plus beau de tous pour accomplir la Feste,
> Joignant à ses accords son admirable vois,
> Desconfit les Titans une seconde fois.[7]
>
> (11. 289-296)

There are only two essential innovations in the conventional feast of *Le Melon*. One is that since organic food has been substituted for the usual menu of nectar and ambrosia, each god is called upon either to contribute a dish of his own, or to offer his services in preparing or serving the banquet. Bacchus of course brings wine, Ceres biscuits and cakes, Neptune oysters, Diana venison, Venus an assortment of aphrodisiacs, and so forth. Those Olympians who do not bring a dish all discharge some office appropriate to their area of expertise: Minerva as the goddess of weaving and artisanry provides the table cloth and place settings, Hercules with his club is doorman, Mars sharpens the knives, the vigilant Mercury oversees all the preparations.

This "innovation" is not entirely without precedent, however. A century earlier Jean Lemaire de Belges, in describing the wedding feast of Peleus and Thetis in his *Illustrations de Gaule et Singularitez de Troye*,[8] had interpolated a number of domestic details very much like those of *Le Melon*. Like Saint-Amant's "Deesse des Fours, des Moulins, et des Plaines" and his "Compere Denis à la troigne vermeille," Jean Lemaire's Ceres and Bacchus bring their own gifts to Thetis' wedding feast: "Certes [sic] la Deesse des bledz, eust desja fourny tous les offices de paneterie. Les gens de Bacchus pareillement eurent fait garnison de toutes sortes de vin, tant pour la bouche que pour le commun." Like Saint-Amant's Priapus ("Le Seigneur des Jardins"), Vertumnus and Pomona, who provide asparagus, green peas, salad and rare fruits, Jean Lemaire's Priapus, "le Dieu des jardins et de fertilité, filz de Bacchus et de Venus, fut verdier ou saulsier. Si fournit la cuisine de toute verdure necessaire, et broya la saulse. . . . Pomona, l'une des Hamadryades, et Frutesa sa compaigne eurent aussi fait finance de toutes especes de fruiterie." Jean Lemaire's Vulcan does not cook a ham and six beef tongues, as does Saint-Amant's "Forgeur écloppé,. . .Patron des Cocus," but like Saint-Amant's Minerva, manufactures the dinner set: "Vulcan, autrement appellé Mulciber, feure des Dieux, fut estably à la garde du buffet, duquel toute la riche vaisselle avoit prins tournure, merveilleuse et supernelle, par ses propres mains." And Cybele, "Mere des Dieux," whose presence at the victory celebration is a source of wonder for Saint-Amant's speaker, is also present at the wedding banquet: "Or feirent les Dieux si grand chere, que jamais ne fut veüe la pareille. Dont Cybele la grand mere des Dieux receut au coeur une joye inestimable, voyant tant de sublimes esprits de sa noble generation tous assemblez en tel triomphe." Lemaire's Pan provides syrinx music rather than a larded lamb, but does so in accordance with the same qualities as Saint-Amant's "Roy des Flusteurs, de qui dans l'Arcadie/Les trouppeaux de Brebis suivent la melodie": "Pan est le Dieu des pastoureaux d'Arcadie. . . . Lors souffla Pan en sa chalemelle de sept buseaux accordez selon l'harmonie des sept Planettes. . . ."

Les Illustrations de Gaule is not a burlesque. It is an encyclopedic summa of mythology which, several decades before Ronsard, attempts to establish a direct lineage between the Trojan royal house and the kings of France. Yet such an abundance of homely detail as we find in the wedding feast of Thetis and Peleus brings the work to the verge of unintentional comedy. Jean Lemaire himself must have sensed this—though too late—in balking at a detailed account of the menu: "Si ne faut pas attendre la description des mets ambrosiens confits en manne celeste, dont les Dieux furent serviz alors: ne aussi l'apprest d'iceux, ou l'ordre du service: car le raconter excederoit pouvoir humain. Mais il suffit d'imaginer." Rather than making the gods merely human, as Homer does with his "inextinguishible laughter of the gods," Jean Lemaire makes them petty and contemptible. The only significant difference between *Les Illustrations* I 29 and the burlesque portion of *Le Melon* is not to be found in content—that is, in the inappropriate pettiness of detail in describing the immortal gods—but rather in tone. Saint-Amant gives precisely the same kind of detailed account that Jean Lemaire does, and even appears to have imitated many of these details directly; but he does so with a correspondingly inappropriate pettiness of style and diction as well.

This brings us to the second of Saint-Amant's innovations in his otherwise conventional feast of the gods. The burlesque diction of *Le Melon* is in fact no more an "innovation" on the part of the poet than is his detailed account of what amounts to a divine "potluck," and it is here that the much-discussed and perhaps over-estimated "Italian influence" can be felt most strongly. Alessandro Tassoni's *Secchia rapita,* which was first published in Paris in 1622 (that is, nine years before the publication of *Le Melon* in the *Suitte des Oeuvres*), is probably the poet's closest stylistic source of inspiration.[9] Like the first part of *Le Melon*, Tassoni's poem relates a petty circumstance (in this case the theft of a bucket) in an unsuitably high style (in this case the heroic style of the Homeric epic). The theft of the bucket, like the rapt of Helen, sets the Modenese and the Bolognese at war, and Tassoni narrates the entire incident in the exalted language of the Homeric and Vergilian tradition. And like the second part of *Le Melon*, Book II of the *Secchia* describes the great Olympian gods in the low style of vulgar farce. Tassoni does not relate a feast of the gods, but rather a divine council modeled after the famous Homeric council in Book I of the *Iliad*. Jupiter "Fè sonar le campane del suo impero/E à consiglio chiamar gli Dei d'Omero." In the next sixteen *ottave* Tassoni then relates the majestic procession of the gods on their way to the Olympian senate, describing with sacrilegious familiarity the bearing and attire of each in succession, and devoting an entire strophe to each. This is clearly the stylistic device adopted by Saint-Amant in cataloguing the contribution of each god to the Olympian banquet. Not only is each god treated in an orderly and logical sequence with vulgar epithets and attributes as in the *Secchia*, but following the rhythm of Tassoni's *ottave*, Saint-Amant devotes precisely *eight* lines to each of the most important banqueters: Jupiter, Juno, Bacchus, Ceres, Neptune, Diana, Vulcan, Venus, Pan and Cybele (11. 137-216).

With Tassoni's style and tone, and Jean Lemaire's subject and detail, Saint-Amant described the conventional victory feast of the Olympians over the Giants, and thereby won the distinc-

tion of having written the first French burlesque poem. The role
of creative genius in this "first" is clearly not very great. But it
is neither the newness, nor the Italian or French lineage of Saint-
Amant's burlesque, that is of primary importance. As always,
Saint-Amant's borrowings and adaptations from earlier literature
are made to serve a new and particular purpose. It is the internal
function of this burlesque narration within the poem as a whole,
not its gratuitous virtuosity, its purely historical significance, or
its superficial debts to other works, that makes *Le Melon* a
valuable poem.

The mythological narration which, as we have seen, is intended as the poet's recompense to Apollo for the gift of the
melon-poem, stands in direct contrast to the first part of the
poem in every respect. The first section is the lyric effusion, in
the present tense, of a lyric "je"; the second section is an epic
narrative, in the past tense, and in the third person. The meter
of the first part is, appropriately, the one most frequently used
by Saint-Amant for light or satirical lyric:[10] octosyllabic couplets like those of *Le Fromage;* the meter of the second part is
likewise appropriately epic: alexandrines like those of *L'Arion.*
To the lyric-epic opposition corresponds an inversion of comic
perspective: the first part exalts a common object belonging to
everyday reality by means of an inappropriately high style
(mock-heroic), while the second part treats an exalted mythological theme in an inappropriately low style (burlesque).[11] The
elevated style of the first part properly belongs to the lofty subject of the second, while the low style of the second is more
suited to the banal subject of the first. Both kinds of disparity
between style and subject have already appeared in *Le Fromage.*
Here they are more clearly distinguished, and placed in direct
opposition to each other.

But the relation between the two parts of *Le Melon* is more
intricate and meaningful than a simple formal contrast between
gift and recompense, lyric and epic, mock-heroic and burlesque.
I mentioned above that the feast of the gods is not described for
its own sake, but as a mere context and setting for the narrator's
main point, which is "ce que je pense,/Et de ce MELON, et de
toy [Phoebus]." Having extended his burlesque ennumeration
of the dishes and duties of each god over 132 lines (slightly more
than the entire octosyllabic portion of the poem), the narrator

at last arrives at his main point:

> Or pour venir au poinct que je vous veux déduire,
> Où je prie aux bons Dieux qu'ils me vueillent conduire,
> Vous sçaurez, Compagnons, que parmy tant de mets,
> Qui furent les meilleurs qu'on mangera jamais;
> Et parmy tant de fruicts, dont en cette Assemblée,
> Au grand plaisir des sens la table fut comblée,
> Il ne se treuva rien à l'égal d'un MELON
> Que Thalie apporta pour son maistre Apollon.
>
> (11. 249-256)

The entire narration, then, merely serves as a term of comparison in describing the excellence of Apollo's melon. The heroic catalog of contributions to the Olympian banquet, in other words, is an exact burlesque counterpart to the anaphoric catalog near the end of the lyric portion of the poem, in which the speaker says that coconuts, apricots, strawberries and cream, Manna, honey, the pears of Tours, etc., etc.,

> Ne sont qu'amertume et que fange
> Au prix de ce MELON divin,
> Honneur du Climat Angevin.
>
> (11. 86-88)

And just as in Part I the melon successively charmed four of the speaker's five senses, so here the Olympian gods are enraptured first by the sight, then the smell, and finally the taste of Apollo's gift:

> Dés qu'il fut sur la Nappe un aigu cry de joye
> Donna son corps de vent aux oreilles en proye;
> Le coeur en tressaillit, et les plus friands nez
> D'une si douce odeur furent tous estonnez:
> Mais quand ce vint au goust ce fut bien autre chose. . .
>
> (11. 265-269)

The "aigu cry de joye" which arises in chorus from the feasting gods corresponds exactly to the ecstatic effusion on the part of the speaker himself, and of which the entire first part of *Le Melon* is nothing more than the faithful transcription. But whereas the taste of Apollo's melon in the lyric part of the poem provoked the speaker to narrate the entire epic part as a recompense to the god of fruit and verse, Apollo's corresponding melon in the epic part itself reduces not only the Muse, but even the female guests, to utter silence:

> Aussi d'en discourir la Muse mesme n'ose:
> Elle dit seulement qu'en ce divin Banquet,
> Il fit cesser pour l'heure aux femmes le caquet.
> (11. 270-272)

The point-for-point correspondence between the two parts of *Le Melon* is carried even further. Before cutting open the fruit of Part I, the speaker expresses the hope that

> . . .au goust il se rencontre
> Aussi bon qu'il a belle montre,
> Et qu'on ne treuve point en luy
> Le deffaut des gens d'aujourd'huy.
> (11. 41-44)

And the speaker's "priere est exaucée." The same problem of being and appearing in matters of human conduct is brought up again in Part II when the second melon also proves to be as excellent on the inside as on the outside. Momus, one of the most common mythological figures in Renaissance moral philosophy, wanted windows to be installed in men's breasts so that they could not dissemble their true sentiments with a hypocritical show. It is Momus himself who proclaims the second melon to be without fault:

> Et ce grand Repreneur, qui d'une aigre censure
> Vouloit que par un trou l'on nous vist la fressure,
> Mome le mesdisant fut contraint d'avouër
> Que sans nulle Hyperbole on le pouvoit louër.
> (11. 261-264)

The most significant point of correspondence between the two parts of *Le Melon,* however, is established only after the speaker's Muse has been dumbfounded by the taste of Apollo's fruit in Part II:

> Phoebus qui le tenoit, sentant sa fantaisie

D'un desir curieux en cét instant saisie,
En coupe la moitié, la creuse proprement;
Bref pour finir le conte, en fait un Instrument,
Dont la forme destruit et renverse la Fable
De ce qu'on a chanté, que jadis sur le sable
Mercure trouvant mort un certain Limaçon,
Qui vit parfois en beste, et parfois en poisson,
Soudain en ramassa la Cocque harmonieuse,
Avec quoy, d'une main aux Arts ingenieuse,
Aussi bien qu'aux Larcins, tout à l'heure qu'il l'eut,
Au bord d'une Riviere il fit le premier Lut.
(11. 273-284)

The world's first lyre was not made by Mercury from a tortoise
shell while Apollo was watching over Admetus' herd (see *Le
Fromage*, 33-60) but from the husk of the melon which Apollo
himself contributed to the feast of the gods. We have seen how
the hyperbolic images at the end of the lyric portion of the poem
(11. 89-100) metaphorically transform the speaker's melon,
Apollo's gift, into the poem entitled *Le Melon*. In the epic portion of the poem, the divine melon, also a gift of Apollo, is
literally and actually transformed into a lyric instrument by
means of which a song can be sung. Part II, then, simply reifies
the metaphor for poesis we have already observed in Part I.

In Part I, the pre-metamorphic melon appealed to only four
of the five senses: smell, sight, touch and taste. The melon of
Part II appealed to only three: sight, smell and taste. The transformation of this second melon allows it now to reach the remaining fifth sense, and in fact to prove even sweeter to the ear
than it had to the eye or the palate:

Ainsi de cette escorce en beauté sans pareille
Fut fabriqué là haut ce Charmeur de l'oreille,
D'où sortit lors un son, par accens mesuré,
Plus doux que le manger qu'on en avoit tiré.
(11. 285-288)

Apollo's audible melon charms the entire feasting assembly:

Là maintes cordes d'Arc en grosseur differantes,
Sous les doigts d'Apollon chanterent des courantes:

> Là mille traits hardis entremeslez d'esclats
> Firent caprioller les pintes et les plats;
> Le plus grave des Dieux en dansa de la teste.
>
> (11. 289-293)

This entire development is merely a replica of the one we have already observed at the end of Part I. Once the first melon has been smelled, seen, felt and tasted, and finally transformed into a "fruict du crû de ma Muse,/Un fruict en Parnasse eslevé," in short, into *Le Melon,* the speaker then uses this "melon" as the medium for a song which he intends to sing for the pleasure of all his fellow banqueters:

> Mais, que tandis, ô chere Troupe,
> Chacun laisse en repos la Coupe,
> Car ce que je vous vay chanter
> Vaut bien qu'on daigne l'escouter.
>
> (11. 113-116)

Similarly, when the second melon has been seen, smelled and tasted, and finally transformed into "le premier Lut," Apollo uses his "melon" as the instrument on which to perform for the entire assembly of feasting gods. Even the subject of Apollo's song corresponds to that of the speaker's. The latter uses his melon-poem as the medium through which to sing the story of the melon's origin, that is, to sing the entire epic portion of *Le Melon* in which the victory celebration of the Olympians is described. Apollo too uses his melon-lyre as the instrument on which to sing the battle for which this very feast is the victory celebration; "le plus beau" of all the gods,

> . . .pour accomplir la Feste,
> Joignant à ses accords son admirable vois,
> Desconfit les Titans une seconde fois.
>
> (11. 294-296)

The first two parts of *Le Melon,* then, are not only absolutely parallel, but typologically equivalent. Each depicts a joyful banquet: the first through the lyric perspective of a first-person monologue, the second through the epic perspective of a third-person narrative. Each describes a melon whose excellence is established by means of a favorable comparison with a long catalog of other delectable foods. Each melon is then transformed into a lyric "instrument": the first into a poem, entitled *Le Melon,* the second into the world's first lyre. And with each of these new "instruments" a song is sung: the speaker's song being Part II of *Le Melon* itself, Apollo's being an account of the battle which preceded and occasioned the feast at which he is singing. As was the case in *Le Fromage,* the mythological development of *Le Melon* contains an exact physical model for the condition and circumstances of the speaker and his words. The origin of Apollo's lyre is exactly analogous to the origin of the poem which describes it: in both cases, a melon is transformed into an instrument of poetry, and in both we are witness to the process by which the subject of the poem becomes the poetic medium itself. The content, or "message," of each section of the poem is metamorphosed, once metaphorically and once literally, into its own form, or "medium," whose only content, then, is its own autogenetic metamorphosis.

With the sublimation of food into song, the epic portion of the poem comes to an end. The speaker's "recompense" to the god of fruit and verse for the gift of a melon-poem, has consisted of the narration of an identical episode in the life of the god himself. Having finished his epic narration, the speaker then returns to his listeners and to the lyric voice and perspective of the first-person singular:

> Voilà, chers Auditeurs, l'effet de ma promesse;
> Voilà ce qu'au Jardin arrousé du Permesse,
> Terpsicore au bon bec, pour qui j'ay de l'amour,
> En voyant des MELONS me prosna l'autre jour.
> (11. 297-300)

Yet the speaker has not yet done precisely what he set out to do, which is to say what he thinks "de *ce* MELON" and of Apollo. The relation between the two melons is rigorously analogical. But this typology of Apollonian melons, while it confirms the real nature of the speaker's "melon" for the reader of *Le Melon,* does not really explain anything at all for the speaker's live audience. What relation between the two melons is perceivable from within the frame of reference of the poem's fiction? The next lines establish a second relation between them:

> . . .je croy que ce fruict, qui possede nos yeux,
> Provient de celuy-là que brifferent les Dieux:
> Car le Roy d'Helicon, le Demon de ma veine,
> Dans le coin d'un mouchoir en garda de la graine,
> Afin que tous les Ans il en pust replanter,
> Et d'un soin liberal nous en faire gouster.
>
> (ll. 303-308)

The genealogy of the speaker's melon establishes an entirely different relation between the melons of Parts I and II. To the typological relation based on analogy is added a strictly linear one based on contiguity. The melon eaten by the speaker of *Le Melon* was grown on Parnassus from the seeds of the same melon which Thalia, the Muse of comedy and banquets, once presented to the victorious Olympians on behalf of her master Apollo. The melon which the speaker transforms into a poem is a scion of the one which Apollo, in precisely the same way, transformed into a lyre. The combination of these two relationships—the coincidence of an analogical and linear relation between the two melons—suggests that the *song,* too, sung by the speaker at his banquet is of the same lineage as the song sung by Apollo at the feast of the gods. The poet's melon—and consequently *Le Melon*—is not any ordinary "fruit" grown on Parnassus and irrigated by the water of the Hippocrene: it was planted there by Apollo himself from the seeds of his very own *lyre.* The poem itself is directly descended from that divine instrument emblematic of *all* lyric poetry. Never did the Renaissance imagine a more direct kind of poetic affiliation with the god of lyric poetry, or claim a closer relationship between its own poetry and the celestial songs of the "Roy d'Helicon."

I remarked earlier that in the burlesque portion of his poem Saint-Amant seems to have followed the example of Jean Lemaire in regard to his detailed account of a feast of the gods, and that of Alessandro Tassoni in regard to tone, style and rhythm. In neither respect does he appear to owe a debt to Charles Sorel. Now that we have observed the complex relation of Saint-Amant's feast to the rest of his poem, all such sources of inspira-

tion appear to be of secondary interest at best. The genius of
Le Melon lies not in this "epic" narrative alone—in its stylistic
virtuosity, its primacy as a burlesque poem, or its "baroque"
wit—but rather in the complex unity of the entire poem and the
interrelatedness of its parts. Saint-Amant's burlesque account
of an Olympian victory feast is of course delightful in itself.
But its primary importance is its integral function within the
poem as a whole, and its role in the generation of an intricate but
unified polyvalence of meaning whose focus—like that of the
three earlier poems I have discussed in the preceding chapters—is
poesis: genres, modes, inspiration and the making of the poem
itself.

As for the mechanism of this complex relation of parts to
each other and to the whole, *Le Melon* follows the example not
of Lemaire, Tassoni or Sorel, but of a far more significant writer,
the poet with whom Saint-Amant most frequently rivaled in his
early poetry, Pierre de Ronsard. We have seen how the lyric and
epic sections of *Le Melon* correspond to the credit and debit
columns of a Parnassian ledger book, and how *Le Melon* itself
is a record of the balanced budget of Apollo's "present" and the
poet's "recompense." Ronsard's poetry often alludes, more or
less explicitly, to the economic system of poetic inspiration on
which Saint-Amant's poem is constructed: in exchange for the
gift of poetic inspiration, the poet uses that gift for the glorification of its divine donor. This kind of poetic potlatch is most
often described in the *Odes*. One of the best examples is to
be found in an early poem, the second *Bocage,* "A son Lut."[12]
Here, in return for the gift of inspiration, the poet sings the
praises of Apollo and the Muses:

> Tandis qu'en l'air je souffleray ma vie,
> Sonner Phebus j'auray tousjours envie,
>   Et ses compagnes aussi,
>   Pour leur rendre un grand-merci
> De m'avoir fait poëte de nature.
>   (11. 21-25)

And conversely, poets pray to the gods for continued inspiration,
only in order to continue their thanks for the renewed gift:

> . . .aux prieres qu'ils font,

L'or aux Dieux criant ne sont,
Ni la richesse qui passe,
Mais un lut tousjours parlant
L'art des Muses excellant
Pour dessus leur rendre grace.
(11. 55-60)

Consequently, when Ronsard asks at the end of his poem:

Dieux! de quelle oblation
Aquitter vers vous me puis-je,
Pour remuneration
Du bien receu qui m'oblige?
(11. 109-112)

the answer—to the degree that grace of any kind can be bought or repaid—is to be found in the glorification of that gift which the entire poem itself constitutes, and which is recapitulated in the very last strophe:

O de Phebus la gloire et le trophée
. . . .
Je te saluë, ô Lut harmonieux. . .
(11. 121-125)

There is a secular corrolary to this system of poetic economy, which is the following: in exchange for the material support which allows the poet to write his great works, the poet bestows immortality upon his patron by including his praise in those very works. In his search for a Maecenas for his projected epic, Ronsard frequently formulated this principle as well, often in shockingly crude terms. Such is the case in his first appeal to Henri II in the *Ode de la Paix* (1550):

Prince, je t'envoye ceste Ode,
Trafiquant mes vers à la mode
Que le marchant baille son bien,
Troque pour troq': toy qui es riche,
Toy, Roy des biens, ne sois point chiche
De changer ton present au mien.
Ne te lasse point de donner,
Et tu verras comme j'accorde

L'honneur que je promets sonner,
Quand un present dore ma corde.[13]

The most intricate elaboration of this system of exchange in the works of Ronsard, however, is to be found in a later poem, one of his most famous, *La Lyre à Jean Belot*.[14] Here, the familiar exchange is not described, but demonstrated. The general outline of this poem is the following:

I.   Ever since the passing of my youth, I had virtually ceased to write poetry. Occasional inspiration would come to me from Bacchus or a Sibyl, but only for a day or two, once every six months or a year. Poetry requires youthful energy and vigor; in my gray old age I did little more than tend my grape vines (11. 1-128)

But as soon as I met you, Belot, I was seized by the sudden desire to sing your praises and immortalize your virtue and liberality (11. 129-156)

You are like those apothecary's jars painted crudely with portraits of men and gods on the outside, but containing healing medicines inside. In this respect you are like Socrates, who brought Philosophy back to its proper place among human affairs (11. 157-208).

Different poets praise different things in you, but all most frequently sing your beneficial influence on French Poetry:

C'est qu'en voyant le Gaulois Apollon
Tout mal en poinct errer par nostre France,
A qui la sotte et maligne Ignorance
Pleine de fard d'envie et de desdain,
Avoit ravi la Lyre de la main,
En sa faveur tu ne t'es monstré chiche,
Faisant ce Dieu en ton dommage riche,
Luy consacrant par un voeu solennel
Ta Lyre courbe, un present eternel,
D'un art cousteux, à fin qu'on la contemple
Pour le present de Belot en son temple.
(11. 209-222)

II.   Description of Belot's lyre, on which the following scenes are represented:

    A.   Apollo singing at a feast of the gods. His song is about the debate between Minerva and Neptune for the patronage of Athens (11. 229-254).

    B.   Marsyas flayed after his music contest with Apollo (11. 255-262).

    C.   Apollo building the walls of Troy with Neptune (11. 263-278).

    D.   Apollo dressed as a pastor watching over Admetus' oxen (11. 279-292).

    E.   Bacchus and a vase containing hundreds of fruits, including a "Pompon aux costes separées" (11. 293-330).

    F.   Mercury, with the shell of a tortoise whose flesh he has eaten, and the entrails of oxen, making

> . . .une lyre au son delicieux,
> Au ventre creux, aux accords delectables,
> Le seul honneur des temples et des tables,
> Et des bons Dieux le plaisir le plus pront,
> Quand le Nectar leur eschaufe le front.
> (11. 331-356)

III.   Such is the lyre which you hung in Apollo's temple, Belot, so that we French could play on it a hymn to the god and to you at the same time. What I myself have been able to play on it, I have dedicated to our friendship,

> . . .present qui te peut suivre
> Apres mille ans, si des Muses l'effort
> Peut surmonter les siecles et la mort.
> (11. 373-384)

In *La Lyre* Ronsard comes close to equating the secular and divine systems of poetic exchange. Belot's liberality to poets is described by means of an image which makes him a personal ally of Apollo in the dispensation of poetic inspiration: the god of poetry himself had lost the symbol of his lyric function; Belot's gift restored to him his power. The relevance of *La Lyre* to *Le Melon* is in the actual mechanics of this exchange. Without Belot's lyre, Ronsard would be unable to sing; with the lyre he *is* able to sing, and he uses Belot's gift as an instrument of thanks to the donor. The poem itself *is*, in effect, Belot's gift, while at the same time it is intended as a recompense to Belot. *La Lyre*, like *Le Melon*, is ultimately an expression of gratitude for its own existence.

But the greatest point of similarity between Ronsard's poem and Saint-Amant's is to be found in the internal relations of its parts. The lyre which Belot has given to Apollo is painted with scenes in which all the most important aspects and episodes involving Apollo's first lyre are depicted: the charm it exercises over the Olympians (feast of the gods), its superiority over wind instruments (Apollo and Marsyas), its magic effect on even inanimate objects (Apollo's role in building Ilium), its relation to wine and food (Bacchus and fruit), its invention (Apollo, Admetus and Mercury), and its function as an epic instrument (celebration of the defeat of the Giants). In describing Belot's lyre, then, Ronsard simultaneously and inevitably describes the history of the lyre which this lyre is meant to replace, from the circumstances and manner of its invention to its eventual part in singing the gigantomachia. The tune which Ronsard plays on Belot's lyre in order to thank him for it is merely a *description* of that lyre which functions at the same time as a *narration* of the history of its predecessor. In a very similar way, Saint Amant's speaker thanks Apollo for the gift of a melon, first by describing it through the medium of the poem into which that melon has been metaphorically transformed, and then by narrating the story of its predecessor, that is, the invention of the lyre and its role in singing the defeat of the giants at a feast of the gods. Not only is each poem intended as a recompense for the gift of the poem itself, not only does each compensating poem consist of a description and history of the "gift" *on* which, and *through* which it is at that very moment being sung, but each is sung on an instrument which in some way replaces Apollo's lyre whose invention each narrates.

The tone of Ronsard's poem is light and playful. The image

for Belot's generosity to poets on which the entire piece is constructed allows for a good deal of wit, and Ronsard exploits its possibilities brilliantly. Yet there can be no doubt concerning the underlying seriousness of the poem's subject. In following so closely the movement and mechanics of *La Lyre,* while at the same time substituting a garden variety melon for a Maecenas' lyre, Saint-Amant seems once again to have adopted an ironic stance vis-à-vis his great forerunner. The "burlesque" of *Le Melon* is directed not only against the highest regions of Fable—the immortal gods and their heroic exploits—but against the exalted Ronsardian conception of the nature and properites of the "lyre" as well.

Le Melon ends with a final ecstatic outpouring in which the two preceding sections are reconciled and fused. The speaker has returned to the first-person lyric stance of the first part, but he has not abandoned the heroic meter of the burlesque part. In its final lines, the poem incorporates both lyric and epic elements in what appears to be a conscious and meaningful synthesis of the two major poetic modes. It is a synthesis in which temporality—both that of the lyric-dramatic monologue and that of the epic narration—has been transcended. Lines 309-332 are indeed entirely static. The series of ejaculations in the first four lines of this final passage is uttered, without reference to the moment and independently of any significant sequence, in a timeless moment of religious ecstasy:

> O manger precieux! Delices de la bouche!
> O doux Reptile herbu, rampant sur une couche!
> O beaucoup mieux que l'or, Chef-d'oeuvre d'Apollon!
> O Fleur de tous les Fruicts! O ravissant MELON!

The last twenty lines of the poem conspire explicitly to deny transience and change by means of a long series of ironic *impossibilia:*

> Les hommes de la Cour seront gens de parolle,
> Les Bordels de Rouën seront francs de verolle,

Sans vermine et sans galle on verra les Pedents,
Les preneurs de Petun auront de belles dents, etc., etc.

. . . .

Avant que je t'oublie.

Yet while these final lines transcend the temporal in their semantic content and sequence, they reproduce for the third and last time a rhetorical movement which we have already observed in each of the first two parts of the poem. Just as the lyric section demonstrated the excellence of the speaker's melon by means of a long anaphoric list of negative terms of comparison ("Ny le cher Abricot. . .Ny la Fraise. . .Ny la Manne. . .Ny le pur aliment. . .Ny la Poire, etc. . .Ne sont qu'amertume et que fange/Au prix de ce MELON"), and just as the epic section established the excellence of Apollo's melon by means of an even longer, nearly anaphoric series of eight-line descriptions of dishes which are also used as terms of negative comparison ("Ce Dieu qui. . .La superbe Junon qui. . .Le Compere Denis. . .La Deesse des Fours. . .Celuy qui sur la Mer. . .Celle qui sur un Mont. . .Le Forgeur écloppé qui. . .La Garce qui nasquit. . .Le Boucq qui contraignit. . .La Vieille au cul crotté. . .Le Seigneur des Jardins, etc. . . .parmy tant de mets. . .Il ne se treuva rien à l'égal d'un MELON"), so in the third synthetic section, a long list of anaphoric *impossibilia* are adduced as negative terms in the proof that the melon's memory will be eternal ("Les hommes seront . . .Les Bordels seront. . .Les preneurs auront. . .Les femmes ne seront. . .Les Corps se plairont. . .Les Amoureux ne seront. . . Les Bourgeois hanteront. . .Les Cabarets deviendront. . .Les Chantres diront. . .Les Quinze-vingts vaudront. . .Les Esprits paroistront. . .Maillet fera, etc. . . .ô MELON. . .Avant que je t'oublie").

A more important correspondence between this final passage and each of the two preceding passages is to be found in the gradual metamorphosis of the "melon" in the last lines of the poem. The fruit of Part I was metaphorically transformed into a poem, and the fruit of Part II was literally transformed into Apollo's lyre. Now that the first melon has been shown to be related to the second by direct kinship, its form is once again sublimated. The exclamations of lines 309-312 allow for only a limited ambiguity concerning the real nature of the thing praised: if "Chef-d'oeuvre d'Apollon" applies somewhat more fittingly to a poem than to a melon, there is little room for equivocation in the epithet "Reptile herbu, rampant sur une couche." By the end of the catalog of *impossibilia*, however, the melon's reality has once again become purely literary:

> Bref, ô MELON succrin, pour t'accabler de gloire,
> Des faveurs de Margot je perdray la memoire,
> Avant que je l'oublie, et que ton goust charmant
> Soit biffé des Cahiers du bon gros SAINT-AMANT.
> (11. 329-332)

Once again, the melon's "goust" has become esthetic rather than gastronomic. This "MELON" has come out of the poet's mouth, not disappeared into it.

But this time the transformed melon is neither the medium of an oral narration still in the process of becoming, as it was at the end of the lyric part of the poem, nor the instrument of a famous song in divine history, as it was at the end of the epic part of the poem. The final section in which the lyric and epic elements of the preceding sections are fused, and in which both lyric and narrative temporality has been transcended, transforms the melon into a *written* poem, into *scripta* which are destined to remain forever on the pages of the poet's note-books. *Tempus edax* may have had a bite of Apollo's melon (11. 259-260); he will not devour this one. The gods "brifferent" the first (1. 304); this will never be "biffé" (1. 332). *Le Melon* ends with the melon's final hypostasis as a written poem, the now-completed *Melon*. Nor are the final claims of "le bon gros Saint-Amant" unjustified, however ironic they may be, for indeed we have in our hands his "cahiers," and we have just savoured the "goust charmant" of his *Melon*.

AFTERWORD

To conclude a study of this kind would be to betray its purpose. The critic's task, and that of the responsible reader of poetry, is not to arrive at a few general statements which are valid for all the works of a poet and which put many poems neatly into one nutshell, not to reduce an entire *oeuvre* to a few paradigms, formulae, deep structures, constants or criteria, not to induce the "poetics" of a poet or to discover the secret of his "creative process," not to draw conclusions concerning the obsessions and determining experiences of a human consciousness through their veiled manifestations in a collection of texts. In short, our real task is not *reductive*. A poem is not interesting or important if it is considered only as an illustration of generalities which transcend it; its only real value is that of an individual work of art which makes its own demands and produces in the responsible and responsive reader its own unduplicated complex of intellectual and emotional responses. We can only claim to be readers of poetry to the degree that we attempt, in each particular encounter with a text, to make our own response adequate to that unique and complex patterning of semantic and allusive elements called a "poem." To the degree that we do otherwise, we are not readers of poetry, but biographers, historians, estheticians, psychoanalysts, cyberneticists, mathematicians, or egoists.

It goes without saying, moreover, that the strenuous and demanding activity we casually refer to as "reading" can never be complete. As much as we learn, as much as we reflect and practice, our response to a good poem will never be entirely adequate or entirely appropriate. Every critical appreciation is merely a progress report, and every reading is merely an "essay."

My intention is therefore not to "conclude" this study in either the logical or the closural sense of the word. A few remarks concerning the way we approach the poems of Saint-

Amant, on the other hand—remarks which do not conclude these essays but may serve as a prolegomenon to future readings—seem to be in order. I began this study by attempting to exorcise an old prejudice which, to one degree or another, has distorted almost all readings of Saint-Amant's poetry, including some of the most intelligent ones. The four essays which followed were based not on a preconception which, even according to external evidence, is clearly inaccurate, but rather on the heuristic hypothesis that Saint-Amant may have been in full control of his art and the poetic tradition, and on the resolve to take his poems seriously before dismissing anything in them as careless or gratuitous. From these essays has emerged an image of Saint-Amant which is very different from that of the undisciplined, unschooled and original "bon Gros," and an image of his poetry very different from the traditional conception of a pre-Romantic or a "baroque" rhapsodic effusiveness. All four of the poems I have attempted to read here are highly allusive to both classical and contemporary texts and conventions; all are centered around the most mysterious aspects of poesis like the origin, mode of production and quiddity of a poetic text; all constitute highly refined experiments with the limits and possibilities of literary genres and of generic mixing; all experiment in a complex and elaborate way with poetic form, unity and closure; and all are in some way self-exegetical.

Given their literary and self-conscious nature, it is undoubtedly significant that each of these four works contains at its very center the image of an Apollonian *kitharoidos* singing or playing, or both. In the grotto of *La Solitude,* the melancholic speaker plays on his lute an imitative canon with Echo:

> . . .par la celeste harmonie
> D'un doux Lut, aux charmes instruit,
> Je flatte sa triste manie,
> Faisant repeter mes accords
> A la voix qui luy sert de corps.

Midway through *Le Fromage* we find Apollo who has left his "violon" to "fluster son soul d'un chalumeau" under an elm tree. Midway through *L'Arion* we find Arion, "tourné vers le Soleil," singing a miraculous hymn to Apollo accompanied by his marvelous lute. And in *Le Melon* we witness Apollo's invention of the lyre and hear his first concert at a feast of the gods. As we have seen, each of these images has a special emblematic value with respect to the text in which it is set. They help to focus our attention on the fact that to a large extent the subject of these poems is poetry, and that their resources of meaning are conventions and works of literature—in short, that these texts are concerned above all else with poesis and the poetic Tradition.

Of all the characteristics we have observed in these four early poems, Saint-Amant's brand of allusiveness is perhaps the most unexpected and the most noteworthy. Saint-Amant was not a Humanist, and he was not erudite in the manner of the Pléiade poets. His allusions are not obscure. But his knowledge of classical and contemporary literature was at least as complete as that of his well-read public. He knew that readers of poetry—and consequently the eventual readers of his own first poems—"possessed" the *Metamorphoses* in the profound and immediate way that today's children "possess" television jingles and popular lyrics. He also knew that readers had both an intimate knowledge and a great reverence of the works of France's last great poet, Ronsard. Unlike the Pléiade poets, who sought to enlighten (and perhaps sometimes to bewilder) their public through references to poets and works most readers had never even heard of, like Anacreon, Terpander and Lycophron, Saint-Amant restricted his allusions to works whose familarity was guaranteed. Unlike the Pléiade, which preached and practiced a kind of *imitation* in which the recognition of a precise source of inspiration rarely plays a role in the understanding of a poem, and which often seems to have no other poetic function than to connote an elevated idea of the poetic art in general,[1] Saint-Amant practiced—without preaching in ponderous prefaces—a brilliant kind of *manipulation* in which the context, connotations and implications of recognizable echoes are *used* to bring an immense wealth of unstated meaning to his poems. And unlike the Pléiade, whose imitations often appear to be unordered except in the most elementary thematic way,[2] Saint-Amant uses his allusions as yet another set of semantic building blocks to supplement words, figures and images in the construction of complex poetic patterns and forms not to be found in any of the works to which allusion is made.

The simpler nature of allusions in *Le Melon* suggests a movement in Saint-Amant's work away from the extremely subtle and complex kind of poetry we find in *La Solitude* and *L'Arion,* and to a somewhat lesser degree in *Le Fromage,* toward a more straightforward and self-sufficient kind of poetry which will blossom in what the poet later came to call the "caprice." Among Saint-Amant's twelve *Caprices,* all of which were published between 1640 (*Le Passage de Gibraltar*) and 1649 (the *Troisiesme Partie des Oeuvres*) are many of the works which we moderns think of as his most "characteristic": the *Rome Ridicule, Le Mauvais Logement, Le Cantal, Pourveus Bacchiques, Le Cidre,* etc. In one of them, *La Petarrade aux Rondeaux,* the poet offers the following description of the genre:

> Et le Caprice avecques sa peinture
> Qui fait bouquer et l'Art, et la Nature,
> Ce Fou divin, riche en inventions,
> Bizarre en mots, vif en descriptions,
> Ce rare Autheur des nobles balivernes,
> Quoy qu'inspiré du Demon des Tavernes. . .
> (*Oeuvres* II, 202)

But we must be extremely cautious with both this flippant definition and our own notion of "characteristic" works. The enormous contrast between what the poet in his 1629 preface and critics from Gautier to Lagny all have to say about the poetry of Saint-Amant on the one hand, and what we actually find in the four poems I have read here on the other hand, should be sufficient warning against an overly complacent approach to these poems. The epistle and the satire (in the original sense of the word) are of course Roman inventions, and Régnier, for one, consistently referred to his own *Satires* as "caprices" three full decades before Saint-Amant published his first. This does not mean that Saint-Amant's *Caprices* and *Epitres héroï-comiques* are imitated, in the sixteenth-century sense, from Horace or Régnier; but neither are they spontaneous inventions which have sprung into existence *ex nihilo.* Saint-Amant undoubtedly arrived at these "new" forms gradually and consciously through the same kind of mastery and manipulation of tradition and the same creative experimentation in poesis which we have found in his very first poems.[3]   It is from the persepctive of these brilliant beginnings, not from the retrospective view of a lingering critical Romanticism, that each of these later poems must be read and re-evaluated.

It is impossible, and perhaps not even desirable, to approach a work of literary art with no preconceptions at all. If the foregoing essays are to have a use other than the intended one of contributing to the on-going search for adequate readings of good poems, then perhaps it is this: for the traditional image of Saint-Amant and his poetry with which students and scholars alike set about reading his poems, a more propitious and accurate one may profitably be substituted. Saint-Amant is not a secondary figure whose place is well below that of Ronsard and Racine in the register of French poets. He is one of those unique geniuses like Monteverdi, whose music is at once the culmination of an entire tradition and the beginning of a new one, and whose daring experiments within an inherited form like the madrigal, for example, resulted in a brave new world which utterly transcends the limits of the adopted form itself, but which our retrospective view domesticates and trivializes with a pat label like "opera."

We must agree with French literary history, then, that Saint-Amant's poetry does not share a place along side that of a Ronsard or a Racine. Its place is rather with the masterpieces of two of Saint-Amant's favorite writers, Rabelais and Cervantes. The lasting greatness of these works, as the young poet certainly realized, is the effect of a double nature. They are fun and amusing, and their appeal is fresh and immediate for each successive generation of readers. But at the same time they are brilliant summas of the literary and cultural traditions of the West, and carefully wrought experiments in literature and literary form. Rabelais and Cervantes are at the same time people's writers and writers' writers; their works are at once among the most popular and the most "intellectual" of our Western heritage. Surely Saint-Amant knew that Ronsard's elitist intellect was not enough in itself to assure the kind of immortality which that poet had sought for himself, and that the shallow and accessible verse of the senses like that of Marc de Papillon or his own friend Guillaume Colletet was even less likely to endure. The four poems I have examined here seem to be the result of an attempt to combine the sacred and profane strains of earlier poetic works into poems which would transcend both.

For over one hundred years readers have loved Saint-Amant as a Quixotic and Pantagrueline poet. Perhaps we should begin to recognize his works as Cervantesque and Rabelaisian in the fullest and most "serious" sense of those words, and read them accordingly.

NOTES TO INTRODUCTION

[1]Théophile Gautier, *Les Grotesques,* nouvelle éd. (Paris: Bibliothèque Charpentier, 1897), p. 156.

[2]Emile Faguet, *Histoire de la poésie française de la Renaissance au Romantisme,* 11 vols. (Paris: Boivin, 1923), II, *De Malherbe à Boileau,* p. 318.

[3]Françoise Gourier, *Etude des oeuvres poétiques de Saint-Amant* (Geneva: Droz, 1961), p. 60. This is the most fundamental characteristic of Saint-Amant's poetry according to Gourier's reading: "Il s'abandonne à sa verve avec une grande liberté d'allure" (p. 67); ". . .cette inspiration primesautière. . .la légèreté avec laquelle le poète s'y abandonne" (p. 143); "Le ton du poème varie. . .avec une liberté complète de la part du poète, qui. . .suit ses 'visions' et le cours de ses pensées sans le moindre effort de composition" (p. 147); "L'art de Saint-Amant réside essentiellement dans l'humeur capricieuse de la présentation" (p. 157); "Toutes ces pièces sont marquées par le même humour changeant, la même composition libre. . .le même style facile et spontané" (p. 240).

[4]Gautier, pp. 156 and 168.

[5]Jean Lagny, *Le poète Saint-Amant (1594-1661): Essai sur sa vie et ses oeuvres* (Paris: Nizet, 1964), p. 64.

[6]Faguet, II, 175.

[7]Christian Wentzlaff-Eggebert, *Forminteresse, Traditionsverbundenheit und Aktualisierungsbedürfnis als Merkmale des Dichtens von Saint-Amant,* Münchener Romanistische Arbeiten, 29 (Munich: Hueber, 1970), pp. 11-28.

[8]See Daniel Bourchenin, *Etude sur les académies protestantes en France au XVIe et au XVIIe siècle* (Paris, 1882; rpt. Geneva: Slatkine Reprints, 1969), especially pp. 179-212; Edward A. Fitzpatrick, ed., *St.*

Ignatius and the Ratio Studiorum (New York: McGraw-Hill, 1933), pp. 208-234; and Juan Luis Vives, *De Tradendis Disciplinis* III, 6.

[9]See Jean Lagny, "Le poète Saint-Amant et le protestantisme," *Bulletin de la Société de l'Histoire du Protestantisme Français,* 103 (1957), 237-266.

[10]"Nous devons nous souvenir que les Français reçoivent alors [au début du XVIIe siècle], dans les collèges, un enseignement tout entier consacré à l'étude des langues et des littératures de l'Antiquité. S'il existe des "modernes," c'est dans la mesure où certains esprits se révoltent contre l'instruction qu'ils ont d'abord reçue," Antoine Adam, *L'Age Classique I: 1624-1660,* Littérature Française, Vol. 6 (Paris: Arthaud, 1968), p. 95.

In his biography of the poet, Jean Lagny makes a convincing argument for supposing that Saint-Amant studied in a college until he was 18 or 20 years old, and that he acquired there "une culture classique au moins ébauchée." Lagny's pages on the question of Saint-Amant's intellectual culture are somewhat narrow in scope and modest in their conclusions, but excellent in their treatment of the documents and testimonials which mention the poet by name. See *Le poète Saint-Amant,* pp. 30-42.

[11]Lagny, *Le poète Saint-Amant,* passim.

[12]Quoted in Lagny, *Le poète Saint-Amant,* p. 121.

[13]Chevreau, *Chevraeana,* II (Paris: Florentin et Pierre Delaulne, 1700), p. 33.

[14]The 1627 edition of Montlyard's translation was published in a beautiful in-folio volume by Saint-Amant's friend Jean Baudoin (and rather scandalously presented in such a way as to give the impression that the translation is in fact Baudoin's own work). This circumstance is one of several reasons for suspecting that whether or not the poet read the *Mythologiae* in the original, he must certainly have been very familiar with the work in translation. Let it be said here that for this and other reasons I have chosen to quote Comes in Montlyard's French translation throughout this study, whereas classical poets—and principally Ovid—are all quoted in the original. The reasons for quoting Latin poetry in Latin rather than in translation will become apparent in my discussion of *La Solitude* below.

[15]This point will become more tangible if we realize that when Saint-

Amant was 18 years old, Du Bellay's death was more recent than Proust's is for us today, Jodelle's death was as recent as James Joyce's, Ronsard's death as recent as Gide's and Eluard's, and Montaigne's death as recent as Camus'.

[16]See Adam, *L'Age Classique I*, pp. 95-98. Not even Saint-Amant escaped this powerful influence: the admiring ode to Théophile published as a liminary piece in the latter's *Oeuvres* of 1621 could have been written in 1550 by Ronsard himself (see *Oeuvres* I, 3-7).

[17]Laumonier XVI, 26. Cohen I, 651. Silver—.

[18]*Les Quatre Premiers Livres des Odes* (1550), "Au Lecteur." Laumonier I, 43-44. Cohen II, 971. Silver—.

[19]Laumonier XIV, 4-6. Cohen II, 996-997. Silver—.

[20]Among recent attempts to deal with the problems of composition in Saint-Amant's poetry, two articles have been particularly successful: David Lee Rubin, "Consciousness and the External World in a Caprice by Saint-Amant," *Yale French Studies*, 49 ("Science, Language and the Perspective Mind"), 170-177; and John D. Lyons, "Saint-Amant's *La Solitude*: The Rhetoric of Fragmentation," *Orbis Litterarum*, 33 (1978), 4-17.

[21]While Saint-Amant's "imitations" have been treated more frequently than any other aspect of his poetry in recent years—particularly his imitations of Berni and the Berneschi—discussions of the subject tend to shed far more light on the poet's own tastes and reading habits than on the poems themselves. This is an area in which literary analysis has lagged woefully far behind biography. The most useful approaches to date are Giovanna Angeli, "Saint-Amant e i rifacimenti visionari dei prototipi berneschi," *Paragone*, 234 (1969), 21-49; and Wentzlaff-Eggebert, *Forminteresse*.

[22]There is one notable exception which has not received the attention it deserves. William Roberts, in his article "Classical Sources of Saint-Amant's *L'Arion*," *French Studies*, 17 (1963), 341-350, has demonstrated that *L'Arion* is composed in part of passages borrowed directly from Herodotus, Plutarch and the *Fasti*. This discovery has tremendously important ramifications which no one, to my knowledge, has taken the trouble to pursue.

[23]Excluded from the admittedly subjective category of "significant"

works are ballet verse (contributions entitled "Bacchus Conquérant," "Junon à Paris" and "Le sorcier amoureux"), liminary poems (an ode to Théophile de Viau, a sonnet to Molière d'Essertines and a madrigal on Giambattista Andreini's *Centaura*), and direct, uncritical imitations (*La Jouyssance, L'Andromède* and *La Métamorphose de Lyrian et de Sylvie*). Though the latter are especially successful poems, they adhere too strictly to a pre-established convention or model to be of any extraordinary historical or esthetic interest.

[24]For all questions of chronology, both in the life and in the works of Saint-Amant, I have relied on Jean Lagny, *Le poète Saint-Amant,* and on the chronological tables at the back of each volume of the Lagny-Bailbé edition of Saint-Amant's *Oeuvres.* For publication dates, the indispensible reference is Lagny, *Bibliographie des éditions anciennes des oeuvres de Saint-Amant* (Paris: Giraud-Badin, 1960), which originally appeared as a special issue of the *Bulletin du Bibliophile et du Bibliothécaire,* 1960, Nos. 3-6, pp. 97-236. See also Claude Abraham, "An Attempt at a Chronology of the Early Works of Saint-Amant," *Romance Notes,* 11 (1970), 591-594.

NOTES ON CHAPTER I

[1]*Oeuvres* I, 33-48. Jacques Bailbé, after Jean Lagny, places its composition before 1620. Claude Abraham situates it between 1617 and 1621. See *Oeuvres* I, 299; *Le poète Saint-Amant*, ch. 3; and "An Attempt at a Chronology," p. 592.

[2]It was reproduced without attribution in Camus' novel *Hermiante* (1623), and in Claude Morlot's pirated edition of the *Oeuvres* of Théophile de Viau (1627), as well as in subsequent editions of Théophile's works (1628). See Saint-Amant, *Oeuvres* I, xx-xxii; Lagny, "Autour de la 'Solitude' de Saint-Amant: questions de dates," *Bulletin du Bibliophile et du Bibliothécaire*, 1955, No. 6, 235-245; and Christian Wentzlaff-Eggebert, *Forminteresse*, pp. 65 ff.

[3]The principal translations by Pierre Dhoges, Henri Golignac and Father François Papus were published in 1646, 1654 and 1662, respectively, but were undoubtedly written much earlier. Some may even have been written before the publication of the first authorized edition of *La Solitude* in 1629. These translations, like the original poem, were both pirated and plagiarized. See *Oeuvres* I, xxii-xxiii; and Lagny, "Autour de la 'Solitude' de Saint-Amant: les traductions latines," *Bulletin du Bibliophile et du Bibliothécaire*, 1956, No. 3, 110-126.

[4]Nicolas Faret's preface to the *Oeuvres* of 1629 is most lavish in its praise of *La Solitude*:

> Et certes, qui peut voir ceste belle Solitude, à qui toute la France
> a donné sa voix, sans estre tenté d'aller resver dans les deserts, et
> si tous ceux qui l'ont admirée s'estoient laissé aller aux premiers
> mouvemens qu'ils ont eus en la lisant, la Solitude mesme n'auroit-
> elle pas esté destruitte par sa propre loüange, et ne seroit-elle pas
> aujourd'hui plus frequentée que les Villes?
> (*Oeuvres* I, 16-17)

A more objective and consequently more valuable appraisal is to be found in the *Mémoires* of Michel de Marolles, who recalls his first meeting with the poet in the following terms: "Ce fut aussi dans le même logis que je vis la premiere fois Monsieur de Saint-Amant, qui s'est acquis tant de reputation par ses beaux Vers, aïant composé dès-lors son Poéme de la solitude, qui fut reçu avec tant d'applaudissement." (quoted in Lagny, *Le poète Saint-Amant*, p. 56).

[5]*Premier Livre des Amours,* "Le plus touffu d'un solitaire bois," 11. 1-7. Laumonier IV, 13. Cohen I, 6. Silver I, 80.

[6]*Ibid.*, "Or que Jupin espoint de sa semence," 11. 12-14. Laumonier IV, 124. Cohen I, 70. Silver I, 249.

[7]*Ibid.*, "Pendant, Baïf, que tu frapes au but," 11. 7-11. Laumonier IV, 129. Cohen I, 72. Silver I, 257.

[8]See Luzius Keller, " 'Solo e pensoso,' 'Seul et pensif,' 'Solitaire et pensif': Mélancolie pétrarquienne et mélancolie pétrarquiste," *Studi Francesi,* nuova serie, 49 (1973), 3-14.

[9]Agrippa d'Aubigné, *Stances,* I, 11. 129-132, in *Le Printemps: Stances et Odes,* ed. Fernand Desonay, TLF (Geneva: Droz, 1952), p. 7.

[10]Du Mas, "Stances," in *Lydie, fable champestre, et Oeuvres meslees* (Paris: J. Millot, 1609), pp. 220-222.

[11]La Roque de Clairmont, *Les Amours de Phyllis,* sonnet 14 ("A la Royne Marguerite"), in *Les Oeuvres* (Paris: Vve Claude de Monstr'oeil, 1609), p. 8. Similar landscapes from the same period can be read in Jean Rousset, ed., *Anthologie de la poésie baroque française,* 2 vols. Bibliothèque de Cluny (Paris: A. Colin, 1961), and in Gisèle Mathieu-Castellani, *Les thèmes amoureux dans la poésie française (1570-1600)* (Paris: Klincksieck, 1975), pp. 358-364 and 401-417.

[12]*Les Grotesques,* p. 168.

[13]Christian Wentzlaff-Eggebert seems to have been the first post-Romantic reader to realize, or at least to consider with any seriousness, the conventionality of *La Solitude.* He has pertinently and cogently demonstrated that many of Saint-Amant's most "realistic" and vivid descriptions are in fact to be found, with only minor variations, in contemporary pastoral literature. See *Forminteresse,* pp. 81-127.

[14]The actual terms of Saint-Amant's line in which the mountain itself is described (1. 26) have their closest Ovidian parallel in a detail from Nestor's account of the battle between the Centaurs and the Lapithae:

> Dictys *ab ancipiti* delapsus *acumine montis,*
> Dum fugit instantem trepidans Ixione natum,
> Decidit in praeceps et pondere corporis ornum
> Ingentem fregit suaque induit ilia fractae.
> *(Metamorphoses* XII, 337-340)

But the circumstances of this scene differ so radically from those of the desperate suicide attempts which Saint-Amant is at such pains to evoke that the possibility of any intended and functional allusion must be dismissed.

[15]This resemblance of diction, though striking, is insufficient grounds in itself for arguing that the Ovidian passage quoted above is either a source or a meaningful reference for Saint-Amant's lines. The uncut forest revered by centuries is a commonplace found frequently in Latin literature, and particularly in Ovid. The encounter between Jupiter and Callisto for example takes place in a "nemus quod *nulla ceciderat aetas*" (*Metamorphoses* II, 418), Cadmus founds Thebes near a Boeotian forest which is described as a "silva vetus. . .*nulla violata securi*" (*Metamorphoses* III, 28), a grove at the foot of the Esquiline hill is described in the *Fasti* as "*multis incaeduus annis* (*Fasti* II, 435), the forest in which Elegeia and Tragoedia compete for Ovid's attentions is a "vetus et *multos incaedua* silva *per annos*" (*Amores* III 1, 1), etc.

[16]The first translation of the *Metamorphoses* into French prose (*Le Grand Olympe;* Lyon, 1532) skirts the problem altogether by rendering the passage thus: ". . .vilains mal gracieux y avoit qui cueilloyent herbes." François Habert's verse translation (Rouen, 1557?) is far more accurate and reproduces the rhythm and sequence of Ovid's lines exactly, but nevertheless renders "ulva" by a more generic French equivalent:

> Un petit Lac au coing d'une vallee,
> Où les vilains du lieu qui travailloient,
> Joncs et Osiers et *herbes* recueilloient.

A later verse rendering by Raimond and Charles de Massac (Paris, 1617) is the only one to offer a literal translation of the passage:

> . . .où des rustres hargneux
> Recueilloient du *feuillu* plaisant au marécage,
> De l'osier, et du jong.

Rather than omit the troublesome word, the Massacs appear to have looked it up in Robert Estienne's *Dictionarium Latinogallicum*, which defines "ulva" as "herbe marine, *feulu de mer*." Nicolas Renouard's popular but approximative prose translation of the *Metamorphoses* (Paris, 1619) betrays nearly as much indifference to such fine points as did the first prose translation which appeared almost a century earlier: "il y avoit des paysans dedans qui coupoient les joncs et les *autres meschantes herbes,* que les lieux marescageux portent."

[17]Wentzlaff-Eggebert has attempted to demonstrate Saint-Amant's particular debt to d'Urfé's *Le Sireine* in this passage, and here again his reading is one of the most convincing and accurate to date.

[18]In a later poem of a very different kind, Saint-Amant describes the ruins of another stately edifice in terms which, despite the differences in style and tone, are curiously reminiscent of those of *La Solitude:*

> Pietre et Barbare Colisée,
> Execrable reste des Goths,
> Nid de Lezards et d'Escargots,
> Digne d'une amere risée:
> Pourquoy ne vous raze-t'on pas?
> Peut-on trouver quelques appas
> En vos ruïnes criminelles?
> (*Rome Ridicule* XIII, in *Oeuvres* III, 11)

[19]One wonders, however, why Saint-Amant's "pauvre Amant" hanged himself in a *castle* if both he and his "Bergere" were strictly rustics.

[20]Françoise Gourier, *Etude des oeuvres poétiques de Saint-Amant* (Geneva: Droz, 1961), pp. 178-179.

[21]Lagny, *Le poète Saint-Amant,* p. 64.

[22]The multifarious correspondences between strophes 3 and 14 allow us to apprehend yet another kind of unity in the ostensibly double subject of strophe 3. In addition to the relation between cliffs and nightingales which textual allusions to the stories of Philomela and Daedalion have

already allowed us to perceive, we can now see that as a symmetrical counterpart to the first seascape strophe, Daedalion and Philomela correspond exactly to the two moments of the Palaemon story, to which clear allusion is made here: (1) the mad suicide leap as punishment for *hubris*, and (2) the metamorphosis into a natural inhabitant of the place.

[23]Letter VII in *Lettres,* ed. Luciano Erba (Milan: Scheiwiller, 1965), pp. 37-39.

[24]Tristan L'Hermite, *Les Amours et autres poésies choisies,* ed. Pierre Camo (Paris: Garnier, 1925), p. 216.

[25]*Ibid.,* p. 56.

[26]John D. Lyons has made a point similar to the one I have been arguing here in an elegant article just published: "Saint-Amant's *La Solitude:* The Rhetoric of Fragmentation," *Orbis Litterarum,* 33 (1978), 4-17. This suggestive analysis argues from a slightly different perspective that in *La Solitude,* "the poet's primary purpose is a resolution in his imagery of the conflicts between his creation and the literary heritage on which he must draw" (p. 16).

[27]If the poem had in fact become what it initially promised to be, the *envoi* would of course have to be addressed either to the cruel and distant lady or, after Petrarch, to the poem itself: "Canzon, s'al dolce loco/La donna nostra vedi. . .," "Canzone, oltra quell'alpe,/Là dove il ciel è più sereno e lieto. . .," etc. (*Il Canzoniere,* 37 and 129).

[28]Joachim Du Bellay, *Deffense et Illustration de la Langue Françoyse,* ed. Henri Chamard, STFM, 4th printing (Paris: Didier, 1970), p. 169 (Livre II, ch. 11).

[29]*Odes* II 2, "A Calliope," 11. 51-54 and 61-64. Laumonier I, 177. Cohen I, 434. Silver III, 125.

[30]*Odes* III 11, "Sur la Naissance de François, Dauphin de France," 11. 1-4 and 16-19. Laumonier II, 29-30. Cohen I, 503-504. Silver III, 210.

[31]*Odes* V 2, "A Madame Marguerite," 11. 37-42. Laumonier III, 100. Cohen I, 583. Silver III, 307.

[32]*Odes* I 10, "A Michel de L'Hospital," strophe 11, 11. 345-348.

Laumonier III, 138-139. Cohen I, 394. Silver III, 67. Saint-Amant himself developed the topos of poetic solitude in one of his earliest circumstantial pieces, the liminary ode to Théophile de Viau. Here the debt to Ronsard and Du Bellay is particularly striking:

> Vous qui dedans *la solitude*
> *D'un bois, d'un antre,* ou d'un estude
> Imaginez vos beaux escrits,
> Lors que la saincte Poësie
> Vous anime, et vous rend espris
> De sa plus douce frenesie.
>   (*Oeuvres* I, 4; 11. 25-30)

[33]Sainte-Beuve, whose critical observations are often among the most perspicacious and useful to be found anywhere, even when they concern works for which he had little or no sympathy, considered this ambiguity in the valorization of solitude to be one of the chief defects of the poem. In his review article on Ch.-L. Livet's then new critical edition of the complete works of Saint-Amant, he had this to say about an ambivalence which he naturally assumed to be unintentional:

> . . .je n'y retrouve ni la solitude du chrétien et du saint, celle dont
> il est écrit «qu'elle bondira dans l'allégresse et qu'elle fleurira
> comme le lis;» ni la *solitude du poëte* et du sage; ni *celle de l'amant
> mélancolique et tendre;* ni celle du peintre exact et rigoureux. Il
> n'y mêle aucune idée morale ni aucun sentiment fait pour toucher,
> et lorsqu'il s'écrie en terminant «Oh! que j'aime la Solitude! c'est
> l'élément des bons esprits,» il ne l'a pas suffisamment prouvé, et
> il a plutôt fait une solitude moitié naturelle, moitié de fantaisie,
> dans laquelle les objets ont tant soit peu dansé devant sa vue, et
> où si d'un côté il ôtait le masque à la nature, il lui en mettait un à
> l'autre joue.»

Causeries du Lundi, 3e édition, 15 vols. (Paris: Garnier, 1857), XII, 173-191 (8 décembre 1855, "Oeuvres complètes de Saint-Amand"), pp. 180-181.

[34]Cesare Ripa, *Iconologia: overo descrittione di diverse imagini cavate dall' antichità, e di propria inventione* (1603; rpt. Hildesheim and New York: Georg Olms Verlag, 1970), pp. 79-80.

[35]*Odes* I 18, "A Joachim Du Bellay, Angevin," 11. 33-34 and 40.

Laumonier I, 146. Cohen I, 421. Silver III, 106.

[36]*Les Regrets* 21, 1. 9.

[37]*Odes* I 18, 11. 25-28. Laumonier I, 145-146. Cohen I, 421. Silver III, 106.

[38]*Odes* I 10, "A Michel de L'Hospital," 11. 451-454, 549-552. Laumonier III, 144 and 149. Cohen I, 397 and 399. Silver III, 71 and 74.

[39]Needless to say, Du Bellay did not "invent" this claim to pure invention any more than Saint-Amant did. It is a common one in Petrarch and Petrarchan verse, as it is in the poetry of the *stil novisti.* Dante, for example, offers the following explanation for the superiority of his own love lyrics over everyone else's:

> . . .I' mi son un che, quando
> Amor mi spira, noto, e a quel modo
> Ch' e' ditta dentro, vo significando.
> (*Purgatorio* XXIV, 52-54)

But whereas Du Bellay's imitation of such claims is not in itself "functional" except in terms of the broadest implications of such borrowings, Saint-Amant's obvious imitation of Du Bellay's diction is multifariously ironic and self-ironic.

[40]Cesare Ripa, *Iconologia,* pp. 76-77.

[1]Only the first poem of the volume, *Le Soleil levant*, can be considered to resemble those of the "serious" section of the 1629 collection.

[2]Tallemant des Réaux, *Historiettes*, ed. Antoine Adam, Bibliothèque de la Pléiade (Paris: Gallimard, 1961), II, 236.

[3]*La Crevaille* will later be augmented by five lines in which the familiar epithet appears:

> Celuy qui forgea ces rimes,
> Dont Bacchus fait tous les crimes,
> C'est *le bon et digne Gros*,
> Qui voudroit que les Abîmes
> Se trouvassent dans les Brocs.
> (*Oeuvres* II, 75 and IV, 192)

The date of this addition is significant: 1658 (*Le Dernier Recueil*). In 1631 Saint-Amant was not yet known as "le bon Gros" except to his own circle of friends. At the very end of his career, twenty-eight years after the composition of the poem, he was naturally inclined to append a trademark which his readers had come to expect in his works.

[4]See Richard A. Mazzara, "Saint-Amant and the Italian Bernesque Poets," *French Reivew*, 32 (1959), 238-240; and Giovanna Angeli, "Saint-Avant e i rifacimenti visionari dei prototipi berneschi," *Paragone*, 234 (1969), 21-49.

[5]Annibal de Lortigue, *Poèmes divers* (Paris: J. Gesselin, 1617), pp. 176-184.

[6]It is true, as Jacques Bailbé remarks in his notes to *Le Fromage*, that Saint-Amant's mythologizing combines elements from two legends which were at one time separate and distinct. But this "conflation" was not Saint-Amant's doing, and was in fact imperceptible to seventeenth-

century readers.   It results from a confusion dating from earliest Latin
mythography, especially evident in Lactantius (*Narrationes Fabularum* II,
11).   By the sixteenth century the conflation had completely absorbed the
two constituent myths, leaving no trace of an original distinction.   Natalis
Comes, who usually records more variants and distinctions in such matters
than anyone could reasonably wish to know, states very matter-of-factly in
both his article on Apollo and his article on Mercury, that Apollo's exile
from Olympus—his punishment for having avenged Aesculapius' death on
the Cyclopes—was the occasion for Mercury's theft of Admetus' herd.   In
the eyes of Saint-Amant's readers there was clearly no question of a significant conflation at all, but of a standard and legitimate myth.

[7] Antoine Oudin, *Les Curiositez françoises.* In a later Bacchic poem,
La Crevaille (1630), Saint-Amant will make a similar pun on "fluste,"
which means not only the woodwind instrument, but a tall drinking glass
as well:

> O que la desbauche est douce!
> Il faut qu'*en faisant Carrousse,*
> *Ma Fluste en sonne le pris;*
> Et que sur Pegase en housse,
> Je la monstre aux beaux Esprits.
> (*Oeuvres* II, 75)

[8] It is interesting to note that the second mythological digression,
successfully negotiated in section IV of the poem, though apparently unrelated, in fact reproduces the essential pattern of this first digression in
section II, to which it corresponds both positionally and functionally.
Rather than placing the cows of Brie under the pastoral guardianship of
Apollo, the speaker will later claim that his cheese has come from no other
cow than the one into which Io was once transformed (11. 110-120). The
cheese, in other words, will be valorized by the attentions of Jupiter rather
than by those of Apollo. But of course Io was taken from Jupiter by his
jealous wife Juno and placed under the watchful surveillance of the hun-
dred-eyed Argus. Mercury, disguised as a goatherd, succeeds in stealing her
back for Jupiter by killing the cowherd-jailer, having first lulled the monster to sleep by playing the *syrinx* and telling the story of its invention.
Both mythological allusions, then, recall a famous cattle theft; the thief in
both cases is Mercury; in both cases the musical instrument which distracts
the cowherd and permits the theft is the *syrinx;* and Pan's "amoureux
martyre," alluded to in the first digression, is the subject of the somniferous
tale recounted by Mercury to Argus, alluded to in the second (See *Meta-*

morphoses I, 622-721).

Though they would appear to have little bearing on the emblematic value of the first digression, these thematic similarities between the two mythological passages do add yet another important dimension to the rigorously symmetrical composition of the poem.

[9]The principal authority for this version is Apollodorus (*Bibliotheca* III 10, 2). A less common version in the Renaissance was that of the Homeric Hymn to Hermes, in which Hermes' invention of the lyre *precedes* his theft of Apollo's cattle. Saint-Amant's playful allusiveness clearly depends on the more intimate relation between cattle and lyres established in the Apollodorus version.

[10]This mythical invention of the lyre was a commonplace in the Renaissance. Saint-Amant playfully subverts the traditional legend in *Le Melon* by asserting that it was Apollo himself, and not Mercury, who invented the first "lut," and that he manufactured his instrument not from the shell of a tortoise, but from the husk of a melon. See chapter 4 below.

[11]Ronsard had played a major role in guaranteeing for future readers the symbolic value of the *kithara* by using the word "lyre" consistently throughout his career to mean not the instrument itself, but the lyric mode, lyric inspiration, all that is sublime in Pindar, Horace. . .and Ronsard.

[12]*La Desbauche* (1623-1624?), which resembles *Le Fromage* in so many respects, will begin with a similar repudiation of the Apollonian *kithara:*

> Nous perdons le temps à rimer
> Amis, il ne faut plus chommer,
> Voicy Bacchus qui nous convie
> A mener bien une autre vie;
> Laissons là ce fat d'Apollon,
> Chions dedans son *violon*,. . .

But unlike *Le Fromage,* the later poem will be explicit, rather than merely allusive, in developing the symbolic value of Apollo's *kithara-violon:*

> . . .Nargue du Parnasse et des Muses,
> Elles sont vieilles et camuses;

Nargue de leur sacré ruisseau,
De leur archet, de leur pinceau,
Et de leur verve poëtique
Qui n'est qu'une ardeur frenetique:
Pegase en fin n'est qu'un Cheval,
Et pour moy je croy, cher Laval,
Que qui le suit et luy fait feste,
Ne suit, et n'est rien qu'une beste.

(*Oeuvres* I, 201-202)

[13]The *syrinx* as a symbol of a lower style in the pastoral mode was as current in the Renaissance as was the *kithara* as a symbol of the elevated lyric style. The "chalumeau" is ubiquitous in sixteenth and seventeenth-century pastoral literature, and an old Parisian folksong recalled much later by Rousseau in his *Confessions* (I 21) bears witness to both the universality and the longevity of its pastoral associations, especially when it is played, as it is in *Le Fromage,* under an elm tree:

Tircis, je n'ose
Ecouter ton chalumeau
Sous l'ormeau,
Car on en cause
Déjà dans notre hameau.

Saint-Amant himself had incorporated lines almost identical to those of *Le Fromage* into the pastoral evocation of a slightly earlier work, *La Jouyssance* (1617-1621):

Tantost nous voyons un Satyre
Assis à l'ombre d'un Ormeau
Faire plaindre son chalumeau
De son agreable martyre.

(*Oeuvres* I, 165)

NOTES TO CHAPTER III

[1]Ed. Félix Gaiffe, STFM (Paris: E. Cornély, 1910), p. 13.

[2]In his preface to the collection of songs entitled *Livre de Meslanges.* Laumonier XVIII, 485. Cohen II, 980. Silver—.

[3]In a poem of the *IX. Livre des poèmes,* entitled "A la Lyre." *Euvres en rime,* ed. Ch. Marty-Laveaux, II (Paris: A. Lemerre, 1883), p. 449.

[4]For a cogent demonstration that Saint-Amant knew and borrowed from all of these classical sources, see William Roberts, "Classical Sources of Saint-Amant's *L'Arion*," *French Studies,* 17 (1963), 341-350. Though debatable in some of its conclusions, this article remains an extremely important contribution to the study of Saint-Amant's poetry in that it proves irrefutably that despite the poet's uncompromisingly modernist pose, he knew his classics and knew how to manipulate them creatively.

Roberts is scrupulous to point out that Saint-Amant would have had to read the *Fasti* either in Latin or in Italian, since the work had not yet been translated into French (p. 344). I am convinced that Saint-Amant had no need of a translation whatever, but I should perhaps point out that a French translation of Ovid's Arion story was in fact available to anyone who did. It is true that the *Fasti* had not been translated as such, but the entire passage concerning Arion *had* been, and it could be found in the very first place any contemporary would have been likely to look for information concerning any mythological subject, that is, in J. de Montlyard's French translation of Natalis Comes' *Mythologiae,* published in 1604, 1607, 1611, 1612 and 1627. For the complete text of this translation, see Appendix I.

[5]Saint-Amant literally pillaged Du Bartas' poem, and William Roberts' study of the classical sources of *L'Arion* (see preceding note) could usefully be supplemented by a similar study of borrowings from the *Cinquiesme Jour* of the *Premiere Sepmaine.* The extent of Saint-Amant's imitation can be surmised from the parallel passages quoted below in Appendix II.

[6]*Oeuvres* I, 109-124. "Bacchus Conquérant," a poem of fifty-four lines written for a *ballet du Roy, Les Bacchanalles,* appeared in 1623 together with other verse for the same occasion by Théophile, Du Vivier, Sorel, Boisrobert, and M. [Malleville?]. *L'Arion* was published separately the same year, and underwent three printings. See Jean Lagny, *Bibliographie des éditions anciennes des oeuvres de Saint-Amant* (Paris: Giraud-Badin, 1960), pp. 7-10.

[7]*Les Regrets* 31. Du Bellay, *Les Regrets et autres oeuvres poëtiques,* ed. J. Joliffe and M. A. Screech, 2nd ed., TLF (Geneva: Droz, 1974), p. 98. In his notes to lines 8-9 of *L'Arion,* Jacques Bailbé rightly points out that the actual wording of these lines is much closer to Du Bartas than to Du Bellay:

> Ains chaque heure du jour il tourne vers la France
> Et son coeur et son oeil, se fachant qu'il ne void
> La fumée à flots gris voltiger sur son toict. . .

That Saint-Amant imitated these lines is all the more likely since they appear early in the same *Cinquiesme Jour* of *La Premiere Sepmaine* in which the Arion legend is recounted, and from which Saint-Amant had plagiarized so many passages (see note 5 above). But the "il" pictured in Du Bartas' image is an unmistakable portrait of Du Bellay himself, as the context of these lines makes clear (11. 135-142), and the portrait of Du Bellay is evoked here as a term of comparison in the description not of Arion, but of fish like salmon and shad which, out of "l'amour de la patrie," leave freshwater streams near the end of their lives in order to die in the sea! Not only does this context have little to do with Arion's return to Greece, but it is very unlikely that Saint-Amant's wording would call to mind for any of his readers this discussion of fresh and salt-water fish. Though Saint-Amant may have borrowed his wording from Du Bartas, he, like Du Bartas before him, used it to help his readers to recall through Du Bellay the homecoming of Odysseus.

[8]*L'Odyssee d'Homere,* translated by Salomon Certon, 2nd ed. (Paris: Nicolas Hameau, 1615), p. 5. These lines correspond to Book I, lines 57-59 of the original Homeric poem.

[9]11. 129-133. Laumonier VIII, 169. Cohen II, 284. Silver VI, 226-227.

[10]I owe the discovery of Erasmus' commentary to M. A. Screech's

valuable notes in his edition of Du Bellay's *Regrets* (pp. 98-99), and several of the other examples of the smoking chimney topos to Henri Chamard, *Histoire de la Pléiade* (Paris: Didier, 1939), II, 245.

[11]Ovid appears to make the same generic use of the word "home" in the passage of the *Fasti* which inspired lines 39-42 of *L'Arion:*

> Nomen Arionium Siculas impleverat urbes,
>   Captaque erat lyricis Ausonis ora sonis;
> Inde *domum repetens* puppem conscendit Arion.
>   (*Fasti* II, 93-95)

[12]Homer, *Les Oeuvres,* trans. Salomon Certon (Paris: Nicolas Hameau, 1615), p. 23. Certon's verse translation of the *Odyssey* was first published in Paris in 1604, when Saint-Amant was ten years old. The translation of the complete works, quoted here, included the *Iliad,* the Homeric Hymns and the *Batrachomyomachia,* and appeared eleven years later, eight years before Saint-Amant published *L'Arion.*

[13]*L'Odyssee,* trans. Certon, 1604, fol. 133^v. In the second edition of the *Odyssey* which was published with *Les Oeuvres d'Homere* in 1615, this passage was modified to read:

> Et de tout leur effort couvrirent l'eau marine
> Haussans les avirons mais quand à bien ramer
> Nous eusmes regagné deux fois autant de mer,
> Lors criant de plus beau. . .
>   (p. 270)

[14]*L'Odyssee,* 1604, fols. 174^v-175^r. *L'Odyssee,* 1615, p. 355.

[15]*L'Odyssee,* 1604, fol. 185^r. *L'Odyssee,* 1615, p. 377.

[16]Laumonier XVI, 90. Cohen I, 674. Silver IV, 68.

[17]Laumonier XVI, 91. Cohen I, 675. Silver IV, 69.

[18]Laumonier XVI, 93. Cohen I, 676. Silver IV, 73.

[19]Other modern poets had imitated traditional embarkation scenes before Saint-Amant, but these imitations rarely had the specific allusive function that we find in the description of *L'Arion.* One such earlier

imitation whose dicton is particularly close to Saint-Amant's is to be found
in Honoré d'Urfé's *Sireine*—the same poem which Wentzlaff-Eggebert con-
siders to have been the principal "source" of *La Solitude:*

> A reins courbez les Matelots
> De rames sillonnoient les flots,
> Ce pendant sur la mer voutee,
> Le vaisseau qui gemit dessous
> L'effort commun, se plaint aux coups
> Dont la vague estoit tourmentee.
>
> L'onde rompüe à l'environ
> Blanchit d'escume l'aviron,
> Puis à menus tortis se roüe
> Apres le vaisseau qui s'enfuit,
> Tout à l'entour on oyt le bruit
> Des flots outragez par la proüe.
>
> Un train d'escume va devant,
> Quelque temps le souffle du vent
> A boüillons sur la vague fole [sic],
> Et puis surpris des tourbillons
> Crevant en cent parts ses boüillons
> Avec eux parmy l'air s'envole.
>   (Quoted by Wentzlaff-Eggebert, pp. 109-110)

[20]Laumonier XVI, 29. Cohen I, 652. Silver IV, 39.

[21]See Ernst Robert Curtius, *European Literature and the Latin Middle Ages,* trans. Willard R. Trask (New York: Harper, 1963), pp. 128-130.

[22]The likelihood of an intended irony in the reified metaphor of
Saint-Amant's dedication seems all the greater when we recall that during
Ronsard's long wait for a sponsor for his poem, both he and his friends
frequently wrote poems about the too-long-awaited masterpiece, and in
doing so they invariably used this same nautical metaphor to evoke its
slow composition. In two *Odes au Roy* first published in 1555, Ronsard
extends the metaphor to its limits in appealing for material support from
Henri II. The dedicatory ode to the entire *Quatre Livres des Odes* ends with
the following lines:

> Les vertus et les biens que je veux recevoir

D'un si puissant Monarque est un jour de pouvoir
Amener ton Francus suivy de mainte trope
De guerriers, pour donter les Princes de l'Europe.
Mais il te faut payer les frais de son arroy:
Car il ne veut venir qu'en majesté de Roy,
Bien qu'il soit fugitif, et qu'il n'ait en partage
Sinon du pere sien l'adresse et le courage.
. . . .
Puis qu'il trouve en mes vers le vent si à propos,
Fay luy enfler la voile, et luy romp le repos
Qui le tient paresseux au rivage d'Epire
Fraudé de son chemin par faute de Navire,
De vivres et de gens: ouvrier je suis tout prest
De charpenter sa Nef et dresser son apprest,
Pourveu que ta grandeur Royale favorise
A ton ayeul Francus, et à mon entreprise.
(Laumonier VII, 9-10. Cohen I, 357. Silver III, 11-12)

The first ode of the *Troisième Livre des Odes* begins in a similar vein:

Comme on voit la navire attendre bien souvent
Au premier front du port la conduite du vent
Afin de voyager, haussant la voile enflée
Du costé que le vent sa poupe aura souflée:
Ainsi, Prince, je suis sans bouger attendant
Que ta faveur royale aille un jour commandant
A ma nef d'entreprendre un chemin honorable
Du costé que ton vent luy sera favorable.
    Car si tu es sa guide, elle courra sans peur
De trouver dessous l'eau quelque rocher trompeur,
Ou les bans perilleux des sablonneuses rades,
Ou l'aboyante Scylle, ou les deux Symplegades:
Mais seurement voguant sans crainte d'abysmer,
Joyeuse emportera les Muses par le mer,
Qui pour l'honneur de toy lui monstreront la voye
D'aller bien loin de France aux rivages de Troye,
Et là sous les monceaux de tant de murs veincus
Deterrer le renom du fils d'Hector Francus:
Lequel en s'embarquant sous ta conduite, Sire,
Au havre de Buthrote à la coste d'Epire,
Deviendra hazardeux au milieu des dangers
Des Gregeois ennemis et des flots estrangers,

Gaignant la mer Euxine, etc., etc.
(Laumonier VII, 24-26. Cohen I, 469. Silver III, 165)

Du Bellay, evidently tired of waiting and skeptical of ever seeing the work completed, takes up the same metaphor to chide Ronsard:

> Ton Francus, cependant, a beau haulser les voiles,
> Dresser le gouvernail, espier les estoiles,
> Pour aller où il deust estre ancré desormais:
> Il a le vent à gré, il est en equippage,
> Il est encor pourtant sur le Troien rivage,
> Aussi croy-je (Ronsard) qu'il n'en partit jamais.
> (*Les Regrets* 23)

The nautical metaphor for poesis became so much a part of the continuing drama of the *Franciade* that it may still have recalled that fiasco to readers of the early seventeenth century.

[23]A comparison of this hymn with the dithyrambic poetry of Ronsard indeed forces us to observe that the inspiration of the two could hardly be more different. Yet Saint-Amant could not have been unaware that Arion was thought to have invented the dithyramb. He knew it from Herodotus, who states the fact unambiguously at the beginning of his digression on Arion: "Arion de Methymnee. . .fut le premier entre les hommes d'alors, selon que j'ay entendu, lequel inventa le chant Dithyrambe, luy donna nom, et le mit en avant" (*Histoire des neuf livres de Herodote*, trans. Pierre Saliat), and from Plutarch, who plays with the notion of an appropriately dithyrambic narration of Arion's adventure (*Le bancquet des sept sages*, trans. Jacques Amyot). Nor could Saint-Amant, who was such a close and avid reader of Ronsard, have been ignorant of what a dithyramb is.

[24]It must be pointed out that these lines are somewhat conventional, and Arion's preluding could just as easily have been suggested by a passage concerning not Orpheus himself, but Orpheus' mother by Apollo, the Muse of *epic poetry*:

> Calliope querulas praetemptat pollice chordas
> Atque haec percussis subiungit carmina nervis.
> (*Metamorphoses* V, 339-340)

[25]It may be felt that the vague reference to Orpheus' end contained

in the four lines concerning "la Lyre d'Orfée" is not sufficient to justify a reading based on the precise details of the Orpheus legend. As an *a priori* defense of this precedure I can only adduce the textual parallels between *L'Arion* and Ovid's account of the Orpheus legend discussed above, and offer positive proof of Saint-Amant's familiarity with the fine points of the legend. The poet alludes more directly to these same details in *La Jouyssance*, whose composition predates that of *L'Arion* by several years (1617-1621). Near the end of this poem, the speaker is playing his lute on the banks of a stream. Birds, beasts, even stones are affected by the music. The last strophe of the poem is uttered by an oak tree which is moved to speech by the sweetness of the lute's accents:

> Orphée aux yeux de Radamante,
> A donc ramené des Enfers,
> Malgré les flames et les fers,
> Sa chere et gracieuse Amante!
> Ce rare exemple d'amitié
> Est donc rejoint à sa moitié
> Par deux fois de luy separée!
> *Et sa teste* où les Dieux tant de dons ont enclos,
> *Ny sa lyre* tant admirée,
> *Ne furent donc jamais à l'abandon des flots.*
> (*Oeuvres* I, 171)

[26]When Saint-Amant reprints *L'Arion* in the *Oeuvres* of 1629 he will alter the somewhat nonsensical penultimate line ("Aprés tant de plaisirs à son merite offers") to read: "Aprés tant de hazards et de malheurs souffers." The revised text gains not only in clarity, but in significance: it reminds us one last time of the homecoming of Arion's epic prototype Odysseus—"le retour aux mille traverses" (*Odyssey* IX 37).

[27]*Les Opuscules d'Homere*, paginated separately in *Les Oeuvres d'Homere, Prince des Poetes*, trans. Salomon Certon (Paris: Nicolas Hameau, 1615). Line numbers following all quotations refer to the original Greek text.

[28]*Moÿse sauvé des eaux*, I, 1-24, in *Les Oeuvres complètes,* ed. Livet (Paris: P. Jannet, 1855), II, 151-152.

[1]*Oeuvres* II, 14-31. *Le Melon* has never been dated, even approximatively. The only certitude is that it was written before 1631. Nothing in fact precludes the possibility of its having been composed before 1629, even though it does not appear in the first collection of the *Oeuvres*. I am inclined to believe that it was written considerably later than 1623, however—that is, well after the three poems considered in preceding chapters.

[2]Giovanna Angeli, "Saint-Amant e i rifacimenti visionari dei prototipi berneschi," *Paragone,* 234 (1969), 21-49. The poem in question is *La Génération de l'homme et le temple de l'âme* by René Bretonnayau (Paris: Abel Langelier, 1583), from which Angeli quotes the following exerpts on pages 29-30 of her article:

> Mais, o Dieu, qu'est ceci? ah, qu'est ce que je sens
> Qui ravisseur m'enleve et desrobbe à mes sens
> Qui embrase mon âme? Et quelle vertu forte
> Mais quelle douce erreur hors de moi me transporte?
> Quelle est ceste fureur qui trouble mon repos?
> . . . .
> Ah, je me pasme d'aize et mon âme qui sort
> N'a plus, n'a plus regret à son corps demy mort.
> C'est, c'est je ne sçay quoy, c'est une joye extrême
> Qui m'affole et chatouille et ravist en moy mesme.

Angeli's article, though brief in its treatment of a large number of Saint-Amant's poems (*Le Fromage, Le Melon, Le Cantal, La Chambre du Débauché, Les Goinfres, Mauvais logement*) is one of the most useful and suggestive pieces of work on Saint-Amant to be found, especially in regard to the question of generic and stylistic mixing in *Le Fromage* and *Le Melon*.

[3]See Saint-Amant's apology to the reader in his preface to the *Moÿse sauvé*:

> Au reste, comme je suis tombé malade d'une maladie tres-périlleuse

> pendant l'impression de ce livre,. . .je n'ay pas eu le moyen d'en
> revoir exactement toutes les espreuves; et par ainsy, il s'y est
> glissé quantité de fautes, tant en la ponctuation qu'en l'obmission
> ou au changement de quelques lettres; *et plus que tout, en mettant*
> *de grandes lettres au lieu de petites, et de petites au lieu de grandes;*
> ce que j'ay remarqué lors qu'il ne s'y pouvoit plus donner ordre.
> Cela se corrigera en une seconde édition.

Oeuvres complètes de Saint-Amant, ed. Ch.-L. Livet, II, 147-148. Few are
the poets who did not blame their printers for all the mistakes, of course,
but Saint-Amant is the only one to my knowledge who ever expressed concern for the case of letters in his text.

[4]Charles Sorel, *Le Berger extravagant,* I (Paris: Toussaint du Bray,
1628), pp. 334-423.

[5]*Hynne de Henry Deuxiesme,* 11. 9-20. Laumonier VIII, 6-7. Cohen
II, 142-143. Silver VI, 67-68.

[6]*Hynne de Charles Cardinal de Lorraine,* 11. 379-382 (11. 455-458
in the first edition). Laumonier IX, 54. Cohen II, 184. Silver VI, 96.

[7]The victory celebrated by this banquet is clearly that of the Olympians over the *Giants.* "Enfans de la Terre" (1. 118) and "mauvais Gar-
çons" (1. 126) are epithets which can apply only to the Giants, and the
participation of Hercules (1. 122) and of Silenus' ass (11. 125-128) are unequivocally episodes of the Revolt. Elsewhere in *Le Melon* Saint-Amant
distinguishes the defeat of the Titans from the revolt of the Giants with
far greater precision than the poets of the Pléiade were wont to do. Cybele-
Rhea is present at the feast since she is, after all, the "Mother of the Gods,"
even though she herself is a Titan, and her allegiance might have lain with
the "Enfans de la Terre":

> Et bien que l'on eust creu qu'*en cest acte rebelle,*
> La Vieille au cul crotté, la terrestre Cybelle,
> Des *orgueilleux Geans* eust tenu le party,
> Auquel en demeura pourtant le desmenty,
> Elle ne laissa pas, quittant Phlegre à main gauche,
> Comme Mere des Dieux d'estre de la desbauche.
>   (11. 209-214)

The distinction between Titans and Giants is made even more explicitly in the lines on Saturn-Cronos, the chief Titan who was deposed long before the revolt of the Giants:

> . . .le vieux Saturne,
> Qui flatté d'un espoir sanglant et taciturne
> Du *complot de Typhon* avoit esté l'Autheur.
> (11. 221-223)

In singing the defeat of the "Titans" (1. 296), then, is Apollo singing an earlier victory? Or is Saint-Amant applying the word "Titan" to the Giants, who are actually the lesser brothers of the deposed Titans? Or is this simply a vestige of the Renaissance confusion of the two? Given the precision of Saint-Amant's references, the second is the most likely hypothesis. But whatever the case, the subject of Apollo's song in *Le Melon* is entirely consistent with his traditional repertoire in classical and Renaissance feasts of the gods.

[8]Jean Lemaire de Belges, *Les Illustrations de Gaule et Singularitez de Troye*, Livre I, chapitre 29, in *Oeuvres*, ed. J. Stecher (Louvain: Lefever, 1882), I, 216-219.

[9]Alessandro Tassoni, *La secchia rapita* (Paris: Toussaint du Bray, 1622). Saint-Amant himself mentions the poem in his preface to the *Passage de Gibraltar*, composed in 1636-1638 and published with *Les Oeuvres, Seconde Partie* in 1643:

> Ce n'est pas. . .que je sois de l'advis de ceux qui croyent comme les Italiens ont fait autrefois à cause de leur *Bernia,* dont ils adoroient les elegantes fadezes, que la simple Naïfveté soit le seul partage des Pieces Comiques. . . . Aussi les plus habiles de cette Nation ont bien changé de sentiment, depuis qu'ils ont veu *la Secchia rapita du Tassone,* où l'Heroïque brille de telle sorte, et est si admirablement confondu avec le Bourlesque, qu'il y en a quelques-uns qui par un excés de loüange osent bien la comparer *à la divine Jerusalem du Tasse.*
> (*Oeuvres* II, 156-157. Italics are Saint-Amant's)

[10]It is used in seven of the thirteen longer poems (i.e., those which are neither sonnets nor epigrams) of the *Raillerie à Part.* Saint-Amant's *serious* lyric pieces of the same period tend to be written in Malherbian strophes of octosyllabic or heterometric lines, rather than in octosyllabic couplets.

[11]This inversion has been nicely observed by Giovanna Angeli, "Saint-Amant e i rifacimenti," p. 30.

[12]Laumonier II, 155-162. Cohen II, 725-728. Silver—.

[13]Antistrophe 8, 11. 369-378 (Antistrophe 10, 11. 469-478 in the first edition). Laumonier III, 33-34. Cohen I, 367. Silver III, 26.

[14]Laumonier XV, 15-38. Cohen II, 321-331. Silver VII, 53-65.

NOTES TO AFTERWORD

[1]Many of the imitations in Ronsard's early odes, for example, seem to connote nothing more than the poet's pretensions for his poem—that is, to convey the implicit statement: "this poem is nobler and more divine than any ever written in France: it is to the French language what Horace's odes were to the Latin language, and Pindar's to the Greek."

[2]Ronsard's early odes sometimes string together—albeit harmoniously and with beautiful results—near translations from two or three different Horatian odes on the same subject, with no attempt to create a meaning or an effect greater than, or even different from, the sum of the Horatian parts.

[3]Since the completion of the present work, a fine article has appeared in which Saint-Amant's *caprices* are placed in their historical context and shown to be far more complex than they are usually assumed to be. See Alice Rathé, "Saint-Amant poète du 'caprice'," *XVIIe Siècle,* 121 (1978), 229-244.

APPENDIX I

The Arion legend as it is told by Ovid (*Fasti* II, 83-116) and translated by
Jean de Montlyard (Comes, *Mythologie, c'est à dire Explication des Fables*).
Lines 101-102 are omitted in the translation.

Quelle mer, quel païs, quelle coste ou province
D'Arion n'a le los entonné? Par la pince
De sa harpe tout court il arrestoit les eaux,
Et bien-souvent le loup poursuivant les agneaux
S'est planté pour ouïr sa voix doux-resonante:
Bien souvent les agneaux d'une crainte bellante
Devant le loup fuyans ont affermi le pied:
Et bien souvent les chiens et lievres vistes-pied
L'on a veu se former dessous un mesme ombrage:
Et le lion joüer avec le cerf volage;
La corneille jasarde, et l'oiseau de Pallas,
L'espervier et pigeon folastrer sans debas.
    Brave Arion, on dit que souvent la Cynthie
N'a pas moins admiré ta douce melodie,
Qu'elle admire escoutant les fraternels accords.
Le nom Arionin retentissoit és bords
De la coste et des bourgs de la gent Sicilide,
Et sa harpe esclatoit en la pleine Ausonide,
Quand pour s'en retourner sur un navire il part
Portant ce qu'il avoit acquesté par son art.
Peut-estre que des vents tu redoutois l'halaine,
Et l'orage grondant, malheureux! mais la plaine
Mieux t'eust valu choisir que ce vaisseau poltron.
Car le glaive en la main devant luy le patron
Se presente assisté de sa brigade armee
Complice du forfaict. Luy d'une ame pasmee
Et panthois leur repond: Las! s'il me faut mourir,
Que sur ma harpe au moins je puisse parcourir
Une seule chanson, ce qu'ils souffrent à l'heure,
Et se mocquent gausseurs de sa longue demeure.

Lors il cerne son chef d'une tresse et chappeau
Qui pourroit honorer, Apollo, ton crin beau.
Il vest sur le loisir que ce delay luy donne,
Un paletoc pourprin, et de ses doigts fredonne
Sur sa Lyre un bel air, semblable à cet accord
Flebile degoisé par l'oiseau chante-mort
Quand il se sent oultré d'une dure sagette.
Avec cet equippage en la mer il se jette,
Et du plongeon qu'il fait s'eslançant à l'envers,
L'onde escarte bien loing le navire bleu-pers.
Alors on dit (quelqu'un ne le croira peut-estre)
Qu'un Dauphin, recourbant le dos, se vint sousmettre
Sous le faix: il s'y sied, son chant paye le port,
Et calme de la mer les vagues jusques [sic] au port.

Parallel passages from Du Bartas' *La Création du Monde, ou la Première Sepmaine* (Book V) and Saint-Amant's *L'Arion*.

Du Bartas

Jà la rive s'enfuit, le tarentain rempart
Se desrobe à ses yeux, desjà de toute part
Il ne void qu'onde et ciel, et sur la plaine humide
Le pilote n'a rien que le quadran pour guide.
Adoncques les nochers (qui sont le plus souvent
Plus traistres que la mer, plus mutins que le vent)
Luy prenent le manteau, le pourpoint luy despouillent,
Pour trouver son thresor haut et bas le refouillent;
Et quand ils l'ont trouvé, sur le bord du vaisseau
Vont tirassans son corps pour le jetter dans l'eau.

(ll. 441-450)

Saint-Amant

Desja le prompt effort d'un gracieux Zephire
Avoit bien loin de terre emporté le Navire,
Et desja pour objet qui s'offrist à ses yeux,
Arion n'avoit plus que la Mer et les Cieux,
Quand ces fiers Matelots, ces perfides courages
Qu'un vil espoir de gain abandonne aux orages
Qui sont le plus souvent bien moins qu'eux inhumains
Au dessein de sa mort appresterent leurs mains.

(ll. 81-88)

Du Bartas

. . Lors, batant doucement
Les nerfs enchante-coeurs de son doux instrument,
Il charme l'ocean d'une telle harmonie,
Que le congre sans peur vit en la compagnie
Du myre aux croches dens, que le muge et le loup
Leur haine hereditaire oublient pour ce coup,
Et la langouste encor, sur le dos d'Amphitrite,
Du poulpe aux pieds larrons les approches n'evite.
(11. 477-484)

«Et d'un veu solennel je consacre à ta gloire
Mon coeur, ma voix, ma main, et ce beau luth d'yvoire.»
(11. 515-516)

La mer à ceste voix sa rage sursoya,
Le ciel, noirci devant, tout son front baloya,
Et les vents, attentifs à si douces merveilles,
Changerent tout soudain leurs bouches en oreilles.
(11. 517-520)

Saint-Amant

Soudain que ces accors sur les eaux s'estendirent,
Mille et mille poissons en foule se rendirent
Autour de ce vaisseau, mais sans bruit toutesfois,
Pour gouster de plus prez une si belle vois:
Là, pour l'entendre mieux l'effroyable Baleine
Aussi bien que les vents retenoit son haleine:
Là, ceux que la Nature a fait naistre ennemis,
Et dont les sentimens furent lors endormis,
Sans qu'aucune dispute y semast des alarmes,
Se laissoient pesle-mesle attirer à ses charmes.
(11. 149-158)

Luy consacrant sa voix, son lut et son butin,
Pour en faire construire un autel à sa gloire.
(11. 244-245)

Là, les Eaux et les Airs demeuroient en repos
De crainte d'interrompre un si divin propos:
Là, le Ciel attentif à ces douces merveilles
Eust bien voulu changer tous ses yeux en oreilles.
(11. 159-162)

Du Bartas

Le dauphin, descouvrant le bord tant souhaitté,
Se tourmente à part soy de s'estre tant hasté,
Et pour plus longuement humer ceste harmonie
Voudroit cent fois plus loin sçavoir sa Laconie.
Toutesfois preferant l'inesperé salut
D'un si rare sonneur au doux son de son luth,
Il le conduit à terre. . . .
(11. 521-527)

 . . .et, ce que plus je prise,
La vie il luy redonne, où la vie il a prise.
(11. 527-528)

Saint-Amant

Le Daufin qui sous luy couloit si promptement,
Pour l'oüir plus long temps, vogant plus lentement,
Nage moins dans la Mer qu'il ne fait dans la joye,
Et découvrant la rive où le Destin l'envoye,
Hesite à l'aborder, tant il sent de douceur
D'estre d'un tel plaisir encore possesseur.
Mais preferant en fin, sans plus le faire attendre,
Le bien de le sauver à celuy de l'entendre,
Il tire droit au port avec legereté. . .
(11. 255-263)

Se voyant mettre à terre au pied du mont-Tenare,
Aprés tant de plaisirs à son merite offers,
Il trouva son salut aux portes des Enfers.
(11. 286-288)

BIBLIOGRAPHY OF PRINCIPAL WORKS CITED

Abraham, Claude. "An Attempt at a Chronology of the Early Works of Saint-Amant." *Romance Notes,* 11 (1970), 591-594.

Adam, Antoine. *L'Age classique I: 1624-1660.* Littérature Française, vol. 6. Paris: Arthaud, 1968.

Angeli, Giovanna. " 'Comique' e 'illusion' nella poesia di Saint-Amant." *Saggi e ricerche di Letteratura Francese,* 10 (1969), 31-95.

—. "Saint-Amant e i rifacimenti visionari dei prototipi berneschi." *Paragone,* 20, No. 234 (1969), 21-49.

Apollodorus. *The Library.* Trans. Sir James George Frazer. Loeb Classical Library. 2 vols. New York: Putnam, 1946, and Cambridge: Harvard University Press, 1954.

—. *Les Trois Livres de la Bibliothèque d'Apollodore, ou de l'Origine des Dieux.* Trans. Jean Passerat. Paris: J. Gesselin, 1605.

Aratus Solensis. See Hyginus.

Auhigné, Agrippa d'. *Le Printemps: Stances et Odes.* Ed. Fernand Desonay. Textes Littéraires Français. Geneva: Droz, 1952.

Aulus Gellius. *The Attic Nights.* Trans. John C. Rolfe. Loeb Classical Library. 3 vols. Cambridge: Harvard University Press, 1948-1954.

Baïf, Jan Antoine de. *Euvres en rime.* Ed. Ch. Marty-Laveaux. 5 vols. Paris: Alphonse Lemerre, 1881-1890.

Berni, Francesco. *Poesie e Prose.* Ed. Ezio Chiòrboli. Florence: Olschki, 1934.

Borton, Samuel L. *Six Modes of Sensibility in Saint-Amant.* Studies in

French Literature, 8. The Hague: Mouton, 1966.

Bourchenin, Daniel. *Etude sur les académies protestantes en France au XVIe et au XVIIe siècle.* 1882; rpt. Geneva: Slatkine Reprints, 1969.

Cartari, Vincenzo. *Le Imagini de i dei de gli antichi, nelle quali si contengono gl'idoli, riti, ceremonie, e altre cose appartenente alla religione de gli antichi, raccolte. . .con la loro espositione, e con bellissime e accomodate figure novamente stampate.* Venice: G. Ziletti, 1571.

—. *Les Images des Dieux des anciens, contenant les idoles, coustumes, cérémonies, et autres choses appartenans à la religion des payens.* Trans. Antoine Du Verdier. Tournon: C. Michel, 1606-1607.

Catullus, Gaius Valerius. *Catullus, Tibullus and Pervigilium Veneris.* Trans. F. W. Cornish, J. P. Postgate and J. W. Mackail. Revised edition. Loeb Classical Library. Cambridge: Harvard University Press, 1962.

Chamard, Henri. *Histoire de la Pléiade.* 4 vols. 1939; rpt. Paris: Didier, 1961-1963.

Chevreau, Urbain. *Chevraeana.* 2 vols. Paris: Delaulne, 1697-1700.

Comes, Natalis. *Mythologiae, sive explicationum fabularum.* Venice, 1581.

—. *Mythologie, c'est à dire Explication des Fables.* Trans. I. D. M. [Jean de Montlyard]. Rouen: Jean Osmond, 1611.

Cotgrave, Randle. *A Dictionarie of the French and English Tongues.* Ed. William S. Woods. 1611; rpt. Columbia: University of South Carolina Press, 1950.

Curtius, Ernst Robert. *European Literature and the Latin Middle Ages.* Trans. Willard R. Trask. New York: Harper, 1963.

Cyrano de Bergerac, Savinien. *Lettres.* Ed. Luciano Erba. Milan: Scheiwiller, 1965.

Dante Alighieri. *La Divina Commedia.* Ed. Charles H. Grandgent. Revised edition. Boston: Heath, 1933.

Dhoges, Pierre. "La Solitude du sieur de Saint-Amant. Solitudo e Gallica Santamani," in *In Grandia Serenissimi Principis ac Ducis d'Anguien Gesta.* Dijon: Pierre Palliot, 1646.

Du Bartas, Guillaume de Salluste. *The Works of Guillaume de Salluste Sieur Du Bartas: A Critical Edition with Introduction, Commentary and Variants.* Ed. U. T. Holmes, Jr., J. C. Lyons and R. W. Linker. 3 vols. Chapel Hill: University of North Carolina Press, 1935-1940.

Du Bellay, Joachim. *Deffense et Illustration de la Langue Françoyse.* Ed. Henri Chamard. Société des Textes Français Modernes. Paris: Didier, 1970.

—. *Les Regrets et autres oeuvres poëtiques.* Ed. J. Joliffe and M. A. Screech. 2nd edition. Textes Littéraires Français. Geneva: Droz, 1974.

Du Mas. *Lydie, fable champestre, et Oeuvres meslees.* Paris: J. Millot, 1609.

Erba, Luciano. "Visione miope e secentismo." *Aevum,* 30 (1956), 495-504.

—. "Realismo e Italianismo in Saint-Amant." *Aevum,* 37 (1963), 285-297.

Estienne, Robert. See Stephanus, Robertus.

Faguet, Emile. *Histoire de la poésie française de la Renaissance au Romantisme.* 11 vols. Paris: Boivin, 1923.

Fitzpatrick, Edward A., ed. *St. Ignatius and the Ratio Studiorum.* New York: McGraw-Hill, 1933.

Fulgentius, Fabius Planciades. See Hyginus and Staveren.

Gautier, Théophile. *Les Grotesques.* Nouvelle édition. Paris: Bibliothèque Charpentier, 1897.

Giraldi, Lilio Gregorio. *De Deis gentium varia et multiplex historia, in qua et simul de eorum imaginibus et cognominibus agitur.* Basel: J. Oporinum, 1548.

Golignac, Henri. *La Solitude du sieur de Saint-Amant, avec la traduction latine.* Toulouse: Jean Boude, 1654.

Gourier, Françoise. *Etude des oeuvres poétiques de Saint-Amant.* Geneva: Droz, 1961.

Herodotus. *Histoire des neuf livres de Herodote.* Trans. Pierre Saliat. Paris: C. Micard, 1575.

Homer. *L'Odyssée d'Homere.* Trans. Salomon Certon. Paris: Abel L'Angelier, 1604.

—. *L'Odyssée d'Homere.* Trans. Salomon Certon. 2nd edition. Paris: Nicolas Hameau, 1615.

—. *Les Oeuvres d'Homere, Prince des Poetes.* Trans. Salomon Certon. Paris: Nicolas Hameau, 1615.

—. *Les Oeuvres.* Trans. Salomon Certon. 2 vols. Paris: Thomas Blaise, 1615.

Horatius Flaccus, Quintus. *The Odes and Epodes.* Trans. C. E. Bennet. Loeb Classical Library. Cambridge: Harvard University Press, 1946.

—. *Satires, Epistles, Ars Poetica.* Trans. H. Rushton Fairclough. Loeb Classical Library. Cambridge: Harvard University Press, 1955.

Hyginus, C. Julius. *Fabularum liber. . .Poeticon astronomicon libri quatuor . . .Fulgentii Planciadis Mythologiarum libri III. . .Phornuti de Natura deorum, sive poeticarum fabularum allegoriis speculatio. . .Albrici philosophi de Deorum imaginibus liber, Arati. . .Phaenomena. . . Apollodori Biblioth., sive de Deorum origine, Lilii G. Giraldi de Musis syntagma. . .* Geneva: S. Camonetus, 1608.

—. See Staveren.

Joukovsky-Micha, Françoise. "La guerre des dieux et des géants chez les poètes français du 16ᵉ siècle (1500-1585)," *Bibliothèque d'Humanisme et Renaissance,* 29 (1967), 55-92.

—. *Orphée et ses disciples dans la poésie française et néo-latine du XVIᵉ siècle.* Geneva: Droz, 1970.

—. *Poésie et mythologie au XVIe siècle: quelques mythes de l'inspiration chez les poètes de la Renaissance.* Paris: Nizet, 1969.

Keller, Luzius. " 'Solo e pensoso,' 'Seul et pensif,' 'Solitaire et pensif': mélancolie pétrarquienne et mélancolie pétrarquiste." *Studi Francesi,* nuova serie, 49 (1973), 3-14.

Lactantius Placidus. See Staveren.

Lagny, Jean. "Autour de la 'Solitude' de Saint-Amant: les traductions latines." *Bulletin du Bibliophile et du Bibliothécaire,* 1956, No. 3, pp. 110-126.

—. "Autour de la 'Solitude' de Saint-Amant: questions de dates." *Bulletin du Bibliophile et du Bibliothécaire,* 1955, No. 6, pp. 235-245.

—. "Bibliographie des éditions anciennes des oeuvres de Saint-Amant." *Bulletin du Bibliophile et du Bibliothécaire,* 1960, Nos. 3-6, pp. 97-236.

—. *Bibliographie des éditions anciennes des oeuvres de Saint-Amant.* Paris: Giraud-Badin, 1960.

—. *Le poète Saint-Amant (1594-1661): Essai sur sa vie et ses oeuvres.* Paris: Nizet, 1964.

—. "Le poète Saint-Amant et le protestantisme." *Bulletin de la Société de l'Histoire du Protestantisme Français,* 103 (1957), 237-266.

La Roque de Clairmont. *Les Oeuvres.* Paris: Vve Claude de Monstr'oeil, 1609.

Lemaire de Belges, Jean. *Oeuvres.* Ed. J. Stecher. 4 vols. Louvain: Lefever, 1882-1891.

Lortigue, Annibal sieur de. *Poèmes divers.* Paris: J. Gesselin, 1617.

Lucianus Samosatensis. *Les oeuvres de Lucian de Samosate.* Trans. Jean Baudoin. Paris: Jean Richer, 1613.

Lyons, John D. "Saint-Amant's *La Solitude:* The Rhetoric of Fragmentation." *Orbis Litterarum,* 33 (1978), 4-17.

Martinon, Philippe. *Les strophes: étude historique et critique sur les formes de la poésie lyrique en France depuis la Renaissance.* Paris: Champion, 1912.

Mathieu-Castellani, Gisèle. *Les thèmes amoureux dans la poésie française (1570-1600).* Paris: Klincksieck, 1975.

Mazzara, Ricahrd A. "A Case of Creative Imagination in Saint-Amant." *French Review,* 31 (1957), 27-34.

—. "Saint-Amant and the Italian Bernesque Poets." *French Review,* 32 (1959), 231-241.

Orpheus. *Orphei Hymni sacri, seu Indigitamenta Apollinis, Latonae, Solis, versibus antiquis latine expressa.* Trans. Joseph Juste Scaliger. Paris: J. Libert, 1614.

Oudin, Antoine. *Curiositez françoises, pour Supplement aux Dictionnaires, ou Recueil de Plusieurs belles proprietez, avec une infinité de Proverbes et Quolibets, pour l'explication de toutes sortes de Livres.* Paris: Antoine de Sommaville, 1640.

Ovidius Naso, Publius. *The Art of Love and Other Poems.* Trans. J. H. Mozley. Loeb Classical Library. Cambridge: Harvard University Press, 1962.

—. *Fasti.* Trans. Sir James George Frazer. Loeb Classical Library. Cambridge: Harvard University Press, 1951.

—. *Le Grand Olympe des histoires poétiques du Prince de Poésie Ovide Naso en sa Metamorphose, oeuvre authentique et de hault artifice.* Paris: 1538.

—. *Heroides and Amores.* Trans. Grant Showerman. Loeb Classical Library. New York: Putnam, 1931.

—. *Les Metamorphoses.* Trans. Raimond and Charles de Massac. Paris: Françoys Pomeray, 1617.

—. *Les Metamorphoses.* Trans. Nicolas Renouard. Paris: Vve L'Angelier, 1619.

—. *Metamorphoses.* Trans. Frank Justus Miller. Loeb Classical Library. 2 vols. Cambridge: Harvard University Press, 1916.

—. *Les Quinze Livres de la Métamorphose d'Ovide.* Trans. François Habert. Rouen: G. L'Oyselet, n.d. [1557?]

—. *Tristia. Ex Ponto.* Trans. Arthur Leslie Wheeler. Loeb Classical Library. Cambridge: Harvard University Press, 1953.

Papus, le Père François. *Solitudo Viri Cl. D. de Sainct Amant, Hexametris Latinis Conversa a P. F. P.* Toulouse: Jean Boude, 1662.

Petrarca, Francesco. *Opere.* 2 vols. Le Voci del Mondo. Florence: Sansoni, 1975.

Philostratus, Flavius. *Les Images, ou Tableaux de platte peinture de Philostrate.* Trans. Blaise de Vigenère. Paris: A. L'Angelier and Vve M. Guillemot, 1615.

Plutarch. *Le Banquet des sept sages.* Trans. Jean Defradas. Paris: Klincksieck, 1954.

—. *Les oeuvres morales et philosophiques de Plutarque.* Trans. Jacques Amyot. Paris: Claude Morel, 1618.

Rabelais, François. *Oeuvres complètes.* Ed. J. Boulenger and L. Scheler. Bibliothèque de la Pléiade. Paris: Gallimard, 1955.

Rathé, Alice. "Saint-Amant poète du 'caprice'." *XVIIe Siècle,* 121 (1978), 229-244.

Ripa, Cesare. *Iconologia: overo descrittione di diverse imagini cavate dall'antichità, e di propria inventione.* 1603; rpt. New York: Georg Olms Verlag, 1970.

Roberts, William. "Berni's *Malo Alloggio* Motif in Saint-Amant." *Studi Francesi,* 27 (1965), 465-471.

—. "Classical Sources of Saint-Amant's *L'Arion.*" *French Studies,* 17 (1963), 341-350.

Rolfe, Christopher D. *Saint-Amant and the Theory of 'Ut Pictura Poesis'.*

Modern Humanities Research Association Dissertation Series, 6. London: The Modern Humanities Research Association, 1972.

Ronsard, Pierre de. *Oeuvres complètes.* Ed. Paul Laumonier. Société des Textes Français Modernes. 19 vols. Paris: Hachette, Droz and Didier, 1914-1974.

—. *Oeuvres complètes.* Ed. Gustave Cohen. Bibliothèque de la Pléiade. 2 vols. Paris: Gallimard, 1950.

—. *Les Oeuvres de Pierre de Ronsard: Texte de 1587.* Ed. Isidore Silver. Published for the Washington University Press. 8 vols. Chicago: University of Chicago Press, 1966-1970.

Rousseau, Jean-Jacques. *Oeuvres complètes.* Ed. G. Petitain. 8 vols. Paris: Lefèvre, 1839.

Rousset, Jean, ed. *Anthologie de la poésie baroque française.* Bibliothèque de Cluny. 2 vols. Paris: Armand Colin, 1961.

Rubin, David Lee. "Consciousness and the External World in a Caprice by Saint-Amant." *Yale French Studies,* 49, "Science, Language and the Perspective Mind," pp. 170-177.

Saint-Amant, Marc-Antoine Girard, sieur de. *Oeuvres.* Ed. Jacques Bailbé and Jean Lagny. Société des Textes Français Modernes. 4 vols. Paris: Didier, 1967-1971.

—. *Oeuvres complètes.* Ed. Ch.-L. Livet. 2 vols. Paris: P. Jannet, 1855.

Sainte-Beuve, Charles Augustin. *Causeries du Lundi.* 3ème édition revue et corrigée. 15 vols. Paris: Garnier, 1857-1872.

Scève Maurice. *Oeuvres complètes.* Ed. Pascal Quignard. Paris: Mercure de France, 1974.

Sébillet, Thomas. *Art poétique fançoys.* Ed. Félix Gaiffe. Société des Textes Français Modernes. Paris: E. Cornély, 1910.

Seznec, Jean. *La survivance des dieux antiques: essai sur le rôle de la tradition mythologique dans l'humanisme et dans l'art de la Renaissance.* Studies of the Warburg Institute, 11. London: Warburg Institute,

1940.

Sorel, Charles. *Le Berger extravagant, où, parmy des fantaisies amoureuses, on void les impertinences des romans et de la poésie.* 3 vols. Paris: Toussaint du Bray, 1627-1628.

Starnes, De Witt T., and Talbert, Ernest William. *Classical Myth and Legend in Renaissance Dictionaries: A Study of Renaissance Dictionaries in their Relation to the Classical Learning of Contemporary English Writers.* Chapel Hill: University of North Carolina Press, 1955.

Staveren, Augustinus van. *Auctores mythographi latini. Cajus Julius Hyginus, Fab. Planciad. Fulgentius, Lactantius Placidus, Albricus philosophus.* Leyden: Samuel Luchtmans, 1742.

Stebbins, Eunice Burr. *The Dolphin in the Literature and Art of Greece and Rome.* Johns Hopkins Diss., 1927. Menasha: George Banta, 1929.

Stephanus, Robertus. *Dictionarium Latinogallicum Thesauro nostro ita ex adverso respondens, ut extra pauca quaedam aut obsoleta, aut minus in usu necessaria vocabula et quas consulto praetermisimus authorum appellationes, in hoc eadem sint omnia, eodem ordine, sermone patrio explicata.* Paris: R. Stephanus, 1543.

—. *Dictionarium propriorum nominum virorum, mulierum, populorum, idolorum, urbium, fluviorum, montium caeterorumque locorum quae passim in libris prophanis leguntur.* Paris: R. Stephanus, 1541.

Tallemant des Réaux, Gédéon. *Historiettes.* Ed. Antoine Adam. Bibliothèque de la Pléiade. 2 vols. Paris: Gallimard, 1960-1961.

Tassoni, Alessandro. *La secchia rapita.* Paris: Toussaint du Bray, 1622.

Tibullus, Albius. See Catullus.

Tristan L'Hermite, François. *Les Amours et autres poésies choisies.* Ed. Pierre Camo. Paris: Garnier, 1925.

Tyard, Pontus de. *Solitaire premier.* Ed. Silvio F. Baridon. Textes Littéraires Français. Geneva: Droz, 1950.

Vergilius Maro, Publius. *Eclogues, Georgics, Aeneid, The Minor Poems.* Trans. H. Rushton Fairclough. Revised edition. Loeb Classical Library. 2 vols. Cambridge: Harvard University Press, 1932.

Vives, Juan Luis. *De Tradendis Disciplinis.* Vol. VI of *Opera Omnia.* 8 vols. Valencia, 1782-1790; rpt. London: Gregg Press, 1964.

Wentzlaff-Eggebert, Christian. *Forminteresse, Traditionsverbundenheit und Aktualisierungsbedürfnis als Merkmale des Dichtens von Saint-Amant.* Münchener Romanistische Arbeiten, 29. Munich: M. Hueber, 1970.